Consumer psychology in behavioural perspective

Consumer research and policy series
Edited by Gordon Foxall

Forthcoming

Morality and the Market
N Craig Smith

Consumer psychology in behavioural perspective

Gordon R. Foxall

Routledge
London and New York

First published 1990
by Routledge
11 New Fetter Lane, London EC4P 4EE

Simultaneously published in the USA and Canada
by Routledge
a division of Routledge, Chapman and Hall, Inc.
29 West 35th Street, New York, NY 10001

© 1990 Gordon Foxall

Typeset by J&L Composition Ltd, Filey, North Yorkshire
Printed and bound in Great Britain by
Biddles Ltd, Guildford and King's Lynn

British Library Cataloguing in Publication Data

Foxall, Gordon R.
 Consumer psychology in behavioural perspective.
 1. Consumer behaviour. Models
 I. Title   II. Series
 658.8'342

   ISBN 0–415–04105–8

Library of Congress Cataloging in Publication Data

Foxall, G. R.
  Consumer psychology in behavioural perspective/Gordon Foxall.
    p.   cm. — (Routledge consumer research and policy series)
  Bibliography: p.
  Includes indexes.
  ISBN 0–415–04105–8
  1. Consumer behavior. I. Title. II. Series: Consumer research
and policy series.
  HF5415.32.F68 1989
  658.8'342—dc20

                                                 89–10543
                                                 CIP

Armande: We'll judge all works, for so our laws decree;
Our laws place prose and verse beneath our rule;
None shall have wit except us and our school;
We'll find flaws everywhere, to our delight,
And see that no one else knows how to write.

Molière

The world is such-and-such and so-and-so only because we tell
ourselves that that is the way it is.

Castaneda (1972)

Knowledge so conceived is not a series of self-consistent theories
that converge towards an ideal view; it is not a gradual approach to
truth. It is rather an ever increasing ocean of mutually
incompatible (and perhaps even incommensurable) alternatives,
each single theory, each fairy tale, each myth that is part of the
collection forcing the others into greater articulation and all of
them contributing, via this process of competition, to the
development of our consciousness. Nothing is ever settled, no
view can ever be omitted from a comprehensive account ... There
is no idea, however ancient and absurd that is not capable of
improving our knowledge.

Feyerabend (1975)

Contents

Figures

Tables

Acknowledgements

The first quotation on page v is from Molière's *Les Femmes Savantes* (Act III, scene 2, 11. 922–6) in *The Misanthrope and Other Plays*, translated by Donald M. Frame, copyright © 1968 Donald M. Frame. It is reprinted by arrangement with New American Library, a division of Penguin Books Inc., New York.

Academic schedules are among the most exacting. I am, therefore, deeply grateful to the four busy academics who took the time to read critically the penultimate draft of this book: Professors Michael Baker, John Dawson, and Paul Peter, and Dr Stephen Lea. Their constructive comments and guidance have been invaluable. My wife, Jean, busier still, also contributed directly by discussing and clarifying many points, and my daughter, Helen, gave much practical help with the preparation of the typescript. I am equally grateful to them. I remain responsible for any errors.

Introduction

It seems to me that the first principle of the study of any belief system is that its ideas and terms must be stated in terms other than its own; that they must be projected on to some screen other than one which they themselves provide. They may and must speak, but they must not be judges in their own case. For concepts, like feelings and desires, have their cunning. Only in this way may we hope to lay bare the devices they employ to make their impact – whether or not those devices are, in the end, endorsed as legitimate.

(Gellner 1985: 5)

This book explores the contribution to consumer research of the experimental analysis of behaviour (EAB), in which the causation of behaviour is attributed to factors external to the individual, and which contrasts with the prevailing cognitive explanations that ascribe observed action to intrapersonal information processing. The book does not advocate a paradigm switch; neither does it assume the superiority of behaviourist explanations over those offered by cognitivism; nor yet does it argue that cognitivism can be superseded by behaviourism. Rather, it is founded on the belief that no single theoretical stance can provide full explanation of complex human behaviours such as those involved in purchasing and consuming. It rests, moreover, on the conviction that the proliferation and active interplay of alternative, competing explanations constitute an important route to scientific progress.

The EAB'S behaviour-based interpretation is founded upon a philosophy of science, radical behaviourism, which explains the rate at which responses are performed by reference to their environmental consequences (rather than their mental precursors). This is not what is implied by the term 'behavioural' when it is generally employed in the marketing context as a synonym for 'psychological' or to refer to the inferred mental antecedents of

1

behaviour – for example, perceptions, attitudes, intentions, and personality traits – which are taken to be the causes of observed action. Nor is it equivalent to the view that behaviourism consists in the quantitative description of trends in consumer behaviour by means of aggregate patterns of brand loyalty or stochastic processes. These descriptive patterns are open to numerous explanations, of which the EAB provides only one interpretation among many.

In the attempt to extend the scope of consumer research beyond the prevailing teleological explanations, the chapters that follow continue an investigation of non-cognitive approaches that began with an account of behaviour-based definitions of the concept of attitude (Foxall 1981a, 1981b). Subsequent research developed the argument that the evidence on attitude-behaviour relationships was as consistent with a behaviour-based interpretation of 'attitude' as with the more common idea that attitudes are intrapsychic causes of choice (Foxall 1983, 1984a, 1984b). Beyond this, a more general examination of the relevance of behaviour analysis to consumer research was incorporated in a paper which proposed a research programme to evaluate the contribution of radical behaviourism to the explanation of choice in this context (Foxall 1986a).

That paper expressed dissatisfaction with the uncritical manner in which many of the tenets of cognitive psychology were loosely accepted as explanations in the marketing and consumer research literatures. It suggested that, within a relativistic perspective (cf. Anderson 1986; Feyerabend 1975), a philosophy of science based on assumptions about the nature and causation of behaviour antithetical to those of the prevailing paradigm would act as a metatheoretical standpoint from which to present a critique of cognitivistic consumer research, revealing its strengths and weaknesses as an explanatory system, through direct comparisons with a viable alternative.

As has been said, the purpose of the proposed programme was not to replace cognitivism with radical behaviourism or, for that matter, anything else. Rather, a relativisitic approach to enquiry was advocated as more likely to advance understanding than the continued prevalence of a single perspective, which, whilst not excluding altogether alternative ways of seeing, was sufficiently strong to predominate at the expense of their not being fully or accurately understood. The starting points are the theory-ladenness of observation and the view that the proliferation of competing explanations is essential to a complete account of behaviour. Given these assumptions, the attempt to select in some ultimate sense from the models comprising the range of psychological perspectives on human behaviour, so that one might be held up as the measure of man whilst the rest are discarded, is as absurd as trying to decide whether a person is described determinatively by either their weight or their height (as though ounces might be superior to inches, or centimetres able in all circumstances to replace kilograms).

It is futile to imagine that paradigms such as cognitivism (which usually attributes a degree of autonomy and subjectivity to the individual) or behaviourism (which assumes that psychology must be objective and empirical) can be 'proved' or 'disproved' in this way. Neither crucial experiment nor philosophical argument can establish or refute such generalizations with finality. The important task is to reject neither but to appreciate the implications of each, first for the other and then for the understanding of consumer behaviour. Hence I have consistently argued that, whilst behaviouristic approaches have been overlooked and deserve the serious, critical attention of consumer researchers, cognitive and other teleological explanations cannot be ruled out of the pluralistic approach intended (Foxall 1986a, 1986b, 1986c, 1986d). This book continues the exploration begun with the analysis of 'attitude'. Its argument is presented sequentially, later chapters building directly upon the ideas examined and conclusions reached earlier. Hence the following *ex ante* summary of the argument may be useful.

Whilst inner-state explanation, exemplified by cognitivism, provided a useful paradigm for the early development of consumer research, to the extent that it now dominates investigation, it threatens to impede theoretical progress in this subdiscipline, not because this paradigm is erroneous but because scientific advance requires a plurality of interacting perspectives.

Chapter one, therefore, has three purposes. First, it discusses the centrality of cognitive explanations in consumer research and supports a critical relativistic approach to open up the field to alternative modes of explanation. Second, it argues for an active interplay of competing explanations to make explicit the strengths and weaknesses of each, and as a prelude to the forging of novel syntheses. Third, the chapter explains why the EAB should occupy a more central position in consumer research and outlines its potential contribution.

Chapter two treats that contribution in greater detail, describing the nature and scope of radical behaviourism as a philosophy of behavioural science, and locating it within the spectrum of available psychological explanations. This chapter also contains an account of the operant conditioning approach to understanding behaviour, illustrating its tenets by extrapolative reference to consumer choice. The purpose of this chapter is to establish the distinguishing character of the EAB in order that its implications for a subdiscipline dominated by cognitive explanations can be assessed. It is also necessary to ascertain (not only in this chapter but also in Chapters 4 and 5) how far the basic model of mankind assumed by radical behaviourists, largely on the basis of animal experimentation, can elucidate consumer behaviour, especially as it is this basic model that has been employed by those marketing authors who have recently portrayed consumer choice in terms of operant psychology.

The interaction of competing paradigms results in the erosion of the 'pure' forms of each, as its basic tenets, otherwise easily taken for granted, are exposed to the critical outlook of another. Hence radical behaviourism provides a valuable standpoint from which to present a critique of the prevailing cognitivism, perhaps eroding its insistence on intrapersonal causation and tempering its excesses as applied in some areas of consumer research.

Chapter three develops the implications of radical behaviourism for current consumer research. The EAB's criticism of 'other realm' theories, based on the notion that behaviour is explicable by reference to prebehavioural states and processes (such as personality traits, information handling, attitudes, and intentions) is illustrated by discussion of the alternative behaviourist approach. First, the highly abstract nature of some recent theories of consumers' innovative behaviour is compared with the parsimonious behavioural account which concentrates on observed new product purchase rather than hypothetical explanatory constructs. Second, several alternative explanations of consumer choice derived from operant psychology are described, from formal theories based on the application of psychological evidence to microeconomic analysis, through the portrayal of consumer choice as a series of responses to marketing stimuli, to a behaviour-based depiction of marketing as reciprocal interaction. The chapter goes on to consider the more direct route to an understanding of the factors that predict and control behaviour offered by experimental operant investigation, and illustrates the principles discussed in terms of a supermarket experiment conducted on the basis of behaviour theory.

No paradigm constitutes a complete and final approach to the explanation of behaviour. The limitations of the EAB as an explanatory system must be understood before its contribution to consumer research can be gauged.

Where Chapter three is concerned with the erosive impact of the EAB on current modes of explanation, Chapter four discusses the weaknesses of the EAB and details how it must be modified through contact with inner-state theories in order to make a convincing contribution to explaining consumer behaviour. This chapter is based on evidence from studies of human operant performance in laboratory settings and in complex social situations. It argues that, in order to benefit from the unique insights of operant psychology, the EAB must be modified to embrace the possibility of the verbal control of behaviour, the situational limitations of behavioural explanations of real world (i.e. non-laboratory) purchasing and consuming, and the informational as well as hedonic effects of reinforcement on the repetition of behaviour.

An important issue raised by this book is the extent to which the EAB can contribute to consumer research before recourse must be made to other explanatory systems. In spite of its limitations, the behaviourist ontology and methodology provide an invaluable addition to current explanations of consumer choice.

Chapter five constructs a Behavioural Perspective Model of consumer choice based on the EAB's location of the causes of behaviour in the environment, but modified according to the critique pursued in Chapter four. The chapter argues that a modified EAB makes available insights into the nature of both consumer and marketer behaviour which are generally overlooked by existing explanations. It also promotes a marketing level of analysis for consumer psychology which recognizes and specifies the marketing mix influences on consumers' brand-related purchase and consumption behaviours. It illustrates the importance of the components of the Behavioural Perspective Model by reference to the modification of consumer choice through so-called 'social marketing' programmes. This does not result in a complete or final explanation of consumer choice in behaviouristic terms, but the analysis undertaken in Chapter five affirms the importance of the EAB as a significant contributor to consumer research which deserves more serious attention than it has hitherto been accorded. The final chapter provides an *ex post* summary of the argument.

Mention must be made of the style I have adopted in presenting this approach. As has been stated, the argument pursued is intended to reflect Feyerabend's advocacy of the deliberate pro-liferation of tenaciously-held competing explanations, the active and critical interplay of which, he maintains, is an essential component of the growth of knowledge. But proliferation and tenacity do not lie easily together within the individual. Prolifera-tion is a function of the scientific community in its entirety, among whose members it is vital that there be a plurality of perspectives, each acting as a means of contextualizing and appraising the rest. Tenacity, in so far as it implies the steadfast adherence to and advocacy of one rigorously-held paradigm, is usually a quality of the individual researcher, or of a small group within that com-munity whose members embrace a common belief structure and set of associated scientific behaviours. My aim in this book is to encourage the proliferation of paradigms in the quest for a more complete understanding of consumer behaviour. The EAB is one vehicle, among several, with which to begin. It is not an end in itself. Yet I am aware that my voice has two registers in that at times I may also appear to be an enthusiastic advocate of the vehicle chosen to stimulate the required theoretical extension. This is unavoidable if a style of exposition which does not exasperate the reader with its constant conscious shifts of view-point (e.g. frequent asides, pointing out that 'An advocate of radical behaviourism would say . . .') is to be adopted. Inasmuch as I come over as a tenacious promoter of the EAB, therefore, it is with the limited aim of drawing critical attention to a necessary but neglected viewpoint in consumer research.

Chapter one

The cognitive consumer – and beyond

What are called the 'causes' of human behaviour turn out, on closer inspection, to be the grounds or reasons for which an agent initiates an action ... Causality in human beings operates through the mind of the agent ... Human beings, unlike purely physical processes, are telic; that is, they pursue ends and purposes, and can and do conceive of the notion of adopting a means to an end.

(Addison *et al*. 1984: 7)

If one had to identify the central fundamental question behind all psychological enquiry, it would be this: *What is the relationship between mental processes and behaviour*? What makes this a difficult question ... is that behaviour is observable whereas mental processes can only be inferred. Psychologists have thus always been faced with the paradoxical problem of how to make observations relevant to the relationship between observables and unobservables.

(Eiser 1981: 3)

The prevailing paradigm

Many myths concerning the nature of managerial behaviour have been exploded over the years by researchers who have taken the trouble to observe managers at work. Mintzberg (1975), for instance, argues persuasively on the basis of his empirical investigations that, whatever managers do with their time, it is not the kind of planning, organizing, co-ordinating, and controlling often attributed to them by management theorists. Some years before Mintzberg's work, Lindblom (1959) noted the practical impossibility of the rational, comprehensive decision-making generally ascribed to (or prescribed for) both administrative and directive executives. It is beyond human capability, he pointed out, to specify all feasible (or even desirable) objectives in advance; some possible strategies are always overlooked, whilst none can be fully examined and appraised; and no-one can know the outcomes of yet-to-be-implemented strategies. The model of managerial behaviour that requires such all-inclusive capacities to obtain, handle, and process information, what Lindblom calls the Comprehensive Model, defies implementation. Yet that model persists: no longer advocated without qualification but held up none the less as an ideal towards which managers are exhorted to advance with whatever degree of rationality they can muster. It endures not only in the literature of managerial prescription but in those of consumer behaviour and marketing.

The most widely-accepted and influential models of consumer behaviour derive in large part from cognitive psychology which is rapidly assuming the status of a dominant, though not exclusive, paradigm for psychological research in general (Gardner 1985; Kassarjian 1982; Mandler 1985). As a result, consumer choice is usually understood as a problem-solving and decision-making sequence of activities, the outcome of which is determined principally by the buyer's intellectual functioning and rational, goal-directed processing of information (Howard 1983). The major comprehensive theories of consumer behaviour (Nicosia 1966; Engel *et al.* 1968, 1986; Howard and Sheth 1969; Howard 1977) invest consumers with extensive capacities to receive and handle considerable quantities of information and to engage in means–ends processing involving comparison and evaluation of alternative brands in relation to the consumer's purposes and aims. None of this ought to be surprising in view of the derivation of these marketing models of consumer behaviour from the same theoretical bases as the earlier models of managerial decision-making founded on reasoned, goal-directed information processing (Jacoby 1983; March 1978; Newell *et al.* 1958; Simon 1959, 1983).

The causal chain common to these approaches to the analysis of consumer choice has been summarized by Howard (1983) as information – attitude – intention – purchase. The achievement of their authors inheres in their skilful expositions of the extended sequence in which information is obtained, classified, and interpreted by the individual prospective buyer and, subsequently, via further mental processing, transformed into the attitudinal and intentional structures that determine such purchase outcomes as brand and store choice and loyalty (Howard 1983; *see also* Bettman 1979; McGuire 1976a, 1976b; Hansen 1976). As the quotations at the beginning of this chapter indicate, this is a predominant form of explanation in social sciences such as economics and psychology; it also pervades much experimental and behavioural economics and economic psychology (Earl 1983; Katona 1975; Lea *et al.* 1987; MacFadyen and MacFadyen 1986; Maital 1982; A. E. Roth 1987; Scitovsky 1976; Van Raaij *et al.* 1988). Formal theories of advertising similarly rely upon the concept of an involved consumer within whom marketer-dominated persuasive communications progressively induce a hierarchy of psychological effects culminating in the purchase of the advertised brand (Colley 1961; Lavidge and Steiner 1961). As is true of the comprehensive consumer choice models, the underlying assumption is that of a 'rational, discerning, and active' consumer, 'devoting attention to the ad, critically perceiving the content (perhaps derogating the source, ignoring some appeals and challenging some arguments), evaluating the personal relevance of the benefits offered, forming an attitude, and executing a purchase' (Atkin 1984: 210).

In both cases, consumer choice is portrayed as an ego-involving sequence of cognitive, affective, and conative changes which precede and predetermine the purchase/no purchase outcome. Indeed, the fundamental premiss is that behavioural change cannot be conceived in the absence of prior, corresponding intrapersonal change. This assumption transcends model-building, as witness the pervasive view among academic and commercial market researchers that attitudinal change is an inevitable precursor of behavioural change (Roberto and Pinson 1973). Prebehavioural modification of the attitudes that are located 'inside consumers' heads' (Schiffman and Kanuk 1983: 210) is generally taken for granted by textbooks on consumer behaviour as part of their accommodation of cognitively-based information processing explanations of choice. Choice itself is portrayed as a mental process initiated by the consumer's awareness of a multiplicity of options. The internal conflict thus generated is reduced by cognitive evaluation of the possibilities available, reasoned consideration of the costs and benefits each entails, and, finally, decision-making (Hansen 1976).

The advertising and marketing models share a mode of explanation founded upon two types of concept: those that relate to an observable, behavioural realm of activity from which the phenomena to be explained are derived, and those that refer to an unobservable, usually mental or conceptual, realm of prebehavioural events, states or processes in terms of which the explanation itself is couched (Moore 1981). This is essentially the stimulus-organism-response model (Tolman 1932; Woodworth 1938) which employs theoretical terms at a nonobservable level of analysis with the intention of rendering observed phenomena intelligible and to account for the consistency of relationships among observables (Mandler 1985). It is most explicit in Howard and Sheth's *Theory of Buyer Behavior* (1969).[1]

The Howard-Sheth theory

The Howard-Sheth theory of buyer behaviour is a sophisticated integration of the various social, psychological, and marketing influences on consumer choice into a coherent sequence of information processing. It aims not only to explain consumer behaviour in terms of cognitive functioning but to provide an empirically testable depiction of such behaviour and its outcomes (see also Howard 1977). It is briefly described here to illustrate the elaborate use of unobservables, representing intervening variables and hypothetical constructs, to account for observed consumer choice. As Figure 1.1 indicates, the theory comprises four sets of variables: *inputs*, stimuli that inaugurate the purchase process; *perceptual constructs*, hypothetical terms that explain the cognitive activity of consumers by reference to internal information processing; *learning constructs*, which signify the products of information processing; and *outputs*, which include not only the act of purchase itself but its perceptual and learning correlates.

The authors distinguish three types of input among the commercial and social stimuli that impact upon consumers: *significative inputs* include quality, price, distinctiveness, service, and availability as they influence the consumer directly through the brand's attributes; *symbolic inputs*, which derive from the same factors as they are portrayed in the mass media and by salespeople, and which influence the consumer indirectly; and *social inputs* – including the family, reference groups, and social class – which are influences that are internalized by the consumer before they can affect the decision process. These stimuli impinge on the consumer's perceptual field to produce *stimulus ambiguity* (feelings of dissonance and uncertainty that can be reduced by a search for further information) and 'perceptual bias' (the result of the consumer's fitting the newly-available information into his or her existing mental set). In the process of learning, the consumer's motives, attitudes, and comprehension of the brand determine the degree of confidence he or she is willing to place in it, their purchase intentions, and actual purchase behaviour (or its absence). The extent to which the buyer is satisfied with the purchase (to which it fulfils his or her goals) feeds back as modifying information that affects attitudes, confidence, purchase intentions, and subsequent activity.

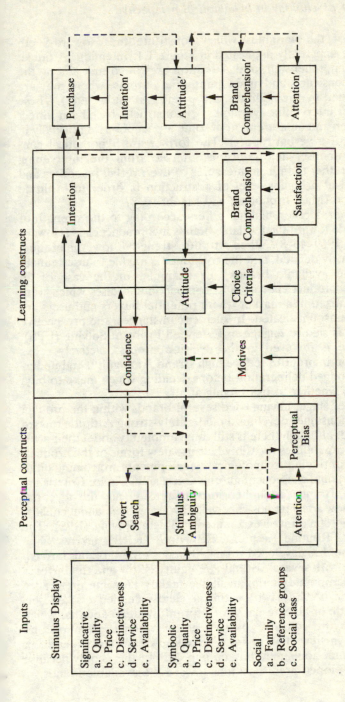

Figure 1.1 A simplified description of the theory of buyer behaviour

Note: Solid lines indicate flow of information; dashed lines, feedback effects

Source: *The Theory of Buyer Behavior* by J. A. Howard and J. N. Sheth, p. 301.
Copyright © 1969 by John Wiley & Sons Inc. Reproduced by permission.

Inputs

Perceptual constructs

Learning constructs

Stimulus Display

Significative
a. Quality
b. Price
c. Distinctiveness
d. Service
e. Availability

Symbolic
a. Quality
b. Price
c. Distinctiveness
d. Service
e. Availability

Social
a. Family
b. Reference groups
c. Social class

Overt
Search

Stimulus
Ambiguity

Attention

Perceptual
Bias

Confidence

Attitude

Motives

Choice
Criteria

Intention

Brand
Comprehension

Satisfaction

Purchase

Intention'

Attitude'

Brand
Comprehension'

Attention'

Some of the variables which constitute the Howard-Sheth theory are apparently duplicated in Figure 1.1: Intention, Attitude, Brand Comprehension, and Attention are found first among the learning constructs and again among the outputs, where they are distinguished by the addition of a prime (Attitude', etc.). These latter are intervening variables – constructs based on direct observation and measurement of some aspect of buying (usually in the form of a verbal report). The former are hypothetical constructs – unobservable concepts inferred from the intervening variables rather than from measures of even verbal responses and postulated at a higher level of abstraction in order to facilitate explanation (MacCorquodale and Meehl 1948).

Consumer decision-making differs according to the strength of the Attitude toward the available brands in a product class (Howard and Sheth 1969: 46–8). When Attitude strength is low, the product class is poorly defined, and the consumer is unable to discriminate among the available brands, for example, in the case of an innovative product class such as compact audio discs which were commercialized in a market where potential buyers and users are relatively unsophisticated. In such circumstances, the prospective consumer is said to engage in Extended Problem Solving (EPS). He or she is involved in the decision process, actively seeks information in order to reduce high Brand Ambiguity, and undertakes prolonged deliberation before deciding which make to buy, or indeed, whether to risk buying at all.

At a later stage, having tried several brands within the product class, the consumer develops a moderately-strong Attitude toward brands and, although there is still some ambiguity about their attributes and capabilities (possibly because new forms of the product, based on continuing technological developments are coming on to the market), and consequent information search, Choice Criteria are shaping up, Brand Comprehension is increasing, and the buyer has come to know a few brands very well, favouring them about equally. This second stage involves Limited Problem Solving (LPS). The third stage, Routine Response Behaviour (RRB), arrives when the consumer has developed strong Attitudes toward brands through experience with several. Brand Ambiguity is low and the buyer is able to discriminate among available makes, showing preference for one (or possibly two) within a clearly-defined evoked set. There is little or no external search for information and that which does reach the consumer is subject to selective attention and perception in view of his or her fund of knowledge and experience. The consumer appears to buy on impulse but this is only because of well-developed predispositions toward the available brands.[2]

Limits of comprehensive modelling

The information processing approach to consumer behaviour has been increasingly criticized in view of the untestability of many of its propositions. Critics have pointed out the lack of correspondence rules enabling decisive empirical investigation of key explanatory linkages, and the arbitrary nature of putative relationships among the variables (Bagozzi 1984; Foxall 1980a, 1980b; Jacoby 1978). Although empirical correspondence is not the only test of a theory's value, and at least one of the comprehensive theories was never intended to be tested in this way, these depictions of consumer decision-making have long been criticized for the high level of abstraction on which they rely and for their inability to describe or predict actual consumer behaviour with accuracy (Tuck 1976).

Where empirical testing has been feasible, the results have been, for the most part, disappointing. The Howard-Sheth model has been the subject of an extensive research project (Farley *et al*. 1974). Of the thirty-seven separate tests performed, only twenty-four generated any positive evidence for the theory; most of these dealt with parts of the theory rather than the whole, and the evidence is 'highly fragmentary, based for the most part on bivariate relationships, even though the hypotheses called for multiple variables.' (Engel *et al*. 1978: 552). None of the relationships tested was confirmed by all the studies which dealt with it and no study shows other than a weak relationship (Holbrook 1974: 250). These findings are in line with the broader evidence showing low correlational consistency between measures of the central prebehavioural components of such theories (notably attitude and intention) and overt purchase choice (Foxall 1983, 1984a, 1984b).

The uninvolved, uncommitted consumer

The whole assumption of an involved, decision-making, and problem-solving consumer has been questioned (Olshavsky and Granbois 1979; see also Driver and Foxall 1984, 1986; Ehrenberg 1972, 1974; Ehrenberg and Goodhardt 1989; Jacoby *et al*. 1977). Even as the comprehensive models were coming into being, Krugman (1965) suggested that television advertising does not create strong pre-purchase attitudes towards purchase but at the most small, possibly undetectable, changes in perception. At this stage, advertising does no more than inaugurate a process of slow and unenduring learning which is not sufficient for consumers to discriminate between the advertised brand and its competitors.

The learning that results from watching televised commercials is, like the learning of things that are nonsensical or unimportant, uninvolving. It is not until the consumer is in a situation where purchase is possible that this perceptual learning comes to the fore and makes brand differentiation possible. If attitudes are formed at all during this process, it is after purchase and consumption have taken place. Even then, because of the low level of personal concern usually evoked by specific brands within a product class, brand attitudes are likely to be extremely weak (Lastovicka and Bonfield 1982).

There is evidence that, under conditions of low brand commitment, the overwhelming majority of consumers make far less use of information than the comprehensive models suggest; show little sign of pre-purchase decision-making based upon the rational processing of information; use brand trial in order to obtain information about and evaluate brands; and, rather than becoming brand loyal, exhibit multi-brand purchasing within a small repertoire of brands with attributes (or characteristics) which are common to all members of their product class (Robertson 1976).

Limited information search and decision-making

Consumer research conducted over the last decade or so suggests strongly that consumers show very limited tendencies for receiving and using information, that they do not as a rule undertake rational, comparative evaluations of brands on the basis of their attributes or make final judgements among brands on the basis of such outputs of complex information processing as attitudes and intentions. From an empirical investigation of consumers' understanding and use of additional information about the nutritional value of food products, provided on the product labels, Jacoby *et al.* (1977: 126) concluded that '*the vast majority of consumers neither use nor comprehend nutrition information in arriving at food purchase decisions*'. An earlier study (Jacoby *et al.* 1974) reached the conclusion that, whilst the increased availability of information led to consumers' reporting greater satisfaction and less confusion, it also resulted in their making less economically rational decisions. This is not to argue against the provision of information: presumably consumers need to be educated in its uses and benefits (cf. Scammon 1975). But it does suggest the idea that consumers are natural information devourers should be qualified.

Consumers' comparatively small use of pre-purchase information is not confined to the situations in which they purchase non-durables such as food. Olshavsky and Granbois (1979) and

Robertson (1976) cite numerous studies which indicate that consumers drastically limit their search for information about durable products like furniture and cars, and services such as those of general practitioners. Most consumers visit a single store, fail to consult advertising, use restricted price information, consider only one make, and employ perceptions of the manufacturer's reputation and packaging rather than making evaluations of the product/service attributes to arrive at judgements of quality. The whole decision sequence assumed in comprehensive modelling appears to be absent from many instances of consumer buying. Situational variables, group pressures, and the physical arrangement of instore displays influence consumer choice at the point of sale. Many purchases of a make or brand seem not to be preceded by a decision process at all, even on the first occasion (Olshavsky and Granbois 1979). As has been noted, there is also evidence that the expected outcomes of rational decision-making – such as strong brand attitudes – are not present even when products have been purchased on many occasions (Lastovicka and Bonfield 1982; Foxall 1983, 1984a).

Product evaluation through trial

Where there is low brand commitment, it is the customer's experience with the brand during a period of trial, which might involve one or several purchases, that determines whether or not that brand becomes part of the repertoire of brands from which subsequent selections are made. Ehrenberg and Goodhardt (1989) present a simplified model of consumer behaviour which contains three phases of purchasing and consuming – awareness, trial, and repeat buying. Simple as this appears, it has proved a valuable device in both theoretical debate and commercial research (e.g. Ehrenberg 1974; Tauber 1981). Repeat buying, which is of enormous significance to the success of consumer goods, is shown as a function of trial purchase and consumption. Trial itself is a function of awareness. The ATR approach emphasizes that awareness of a new brand, and any other mental state it engenders, is not alone sufficient to guarantee the adoption (repeat purchase) of the advertised brand. Rather, awareness results at best in curiosity and trial, and it is only when the brand is in use that evaluations and comparisons are possible.

Multi-brand purchasing

Most non-durable product classes comprise several brands which are so similar to each other in terms of their basic attributes that consumers do not discriminate among them. Thus it is hardly surprising that consumers do not on the whole show total loyalty to any one brand but select from a small set of tried and tested brands which are close substitutes. There is a great deal of evidence that consumers behave in this manner. The markets for established non-durable products are characterized typically by more or less stable sales, at least in the short to medium term; the buying behaviour of individuals usually involves several brand choices but the aggregate level of market sales and brand shares is stable and predictable. Customers may change brands often – the vast majority frequently do make substitutions – but not in the sense of irrevocably switching brands, never again buying that which is 'rejected' (Ehrenberg 1972). Buyers of a given product class typically choose several brands over a sequence of purchases. Some consumers are totally loyal in the sense that they buy only one brand and never try its competitors but they make up only a small proportion of most markets. There is no evidence, however, that the majority of consumers are brand loyal in the sense of always purchasing a particular brand.

Various attempts have been made by academic consumer researchers to account for the frequently-encountered uninvolved, uncommitted consumer. Sequences other than cognition-affect-conation have been shown to describe some, perhaps most, consumer choice (e.g. Ray 1973a; Van Raaij 1984) and some authors have stressed the direct and indirect effects of situational factors (Belk 1974, 1975; Branthwaite 1984; Kakkar and Lutz 1981; Leigh and Martin 1981; Troye 1985). At the level of practical marketing, the inadequacies of cognitively-based market research to predict such aspects of consumer behaviour as innovative brand choice have been noted (Foxall 1984c, 1984d; Tauber 1981), and this has even led to questioning of the validity of customer-orientation as the basis of the marketing approach to management (Oxenfeldt and Moore 1978). Within this context, Kassarjian (1978) proposed that simpler, behaviouristic models of behaviour might capture the realities of consumer choice more accurately than the prevailing information processing approaches. An issue that arises, however, is how the extension of the range of explanations of consumer behaviour might proceed. Even if it were desirable, outright paradigm switching is rare in the social sciences, and does not in any case appear to be called for here. The following discussion assesses the role of the information processing approach in consumer research and argues for its critical retention rather that its overthrow.

Scientific progress

The strength of cognitive explanation

Evidence of the limitations of comprehensive modelling deserves to be taken seriously since, despite the values of the information processing theories, their inability to match observed consumer choice in some circumstances may indicate a level of analysis which they are incapable of handling, or a category of behaviour which they cannot readily accommodate. But the concerns of this book do not arise primarily from the lack of correspondence between cognitive consumer theory and observed patterns of consumer choice; a model may perform useful functions irrespective of the predictive validity of the theories derived from it, and it is always possible that superior techniques of measurement will emerge to justify the model. Nor do the problems raised here undermine the legitimacy of the cognitive model *per se*, though the looser uses of its method of explanation in the consumer behaviour and marketing literatures will be noted.

The objection pursued here is not that the comprehensive models and the inner-state explanations upon which they rely are flawed in some ultimate sense, requiring that they be rejected unanimously; rather, attention is turned to the consumer research community's reluctance to acknowledge actively that they are incomplete and to researchers' effective disregard of models founded upon the environmental determinants of purchase and consumption. Hence the concern is with the strength of the prevailing paradigm and the implications of its success for scientific progress in consumer psychology. Cognitivism's strength and resilience are apparent not only from its dominant influence on the development of marketing models of consumer behaviour, but also from its capacity to withstand the forceful criticisms levelled against it and, more subtly, to accommodate, absorb, and render harmless alternative perspectives, even those abundantly supported by empirical data which are, none the less, based on antithetical assumptions about the nature of human behaviour and its causation.

In spite of criticism, therefore, cognitively-based explanation in consumer research has survived fundamentally unscathed; to judge from the major journals in the field, as well as from professional periodicals, it may even have been strengthened further in the process. The comprehensive theories have been modified without deviating from the basic philosophical stance on which cognitivism is built (cf. Howard 1977, 1983 with Howard and Sheth 1969; and Engel *et al.* 1978 with Engel and Blackwell

1982, and again with Engel *et al.* 1986). As discussed further on p. 27, the capacity of the paradigm to ward off the trenchant criticisms inherent in radical behaviourism is additional evidence of its tendency to obliterate the opposition without debate.

There are, of course, good reasons for the strength of cognitivism as an explanatory device. Its closeness to the common-sense explanations of everyday discourse make it an intuitively attractive means of offering explanations of everyday behaviours such as purchasing and consuming; and the ability of consumers to describe their experiences in terms of their attitudes, wants, needs, and motives ensures that an explanation proceeds in the same terms as the description of what is explained. Moreover, a strong paradigm has undoubtedly had advantages for consumer researchers, especially in so far as it brings a measure of unity and consensus to a still young field of inquiry. In addition, the extensive use made by other social science and humanities disciplines of cognitive explanation has assisted the conceptual development of this line of consumer research by making possible the borrowing of theoretical and methodological inputs.

Yet it is the very success of the cognitive approach, manifested in its ability to avoid the critical evaluation of its fundamental assumptions, which now inhibits certain forms of theoretical progress, notably those that would benefit from a more robust and accurate acceptance of alternative explanatory systems. The answer is not to advance limited criticisms of cognitivism in practice, but to compare it critically with alternatives based on varying assumptions, a process which ought to be made easier by the recent recognition by many consumer researchers of the theory-ladenness of observation and their acceptance of the need for a relativistic perspective on consumer research. The broad intention pursued here is, therefore, to uncover strengths and weaknesses, not only of the prevailing paradigm, but of that with which it is critically compared.

Theory-ladenness

Questions of theory and metatheory are still widely considered to be irrelevant to, or even obstructive of, useful market research and the effective practice of marketing. Applied researchers and marketing practitioners often avoid what appears to be no more than academic speculation, preferring to 'let the facts speak for themselves'. But observation/practice on the one hand and theory/ metatheory on the other are inextricably linked (Kuhn 1970a; Popper 1972). Observation, no matter how casual, cannot be other than selective, reflecting a point of view; and even the most basic descriptions are invariably interpretations too, 'interpretations in the light of theory' (Popper 1980: 107; 1972: 46). Facts are not, on this view, logically prior to theoretical assumptions but are generated by them, even though at the earliest stages of an investigation those assumptions may be vague and difficult to articulate, rather than full-blown scientific theories. Popular notions notwithstanding, scientific advance does not consist in the production of successively more accurate descriptions of a subject matter that is entirely independent of the conceptions of scientists (Feyerabend 1970; Kuhn 1970b; Lakatos 1970). Whatever the nature of reality, our conceptions of it are inevitably partial and multiple, depending upon our several viewpoints and intentions.

It follows from acceptance of the theory-ladenness of observation that even the most casual observer is influenced by some framework of assumption through which 'facts' are constructed, that is, by what has become known as a scientific paradigm. Kuhn (1970a) refers to a paradigm as 'what the members of a scientific community share ... some implicit body of intertwined theoretical and methodological belief that permits selection, evaluation and criticism.' Although Kuhn's use of the term has had its ambiguities (Masterman 1970; cf. Kuhn 1970b), it suggests a frame of meta-theoretical reference within which theory is derived, by which empirical investigation is governed, and through which theory and observation are related in the process of explanation. The paradigm within which normal science proceeds acts as an official ideology which is not questioned by investigators except at infrequent times of crisis, when hitherto acceptable explanations are patently unable to provide an account of the observable that the scientific community as a whole can agree upon. The subsequent search for an alternative paradigm ends only when another generally approved framework of assumption, conceptualization, and analysis, a professional *Weltanschauung* which generates appropriate scientific puzzles, is sufficiently established to permit the resumption of normal science (cf. Lakatos 1970).[3]

Scientific relativism acknowledges the inevitability of a plurality of paradigms and methods in social research. Such research is theory-laden if only because the limited and personal as well as the professional aims of investigators, variously shaped by their social and professional environments, determine not only the theoretical and methodological standpoints from which their work is undertaken but also, to a degree, what they observe from those standpoints. The understanding that the behavioural scientist, theoretician, or empiricist, constructs or invents rather than discovers the social world under investigation has steadily gained ground among consumer researchers during the 1980s (e.g. Anderson 1983; Bagozzi 1984; Peter and Olson 1983). The decade has witnessed repeated calls for the extension of the range of methodological and ontological perspectives available to the scientific community of consumer researchers (for example, Brinberg and Lutz 1986; Brown and Fisk 1984; Kassarjian 1978, 1986; Olson 1982). It has also been argued persuasively that there is room for all styles of scientific endeavour reflecting the investigative and interpretive idiosyncrasies of individual researchers, and something to be gained from every paradigm's peculiar ways of seeing and, correspondingly, not seeing (Hirschman 1985a).

Critical relativism

The natural proliferation of theoretical perspectives suggests that there can be no absolute standard for determining the contribution of one paradigm to scientific advance compared with that of another. After all, there are only limited criteria, useful in some research contexts but inexpedient in others, for the intra-paradigmatic comparative evaluation of alternative explanations (cf. Bell and Kristol 1981; Borger and Cioffi 1970; Chapman and Jones 1980; Goodson and Morgan 1976; Lakatos and Musgrave 1970; Robinson 1962). What attention has been given to the theoretical development of cognitive consumer psychology has been focused for the most part upon increasing its internal efficiency: researchers have been encouraged, for example, to give greater attention to the demonstration of construct validity in their empirical work, to the establishment of correspondence rules in theory construction, and to related neglected concerns (Bagozzi 1984; Jacoby 1978).

Attention has also been accorded the criteria by which competing hypotheses within a given theoretical structure might be judged, including parsimony, predictive validity, clarity, empirical support, fruitfulness, and logical precision (Goodson and Morgan 1976; Paxton 1976). There are often disagreements over whether any of these deserves general pre-eminence and the need to trade one off against another (e.g. Midgley 1984; Silver 1984), but there is some evidence of the value of each under specific circumstances (Valentine 1982). However, in view of the existence of a multiplicity of competing explanatory frameworks, each founded upon a different ontology and methodology, one of the problems of ensuring scientific progress is that of critically comparing whole paradigms one with another.

It is surprising then that, for all their emphasis on pluralism, calls for relativism in consumer research lack any seriously developed sense of the dynamic contribution to the growth of knowledge made by the deliberate clash of entrenched positions. On the whole, they have tended to ignore the need for an active interplay of competing paradigms, the consequent disordering and subsequent reordering of explanations stimulating the emergence of new integrations and syntheses as well as clearer understandings of the original paradigms. Instead, whilst the predominant approach has been to welcome diversity for its own sake – indeed, not only to tolerate but to celebrate the aim of extending the number and scope of distinctive explanations – the outcome has been to encapsulate those available, each within its own ontological outlook, separating it thereby from the rest. Anderson (1986), for example, critically examines four positivistic paradigms derived from cognitivism, behaviourism, structuralism, and economics, apparently ignoring the possibility that in the capacity of one explanation to impinge critically upon another lies a crucial component of scientific advance. Indeed, Anderson argues that fusion between these programmes is impossible precisely because the explanatory variables they severally employ are not equivalent. Expressions of attitude and intentions, for instance, which are held by cognitivists to cause behaviour are construed by radical behaviourists as internal verbal behaviours, epiphenomenal effects of causative environmental stimuli rather than internal causes of overt action (cf. Mandler 1985; Skinner 1945).

But the equivalence or otherwise of the explanations provided by these variables ought surely to be decided through critical examination of the roles they perform in specific instances of theory and research rather than by abstract reasoning applied to every variable in all paradigms. The premature assumption of what Anderson calls the 'disjunction at the ontological level' allegedly displayed by these various sources of explanation can easily preclude interaction and reduction, leaving an impression of an inevitable plurality of explanations that are forever clinically separated from one another.

Active interplay

By contrast, Feyerabend (1970) maintains that scientific progress (however conceived by the investigator) requires not only the proliferation of incompatible, even incommensurable, explanations but also the 'active interplay' of these methodologically contradictory approaches. Competing theories are spawned, on this view, not intermittently during the crises which precede periodic overthrows of one paradigm by another (Kuhn 1970a), but continuously. The normal science component of an intellectual community's work does not rule out the active influence of alternative, potentially subversive theoretical systems; rather, the normal and revolutionary components coexist and their usual relationship is that of the dynamic interaction of tenaciously-held but competing viewpoints. 'Science as we know it', Feyerabend writes, 'is not a temporal succession of normal periods and periods of proliferation; it is their juxtaposition.' Hence the true relationship between normal and proliferative modes is 'one of simultaneity and interaction' (Feyerabend 1970: 209).

It is not necessary to embrace Feyerabend's advocacy of 'epistemological anarchy', or to contend with him that 'anything goes', in order to profit from his essential point that scientific progress depends to an extent on a deliberate proliferation of theoretical perspectives and their mutual encounter, from which flow novel explanations, the resuscitation of unfashionable theories, the forcing into the open of taken for granted assumptions that underlie accepted theories and the critical comparison of a widely-accepted theory with counter-intuitive alternative explanations. No paradigm has a monopoly on validity, methodological purity and completeness, or wholeness; none is infallible or capable of containing the entire truth; any unquestioned paradigms are held through prejudice rather than understanding (Feyerabend 1987; Jary 1988).

Furthermore, an 'active interplay of various tenaciously held views' is necessary, given the theory-dependency of observation and empirical evidence, to an assessment of the strengths, weaknesses, and scope of each paradigm. It stimulates the generation of novel data, and provides critical insight into the reality of the tenets of an otherwise unquestioned theoretical approach. Since no theory, taken alone, can account for all of the observed facts, additional explanations should be welcomed rather than avoided or refuted according to arbitrary rules of scientific method that in fact restrict intellectual enterprise (Feyerabend 1975: 30–2).

It is interesting in view of these sentiments to note that several recent advocates of relativistic pluralism in consumer research (e.g. Anderson 1986; Deshpande 1983; O'Shaughnessy and Holbrook 1988) have tended to view their mission as wholly 'post-positivistic', some of them proposing the development of subjectivist, interpretivist accounts apparently to the exclusion of systems based on the search for objectivity (or, more accurately, intersubjectivity) such as cognitivism and behaviourism. However, the argument pursued here is based on the view that all sources of explanation are essential to as complete an understanding of consumer behaviour as is currently humanly possible, and that such completeness will suffer if any is arbitrarily ignored. This is not, of course, to argue against semiotic, hermeneutic, or other interpretivist approaches, but for comprehensiveness and the active interplay of all competing paradigms. It rejects the view that 'relativism' is synonymous with 'post-positivism' or in any way an antonym of positivism.

This is not meant to lead to either an uncritical eclecticism or the exclusive adoption of positivism, but it strongly emphasizes that consumer research ought not to exclude any available explanation from its intellectual mêlée. An understanding of relativism that embraces only 'post-positivist' explanations is, therefore, not consistent with the critical relativism advocated in this book which rules out no methodology or ontology from the quest for a comprehensive understanding of consumer behaviour. Nor does it imply that the individual researcher ought to embrace each and every source of explanation. Not only is the necessary cognitive capacity unavailable: even if an individual could simultaneously hold a large number of paradigms in preparation for so comprehensive an information processing task as this would imply, he or she would find it impossible to assess critically either the theories they presented or the data generated by them. The principle of tenaciously held individual views is as essential to a progressive active interplay as proliferation (Feyerabend 1975). It is the discipline, not the individual which ought to contain a multiplicity of explanations. It is the scientific community which must provide the forum for their critical interaction.

Paradigm erosion

Because no single paradigm can provide a full explanation of human choice, not only is a degree of natural proliferation of explanatory systems inevitable but so also is a tendency towards their synthesis to produce novel theories. Active interplay of the sort intended here does not leave the mutually-impinging paradigms where it found them: social science advances through 'paradigm erosion' (Foxall 1984a, 1987a). The integration of existing paradigms to produce new syntheses is seen as a consequence of the perennial jostling for position of competing philosophical and methodological ideas and ideologies in a social scientific system that contains opposed interests, viewpoints, and standpoints. This is especially likely when theories generated within an established paradigm are judged for one reason or other to offer inadequate explanations of observed phenomena.

For instance, when existing theories are disconfirmed by failure to predict with required accuracy, their assumptions are questioned and theories based on antithetical bases of assumption may be preferred; or, new technologies of data gathering and analysis may lead to novel observations which support alternative explanations (such as the emergence of the heliocentric view of the universe); or, a new theory might provide a means of extending the scope of current explanations to new orders of observed phenomena (as in the application of risk analysis to the study of consumer behaviour: Ingene and Hughes, 1985). In all of these cases, the appropriate analogy is that of constant erosion of the existing wisdom through its interaction with disparate concepts rather than that of intermittent revolution. An interesting outcome of such erosion is that, whereas paradigms can usually accommodate alternative viewpoints, eventually a fragmenting of the scientific community seems inevitable, separating the 'purists' who continue to accept one or other of the conventional approaches, from the 'innovators' who accept the new theory or synthesis.

Relativism that provokes such erosive interaction of paradigms contributes in three ways to scientific progress. It provides (a) critical standpoints by which prevailing theories may be judged, leading to new understandings of both the possibilities and limitations of all theories considered; (b) new syntheses of existing theories as well as new theories; (c) new data and interpretations of data. As a result, it makes available the means of ascertaining whether Theory A' is (i) superior to Theory A in some respect (for example, explains more observations, leads to the collection of novel data), (ii) equivalent to Theory A (its hypotheses amount to the same thing irrespective of terminology), or (iii) part of a wider synthesis with Theory A in which both work in complementary fashion to arrive at a more comprehensive explanation. In the process, the explicative power of each contributing paradigm is both enhanced and circumscribed as a result of comparative interaction with the others.

Examples of paradigm erosion

'Creeping cognitivism'

A current example of paradigm erosion is the cognitivist challenge to behaviourist explanation adopted by certain operant psychologists to account for the experimental performance of animals.

Some descriptive behaviourists, the distinguishing feature of whose scientific community is the avoidance of causal reference to intrapsychic events to explain objectively observed behaviour, explicate observed patterns of choice in laboratory animals in terms of the subjects' cognitive structure and functioning (Blackman 1983a; Hulse *et al*. 1978; Lowe 1983; this is interesting not because it is novel – Tolman (1932) – but for its resurgence). The consequent split in the scientific community, between those of its members who rigorously retain the radical behaviourist philosophy to explain animal behaviour and those responsible for the 'creeping cognitivism' that casts the same events in mentalistic terms (Blackman 1983b), illustrates both the partial erosion of the operant paradigm and its capacity to be stretched by the incorporation of alternative concepts in the formation of a novel synthesis (Morris *et al*. 1982; Branch and Malagodi 1980; Knapp 1982; Michael 1980; Trice 1983).

'Behavioural economics'

A second example is the integration of concepts from economics with the experimental analysis of behaviour in the subfield known as 'behavioural economics'; researchers in this area have successfully employed the techniques of one discipline to test hypotheses derived from the other and to extend the scope of both. While some economists and psychologists have gladly embraced the synthesis, the majority in each camp have retained their original disciplinary allegiances by ignoring or trivializing the new findings (Castro and Weingarten 1970; Hursh 1980; Scitovsky 1976). However, presumably because the findings have not threatened either of these well-established disciplines but rather strengthened both, the result has been a fruitful integration of concepts rather than a disruptive incursion into one or other; as a result, dissenters have viewed the experimental evidence as superfluous rather than illegitimate (Kagel 1987).

'Cognitive behaviour modification'

A third example (described further in the Appendix) is that of cognitive behaviour modification which incorporates techniques derived from both cognitive and behavioural therapies as a means of effecting personal adjustments. In this case, the scientific community has split into two broad camps of 'purists' (therapists and theorists who prefer one or other of the original therapies and its accompanying explanation of behaviour change), who can be clearly distinguished from the 'integrationists' (who embrace a synthesis of both techniques and explanations) (Dush *et al*. 1983; Mahoney and Kazdin 1979; Meichenbaum 1978; Wilson 1982).

Rationale

The purpose of this book is to explore the role of active interplay in a critical relativist consumer research, thereby promoting the erosion not only of the dominant cognitive paradigm, but also of the contending behaviourist paradigm, in pursuit of a more theoretically refined subdiscipline. The chosen vehicle for this discussion is the experimental analysis of behaviour (EAB), a paradigm that comprises three broad elements (Skinner 1938, 1974). The first is a philosophy of science, radical behaviourism, which explains behaviour by reference to its environmental consequences, denying causal significance to intrapersonal (mental, neural, or hypothetical) events. The second is an empirical/experimental technique, operant conditioning, in which the rate of emission of a response is brought under the control of antecedent and contingent stimuli. And the third is a research strategy, based on inductive generalization, and involving the intensive analysis of the behaviours of single subjects (Blackman 1974, 1981).

The EAB is not the only paradigm available for the purpose of critically examining the prevailing wisdom. Marxism, psycho-analysis, and other varieties of behaviourism are just a few of the alternatives which have both been explored already by consumer researchers and which may yet play a fuller role in the critical interplay of explanations. This book concentrates upon the EAB for several reasons. First, radical behaviourism and operant psychology are founded upon postulates about human nature and its analysis which are not just different from but diametrically opposed to those of the cognitive paradigm. They are, in addition, components of one of the most carefully articulated and empirically tested psychological paradigms. As a result, they are capable of stimulating an active clash of explanations, each paradigm having far-reaching implications for the other. Second, the EAB is concerned with instrumental behaviour and thereby shares an affinity with marketing which makes it particularly suitable for the analysis of economic behaviour. Third, whilst operant psychology has made some impact upon marketing and consumer research during the 1980s, it has not received critical philosophical attention from academics in these fields. In view of the expanding interest in non-cognitive explanations of consumer choice among a relatively small number of researchers, this last assertion requires further comment.

The role of the EAB in a relativistic perspective on consumer research is especially pertinent in view of the strength of the prevailing cognitivist paradigm which currently constitutes the normal science component of consumer psychology (Hirschman

1985b; Kassarjian 1982). The Recent attempts to challenge the pre-eminence of this prevailing model by extending the range of social scientific paradigms available for consumer research have come from intellectual sources that, like cognitivism itself, emphasize intrapersonal influences on choice (for example, Hirschman and Holbrook 1986). Whilst there is no intention here of criticizing this, it is important to stress that a relativistic approach should provide challenges to orthodoxy that derive from theoretical standpoints based unequivocally upon alternative models of human nature and behaviour. The antipodal explanation provided by the EAB and, in particular, its philosophical basis, radical behaviour-ism, is particularly relevant to this quest for the following reasons.

First, accounts of the EAB in the marketing and consumer behaviour literatures have been largely confined to discussions of operant conditioning. In the absence of formal recognition of the radical behaviourist ontology and methodology by which operant conditioning phenomena have generally been interpreted, such accounts have proceeded atheoretically. Several authors have chosen to concentrate upon the marketing and promotional im-plications of operant conditioning: whilst this is in itself a noble concern, it is of limited relevance in a critical relativist research programme. As a result, little mention has been made of the contrasting models of human behaviour presented by descriptive behaviourism and cognitivism, and their distinct implications for one another and for understanding, predicting, and influencing choice. This atheoretical stance is also evident from the way in which several consumer behaviour texts have dealt with be-havioural learning, locating it within accounts of information processing alongside descriptions of cognitive learning, apparently assuming them to be complementary components of learning processes or perhaps viable alternatives within an overarching cognitivistic theoretical framework.

Second, discussions in these literatures have often seriously misrepresented the character of radical behaviourist explanation by denying its rejection of mental causation. Several authors of texts and of empirical and theoretical papers include 'attitudes', 'wants', and 'motives' without explanation as part of their accounts of operant conditioning (for example, Engel *et al*. 1986; Berry 1969; Berry and Kunkel 1970; Kunkel and Berry 1968). Others deliberately blend cognitive and operant concepts for convenience but without theoretical or methodological reason (Loudon and Della Bitta 1983). As a result, central concepts of the operant conditioning framework, such as negative reinforcement, have been misdefined (e.g. Engel *et al*. 1986; Nord and Peter 1980;

Rothschild and Gaidis 1981; Schiffman and Kanuk 1983. The same is true in psychology: *see* Todd and Morris 1983). Some authors have committed themselves to forms of learning theory that formally incorporate cognitive as well as environmental variables, such as social learning theory and, whilst this represents an understandable simplifying choice, it is again essentially atheoretical, no reasons other than personal preference being adduced to justify it. In view of all of these misrepresentations and analytical choices, the full impact of a rigorously descriptive behaviourism on consumer research has been avoided. Its contribution to relativistic consumer research remains to be gauged.

Third, consumer behaviour texts and discussants of operant conditioning in the marketing literature have taken over uncritically the assumption that principles of operant conditioning established in animal experimentation can be applied directly in accounts of human consumer choice. In extrapolating directly from the experimental research findings on animal operant behaviour to the human context, consumer researchers have ignored recent results from experiments on human operant performance which have broader implications for consumer research than animal studies. As a result of this empirical research, the degree to which human behavioural change is subject to direct exposure to reinforcement contingencies is the subject of considerable debate among psychologists (Kagel 1987; Lowe and Horne 1985; Pierce and Epling 1983). It is essential, therefore, that consumer researchers appreciate the limitations as well as the contributions to explanation inherent in the EAB paradigm.

The comparative and critical evaluation of research paradigms for consumer behaviour cannot, of course, be confined to a debate between cognitivism and radical behaviourism. But these issues support the view that that debate is a useful starting point. In exploring the philosophical foundation of operant conditioning on the basis of an accurate representation of its ontology and methodology, and examining the implications of research on human as well as animal operant performance, this book seeks to elucidate the relevance of the EAB for marketing and consumer research. However, despite the ability of the EAB to integrate viewpoints from economics, psychology, and marketing, its explicatory and integrative potential can be easily overlooked. In exploring the nature and boundaries of that potential, this book first compares and contrasts an EAB approach to consumer research with the prevailing cognitivism, drawing attention to the explicatory and empirical benefits of a behavioural analysis. It goes on to consider the deficiencies of the EAB as a comprehensive paradigm for the study of human choice. Not surprisingly in a relativistic framework, the belief that concepts of intrapersonal causation can be entirely abandoned in favour of reliance upon the explicative power of environmental variables is shown to be untenable. Consumer and marketing research depend upon both types of variable and require elements of both types of explanation. However, the book demonstrates that the neglected behavioural dimension offers insights into marketing behaviour which should no longer be denied by investigators.

The concept of paradigm erosion implies that scientific (sub) communities representing each of the possible perspectives will emerge or be maintained in the process of active interplay. It is, therefore, to be expected that both 'pure' radical behaviourist and 'pure' cognitivist views will survive this kind of debate and may actually be strengthened thereby. But, while acknowledging that both of these views will remain available, intact, to consumer researchers who wish to employ them as distinctive paradigms in their own right, it is likely that the interaction of cognitive and behaviourist metatheories will additionally produce both full syntheses and more limited theoretical modifications of existing explanations derived from the influence of one paradigm on another, increasing in the process their applicability to the analysis of consumer behaviour. The analysis which follows, leads to an example of the second of these possibilities: the Behavioural Perspective Model developed in Chapter 5 remains faithful to the general analytical framework of the EAB but modifies it theoretically in order to take account of the criticisms presented by inner-state theories. The outcome of this limited synthesis is a behaviour-based approach which retains the unique insights of the EAB but avoids the worst excesses of descriptive behaviourism through sensitivity to the undeniable claims of inner-state theories.

In the spirit of relativism, the following chapters ask 'How far can we go with operant psychology before we have to turn to other forms of explanation? And what can we learn from this paradigm about the nature of consumer choice?' This is not a question of testing competing hypotheses or theories by reference to some relevant but limited criterion such as parsimony, but that of contrasting alternative philosophies of explanation in order to discover the implications each holds for the other. The quest is not for a single, unified theory of consumer behaviour: rather, the intention is to increase the range of explanatory possibilities. This procedure avoids the extremes inherent in the first two quotations at the beginning of the book: the shackled intellectual imperialism imposed by savants, and the uncritically subjectivist view that there is no world of investigation at all independent of human imagination. By extending the range of intellectual tools available to consumer researchers, the book attempts to avoid a situation in which, equipped only with cognitive outlooks, consumer researchers see all behaviour as either the outcome of information processing or attributable to abstract constructions of innate traits of character.

Chapter two

The experimental analysis of behaviour

It is clear that the behavioral sciences have not yet fulfilled their promise. There are economists who question whether there is a science of economics, and if we can judge by international strategies in the world today, governments make little use of political science. Anthropologists, sociologists and social psychologists grow increasingly uneasy about their fields. ... In most of these fields there is no shortage of facts, and efforts are continually made to discover meaningful relations among them, mathematical or otherwise. What is missing is a coherent theory of human behavior.

(Skinner 1978: 94)

Introduction

The experimental analysis of behaviour is so closely related to the work of B. F. Skinner that it is sometimes known as 'Skinnerian psychology'. Whilst he does not write as *the* behaviourist (Skinner 1974), however, and significant theoretical and experimental contributions to the EAB have been made by others, this chapter treats radical behaviourism and its experimental base principally from the point of view of Skinner's writings.[1] It is, after all, his thought which is employed in Chapter three to present a critique of the prevailing cognitive approach to consumer choice, which is itself criticized in Chapter four, and which, modified as a result of that criticism, provides the basis of an alternative model of consumer behaviour in Chapter five. It is essential, therefore, at the outset to understand clearly and accurately the foundations of Skinner's contribution and its place in psychological theory. The three elements that combine to form the experimental analysis of behaviour (EAB) – radical behaviourism, operant conditioning, and a single-subject research strategy – are logically separable (Blackman 1974). For instance, many experimental psychologists employ techniques derived from Skinner's (1938) methodology without subscribing to the philosophy of science denoted by radical behaviourism (Skinner 1963b: 951; 1974). But they combine to form a unified paradigm for psychological research and explanation. Indeed, the EAB is probably the most fully developed framework of conceptualization and analysis in the behavioural sciences.

This chapter is primarily concerned with the first two elements listed above: the proposition that behavioural science should focus on the explanation of observable behaviour in terms of contingent environmental stimuli; and the process whereby rate of responding is brought under the control of consequent stimuli (reinforcers and punishers) in the presence of antecedent signals that particular outcomes will follow the performance of specific actions. The third component, the derivation of generalizations about behaviour from the study of small numbers of subjects (rather than the testing of deductive hypotheses through the comparison of inter-group statistical differences), is already a component of qualitative marketing research and transcends the present account. Therefore, while it is recognized that operant analysis implies methodological individualism, the book does not explicitly deal with its emphasis on a single-subject research strategy. The following section discusses the distinguishing features of radical behaviourism, locating its unique approach within the spectrum of psychological explanations, and the nature of operant conditioning, illustrated wherever possible in terms of consumer choice.

Radical behaviourism

Epistemological location

Psychology contains a range of theoretical and metatheoretical positions extending from the entirely objective, whose adherents attempt to apply the methods of the physical sciences directly to the analysis of animal and human behaviour, to the wholly subjective, which derives its subject matter from the taken for granted world of personal experience. Between these behaviouristic and phenomenological poles, the continuum of available explanations represents numerous hybrids (Marx and Hillix 1979; Hillner 1984; Leahey 1987, for example). This situation is broadly analogous to the range of neoclassical microeconomic models in which the theories of pure monopoly and pure competition are the limiting cases. Some economists are unwilling to extend the repertoire of micro-theory beyond these (e.g. Friedman 1953;

Stigler 1949), arguing that they are sufficient not only for the analysis of the extreme market structures from which they take their names but also for the understanding of intermediate real-world market structures. Other economists, such as Chamberlin (1933) have, nevertheless, devised specialized models for the study of these mediating forms of monopolistically competitive markets.

Among psychological paradigms, descriptive behaviourism represents one limiting case containing research programmes for the analysis of behaviour exclusively in terms of heredity and environment; as noted, an equally extreme phenomenology describes the other limit. Between these counterpositions lie models that rely more or less upon behaviouristic objectivism or phenomenological subjectivism, giving various weightings to the importance of intrapsychic factors such as information processing and the formation of values, and environmental influences such as physical cues and rewards. (In contrast to these psychological theories, the polar theories of microeconomics are cast in terms of the same variables – costs, revenues, maximization, etc. – and the same underlying model of human nature, 'economic man'. The psychological theories at different points in the spectrum posit distinct models of man and emphasize the need to measure quite different variables. Moreover, each theory attempts to embrace the entire gamut of human nature and behaviour.)

Figure 2.1 indicates the range of psychological theory with which this discussion is principally concerned, distinguishing them according to the extent to which their underlying models attribute the causation of behaviour to intrapersonal (usually cognitive) or extrapersonal (environmental) influences. Radical behaviourism is distinguishable both from cognitivism and from other behavioural theories, primarily, as will be seen, in its treatment of private or 'within-the-skin' events and processes.

The essence of behaviourism is its exploration of the nature of a psychology based on objectivity and empiricism, 'an elaboration of what it means for psychology to be a natural science' (Zuriff 1985: 8). By objectivity, Zuriff implies that the science should proceed independently of the subjective prejudices, tastes, and private opinions of the scientist, that findings be precise, unambiguous, and replicable. Empiricalness requires that psychological facts be 'derived through the senses, preferably through careful perception, and ideally through experimentally controlled observation' (pp. 8–9). But behaviourism comes in several varieties. Hillner (1984) proposes five dimensions on which the various behaviourisms – including 'cognitive behaviourism' which subsumes the information processing paradigm, and which in some forms is

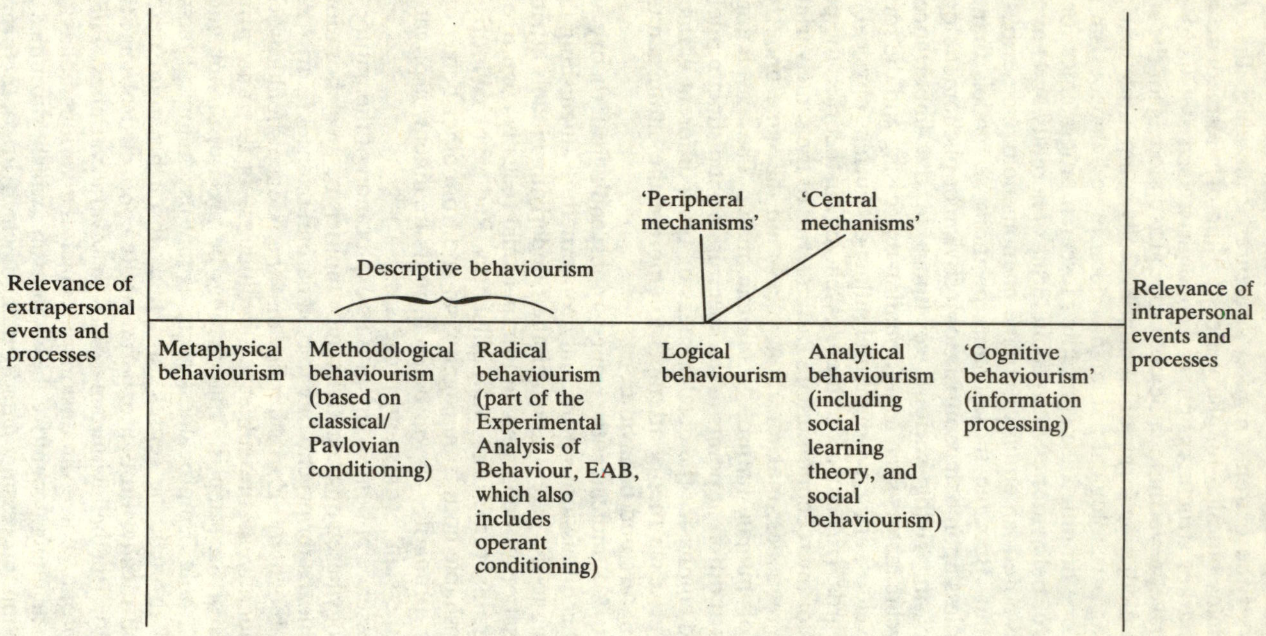

	Descriptive behaviourism		'Peripheral mechanisms' 'Central mechanisms'		
Metaphysical behaviourism	Methodological behaviourism (based on classical/ Pavlovian conditioning)	Radical behaviourism (part of the Experimental Analysis of Behaviour, EAB, which also includes operant conditioning)	Logical behaviourism	Analytical behaviourism (including social learning theory, and social behaviourism)	'Cognitive behaviourism' (information processing)

Relevance of extrapersonal events and processes

Relevance of intrapersonal events and processes

Figure 2.1 Varieties of behaviourism

exempt from the principles of objectivity and empiricalness – can be usefully distinguished and comparatively defined. These are: the nature of mind-body relationships; the relevance of mind/ consciousness; the location of the primary determinants of behaviour; the primary locus of internal mediators; and the reducibility of central mediators to behavioural terms.

The nature of mind-body

Whereas *metaphysical behaviourists* deny the existence of mind and adhere to a strict monism, *descriptive behaviourists* acknowledge the existence of intrapersonal ('mental' events in other explanatory systems) events but treat them as epiphenomenal, that is, collateral products of the external causes of behaviour and not as causes in their own right.

Relevance of mental events

Mental epiphenomenalism is not concerned with cognition as such: it assumes no nonphysical 'mind stuff' but assumes that the epiphenomena are physical and material. *Methodological behaviourists* investigate behaviour without reference to consciousness or mental events, believing that while they exist they are outside the scope of a scientific analysis because their private nature puts them beyond the public verification which is the hallmark of natural science. Hence Watson's (1913: 158) claim that

> Psychology as the behaviorist sees it is a purely objective experimental branch of natural science. Its theoretical goal is the prediction and control of behavior. Introspection forms no part of its methods, nor is the scientific value of data dependent upon the readiness with which they lend themselves to interpretation in terms of consciousness.

Radical behaviourists would agree with much of this but argue that so-called mental processes – for which Skinner (1974) substitutes the term 'within-the-skin' events – are of empirical interest and that, although not causative, they are important dependent variables that must be explained by a science of behaviour.

Location of primary determinants of behaviour

Descriptive behaviourism (a category which includes both Watson's methodological behaviourism and Skinner's radical behaviourism) attributes behaviour entirely to external environmental causes; its 'immediate' interpretation eschews the idea that internal mediators can explain responses. *Radical behaviourism's* dependent variable, the effect it seeks to explain, is observed behaviour; its independent variables, the causes of observed behaviour, are consequential stimuli located in the environment, that is, external controlling conditions, of which behaviour is the function (Skinner 1953a: 35). *Logical behaviourism*, on the other hand, gives a place to internal mediators of stimuli and responses; its 'ultimate' interpretation permits the explicative incorporation of intervening variables and hypothetical constructs (MacCorquodale and Meehl 1948).

Primary locus of internal mediators

Logical behaviourists differ according to the location they ascribe to internal mediators. Hull (1951, 1952) and Guthrie (1935) claimed that mediators were confined to 'peripheral mechanisms' such as the muscles and glands, whereas Tolman's (1932) *purposive behaviourism* is based on the functioning of 'central mechanisms', cognitive processes such as cognitive maps, expectancies, and hypotheses.

Reducibility of central mediators

Finally, some 'central mechanism logical behaviourists' claim that cognitive events can be reduced to behavioural or peripheral terms (*analytical behaviourists*) whilst others (*cognitive behaviourists*) deny this, claiming that cognitive processes are not the result of conditioning or appropriational learning but are the primary, irreducible determinants of overt behaviours. They claim, therefore, that intrapersonal cognitive events and processes are causative (independent) variables in their own right (Hillner 1984: 107). This latter position is that which has guided the development of information processing models of human choice and decision-making for over three decades and which has profoundly influenced management science and economics as well as psychology and marketing (Jacoby 1983; T. P. Roth 1987; Simon 1983).

'Radical epiphenomenalism'

In rejecting teleological explanations, radical behaviourism denies that an organism acts in a given way with the intention or expectation of producing particular consequences or reaching predetermined goals, or that it acts purposefully or in line with attitudes, intentions, or other outputs of an information processing system or with traits of personality (cf. Dennett 1988; Fodor 1988; Searle 1983, 1984). Rather, a behavioural response is explained when the factors that control its rate of emission have been identified such that the response can be accurately predicted and controlled (Skinner 1950). In sum, 'by arranging a reinforcing consequence, we increase the rate at which a response occurs; by eliminating the consequence, we decrease the rate. These are the processes of operant conditioning and extinction' (Skinner 1963a: 508). But, as Skinner goes on to explain, a response and the consequence that is contingent upon its performance are only temporally related: the response produces the consequence only in the sense that the consequence follows it. Radical behaviourism is a form of operationism, defined by Skinner (1945: 270) as 'the practice of talking about (1) one's observations, (2) the manipulative and calculational procedures involved in making them, (3) the logical and mathematical steps which intervene between earlier and later statements, and (4) *nothing else*'. More particularly, the nature of radical behaviourist explanation which distinguishes it from other philosophies of science can be summarized in four basic tenets derived from Skinner's (1945, 1953a, 1963b, 1974) work (Creel 1980).

First, it assumes that private events, whilst real, are non-causative. What individuals report as feelings that arise when they behave in a particular way (for example, feelings of confidence when buying familiar products) do exist but consist literally of the individual feeling physical events within his or her body. The timing of these events, coming just as the behaviour is performed, easily gives rise to the notion that they are the causes of behaviour but they are actually no more than collateral products of the contingencies of reinforcement that occasion and strengthen the purchase response (Skinner 1974: 47; 1971). Such within-the-skin phenomena are not 'unobservables': although they are not publicly available, they are observable, in the case of human beings, by the individual who feels them and learns to identify them verbally, accurately or inaccurately, to other people who have been responsible for his verbal conditioning or who have been similarly conditioned to the 'meanings' of words and gestures. A scientific analysis should, Skinner argues, include and account for these private events in the same terms it employs to explain public behaviours, that is, on the understanding that they are never other than dependent variables the causes of which are to be found within the environment rather than within-the-skin.

Second, events occurring within-the-skin have no non-physical properties, having 'the same kinds of physical dimensions as public events' (Skinner 1945) and distinguished only by their limited accessibility. For this reason, radical behaviourism is sometimes equated with metaphysical behaviourism (Marx and Hillix 1979; Leahey 1987); however, whilst metaphysical behaviourism rests primarily upon a dogmatic assertion, radical behaviourism is essentially empirically-based (Eysenck 1972: 291).

Third, although Skinner embraces the epiphenomenological view that private events are collateral products that do not determine behaviour, he is not an epiphenomenalist in the classic sense since he rejects the dualistic idea that private events are non-physical. Creel (1980: 35) refers to the Skinnerian view as 'radical epiphenomenalism'.

Fourth, private events are, to the radical behaviourist, inaccessible: experienced feelings, dreams, memories, and so on, are not empirically available for scientific analysis including physiological investigation (though they remain relevant and require explanation).

Mode of explanation

A response which acts upon the environment and produces consequences is known as an operant response; consequences which increase the subsequent rate of emission of such a response in similar circumstances are known as reinforcers; those which reduce its rate of performance, as punishers (Skinner 1974). The setting for reinforcement (or punishment), contingent upon the emission of an operant, is frequently marked by prebehavioural stimuli that have been repeatedly paired with the performance of the response in question and its consequences. These antecedent stimuli tend in due course to mark the occasion for discriminated behaviour on the part of the individual, that is, he or she comes to emit the previously reinforced response only when this stimulus (or a similar stimulus) is present; or to avoid making the previously-punished response. These elements of the situation which signal the opportunity for reinforcement (or punishment) are known as discriminative stimuli.

This summary of the radical behaviourist paradigm is a description of the 'contingencies of reinforcement', that is, (i) the specific behaviour (response) in question, (ii) the situation (setting conditions) in which it occurs, (iii) those of its consequences that affect the rate at which the response subsequently occurs, and (iv) the relationships among them. The paradigm thus comprises the following 'three-term contingency' (Skinner 1953a: 110):

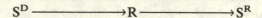

$$S^D \longrightarrow R \longrightarrow S^R$$

where S^D = discriminative stimulus
R = response, and
S^R = the reinforcing stimulus.

This is not an automatic sequence, however. The presence of a discriminative stimulus increases the probability that a response belonging to the relevant operant class will be emitted, but such occasions only predispose, they do not compel (Skinner 1953b, 1971). Nor is the assumption of a relationship between response and consequence indicative of teleological explanation. The organism does not behave in a particular manner because it plans, intends, or purposes to obtain a reinforcing consequence. Rather, radical behaviourism explains the rate of current responding, directly and parsimoniously, by reference to the consequences that have followed such behaviour in the past. The probabilistic nature of the relationships described by the three-term contingency is emphasized by Blackman (1983a) who summarizes the paradigm as:

$$A \; : \; B \; : \; C$$

where A = antecedent conditions
  B = behaviour, and
  C = consequences.

The colons infer a correlational relationship in each case: as Blackman points out, particular consequences may follow behaviour only occasionally or after delay; but they may fail to reinforce the response or may decrease rather than increase its rate of emission. The usual representation of the contingencies in terms of a progression from S^D to R to S^R is, therefore, one of several possible subsets of Blackman's A:B:C, that in which the antecedent conditions act as discriminative stimuli and in which the consequences of responding reinforce the operant.

The identification of the environmental factors which affect the rate at which behavioural responses occur provides, as noted above, an explanation of the behaviour (Skinner 1950). But, in the experimental analysis of behaviour, explanation and technology run together: the aim and the test of science are the ability to predict and control, and explanation follows from the performance of these functions rather than the development of theories that infer the mental precursors of what is observed. Hence

Behavior which operates upon the environment to produce consequences ('operant' behavior) can be studied by arranging environments in which specific consequences are contingent upon it. The contingencies under investigation have become steadily more complex, and one by one, they are taking over the explanatory functions previously assigned to personalities, states of mind, feelings, traits of character, purposes and intentions (Skinner 1971: 18).

Some definitional elaborations

Operants on the one hand and reinforcers/punishers on the other are defined in mutually dependent ways: responses should not be labelled operant unless their rate of emission is influenced by their consequences; no event is a reinforcer or punisher unless it consistently affects the rate of emission of a preceding response. So reinforcers/punishers are functionally defined in relation to operants; that is, they are said to reinforce or punish because they are related to changes in the rate of performance of actions, not because they are intrinsically rewarding or painful. This does not necessarily imply a circular definition since not all responses produce reinforcing or punishing consequences; some stimuli produce changes in the rate of responding, while others do not. Those that do are known as reinforcers/punishers; those that do not, are known as neutral (Skinner 1938: 62; Meehl 1950). Further, the fact that reinforcers can be independently defined by empirical means, described in more detail later in this chapter, also serves to redress the charge of circularity (Premack 1965, 1971).

Note also that the elements of the three-term contingency refer not to individual examples of stimuli and responses but to classes thereof. Several somewhat different responses comprise an operant when each response is controlled by the same contingencies (Skinner 1969). Purchasing a retailer's 'own label' versions of a food product and shopping at a down-market store are behaviours which have very different topographies; yet they may belong to the same operant class if they are reinforced by the same outcomes, say, economy and convenience. However, the same response (say, buying a tie) belongs to different operant classes when, in varying contexts, it is controlled by different contingencies (as in personal vs. gift buying).

Reinforcement of a single operant response means that not only is repetition of that particular response more probable (if similar conditions recur), but that the emission of any member of the operant class to which that response belongs becomes more probable. So, purchasing one 'own label' item may be followed by purchase of others as long as the first led to reinforcing consequences such as a pleasant consumption experience. Similarly, the original discriminative stimulus which marked the opportunity for reinforcement is one of a class: presentation of other members of this class also increases the probability of that response's being repeated (though it will only be maintained in the new circumstances if it is followed from time to time by reinforcing stimuli).

Moreover, any of the reinforcing stimuli belonging to the same class as the original reinforcer may now strengthen the operant in question. These phenomena will be further discussed in the next section in terms of stimulus and response generalization.

Operant conditioning

The philosophical stance of radical behaviourism leans directly upon the findings of operant conditioning experimentation. The basis of the functional relationships among stimuli and responses has been briefly mentioned in the description of that stance provided above. The following, more detailed account of operant phenomena is intended to facilitate further discussion of the paradigm in the context of consumer choice.

Reinforcement

Certain consequences of a behavioural response are followed by an increase in the rate at which the response (or another member of its class) occurs. When such a consequence is contingent upon the performance of the response, it is termed a reinforcer. Positive reinforcement occurs when the reinforcer is accepted (physically: not by mental assent) by the individual. A thirsty person's drinking is said to be positively reinforced because the probability of such behaviour being repeated in similar circumstances thereafter is increased. The drink is not described as reinforcing because of any of its intrinsic qualities – for example, flavour – but simply because of its effect on the rate of response, the sole dependent variable in operant research.

Much consumer choice is explicable in these terms, including brand choice, and store patronage: for example, a store logo can be a discriminative stimulus for pleasant service, this reinforcer being contingent upon entering the shop and speaking to an assistant. Similarly, a brand name of a food item may signal certain reinforcing flavours which are consequent upon consuming the product. Negative reinforcement occurs when the behavioural response which is strengthened operates on the environment to remove or avoid a consequence. For example: a customer is likely to walk past a store where her complaints have met with abusive outbursts on the part of the salesperson. Walking past and shopping elsewhere avoid such aversive consequences and are said to be negatively reinforced: that is, their rate of repetition is increased by avoidance/escape rather than by approach.

Primary reinforcers are unconditioned or unlearned: food is

reinforcing to a hungry animal automatically and not as a result of learning. Examples of primary reinforcers are food, water, variety, and sexual contact; social attention can be a powerful reinforcer and may be more significant than metabolic reinforcers such as food and warmth (Harlow 1962; Harlow and Zimmerman 1959). Secondary reinforcers are learned or conditioned: whilst they initially exerted no reinforcing effects on behaviour, their repeated pairing with a primary reinforcer resulted (via one or other form of conditioning) in their exerting a reinforcing effect in their own right. Secondary reinforcers include tokens, such as money[2] and educational certificates, which are frequently paired with several primary reinforcers (food and approval, for instance) and are contingent upon the performance of many responses. Money in particular is an extremely important secondary reinforcer because it is generally exchangeable for a wide range of primary reinforcers.

Reinforcement versus reward

The EAB makes a vital conceptual distinction between rewards and reinforcers which is relevant to the behavioural analysis of both consumer and marketer action. Although these terms are often treated as synonyms in imprecise accounts of the EAB, they differ decisively in their respective implications for explanation. A reware is a prize, recompense, or bonus received by an individual; it may or may not be a reinforcer, that is, an event or entity that affects the rate at which a particular (operant) response is emitted. The difference in function is clear from the observation that an individual is rewarded, whilst a response is reinforced.

Although marketers provide consumers with numerous actual and potential rewards – in the form of product/brand attributes, entertaining advertising, additional sales promotions featuring gifts, competition entries, attractive and useful packaging, money-off or money-back offers, and so on – not all of these reinforce consumers' behaviour. Many of the reinforcers linked to sales promotions reinforce brand purchase (and, therefore, consumption) in the short term (usually the duration of the campaign). However, the brand features obtained in the process do not vary in substance from those provided by other brands within the same product class and, therefore, do not differentially reinforce revealed preference for the promoted item in the sense of changing the long term probability of consumers' brand purchases.

Punishment

A punisher is a contingent consequence which is followed by a decrease in the frequency of operant response. Punishment may consist in the presentation of an aversive stimulus or the removal of a positive event immediately after the emission of a response. The purchase of a brand which has aversive consequences – for example, frowns from the neighbour with whom one is shopping – is punished by that consequence. The removal of a benefit previously paired with a purchased brand – for example, a bonus sample of a related product as part of a short-term promotion – is a punisher when repurchase of the brand is reduced once the promotion is withdrawn.

Negative reinforcement is often confused in the consumer behaviour and marketing literatures with punishment, presumably because both involve aversive consequences. The term 'reinforcement' always refers to a strengthening of behaviour: negative reinforcement occurs when a response that leads to the avoidance of or escape from an aversive stimulus is thereby emitted more often, for example, when taking an aspirin removes a toothache, and is repeated when the tooth aches again. In punishment, the individual suffers the aversive consequences contingent upon a response and, as a result, the probability of his or her emitting the same response again is reduced. Punishment of one response often leads to the emission and subsequent strengthening of alternative, avoidance or escape behaviours which are negatively reinforced.

A behavioural taxonomy of commodities

Alhadeff (1982) identifies three types of commodity on the basis of the positive or aversive stimuli they represent or remove. *Primary commodities* are positive primary (i.e. unconditioned) reinforcers such as basic food products like bread which offer no more than the nutrients necessary for life; their capacity to reinforce stems from the consumer's biological inheritance (Alhadeff 1982: 16). *Secondary commodities* are positive conditioned reinforcers which receive their power to strengthen behaviour as a result of having been paired with primary reinforcers. They vary, therefore, from consumer to consumer according to reinforcement history. They typically include books, certain furnishings, motor cars and the branded, highly differentiated forms of some primary commodities such as rare or elaborate foods and drinks designed to confer status on those who serve them.

Escape/avoidance commodities are positive, conditioned reinforcers, the acquisition and/or use of which results in escape from or avoidance of aversive consequences. Escape, which is followed by the removal of an aversive stimulus, is effected by purchase and consumption behaviours that are negatively reinforced. Escape/avoidance responses and the commodities on which they depend are widespread. Fennell (1987: 3–4) draws attention to the frequency with which purchase and consumption responses are negatively reinforced as in

> removing aversive stimulation associated with headache, various forms of minor pain, cold, dirt on fabrics and surfaces, wear and tear caused by mechanical friction and the elements, various kinds of anxiety – in a word, the unpleasant stimulation that is the daily lot of humans and for the control and avoidance of which people allocate some substantial portion of their resources. Marketers identify aversive conditions through the usual forms of marketing research and participate in developing goods/services to deal with them. To say [as have some discussants of operant behaviour in the marketing literature] that few examples of negative reinforcement are found in marketing is simply inaccurate. The true state of affairs is that much marketing activity is directed to developing a productive response to conditions that users want to escape or avoid.

Extinction

A response which is no longer reinforced, either positively or negatively, tends to extinguish, that is, not to be emitted any more by the individual. The removal of the reinforcer, in this case, is not contingent upon the response and, therefore, neither punishment nor negative reinforcement is involved. For example, after suffering damage to his taste buds, a consumer's eating spicy foods is no longer reinforced; purchase and consumption of these foods would, after a time, cease (extinguish).

More complex behaviours

Chaining

Discriminative stimuli, via constant pairing with a primary or secondary reinforcing stimulus, become conditioned reinforcers in their own right. The radical behaviourist explains complex behaviours in terms of sequences of three-term contingencies in which each discriminative stimulus not only signals the availability of a further reinforcement contingent upon the performance of an operant behaviour, but reinforces the preceding operant.

For example, shopping at a supermarket may entail (i) writing out a shopping list, (ii) leaving home, (iii) driving and parking, (iv) entering the store, (v) selecting the required items, (vi) taking them to the checkout, and (vii) paying for them. Only the last of these is obviously reinforced (by the receipt of the primary reinforcers purchased). However, the behaviourist explanation of the sequence of actions suggests that each response, by being paired with the conditioned reinforcers, becomes a conditioned reinforcer in its own right, with the exception of the initial response which becomes a discriminative stimulus (it has no prior response to reinforce). Thus, whilst only the final response in the sequence appears to be reinforced, the preceding action (taking the goods to the checkout) becomes a discriminative stimulus for the reinforcement of that final response. Taking the goods to the checkout, through pairing with immediately antecedent actions such as brand selection, becomes a reinforcer, too. The chain of events is, therefore, analysed in reverse order. Chaining indicates why, in human learning, reinforcement often appears to be delayed (Skinner 1953a: 224).

Shaping

Complex new behaviours do not generally appear spontaneously. Sometimes a final response may be explained as appearing after preceding acts which taken together constitute a chain of successive approximations of the terminal behaviour, each reinforced in turn. This process, 'shaping', is not a matter of forming a habit (cf. Rothschild and Gaidis 1981), which implies that an existing response is frequently repeated, but of learning a new terminal response through performing a sequence of prior actions that build toward it as a result of differential reinforcement. For instance, before doing all of his or her monthly grocery shopping at a one-stop hypermarket, the buyer may emit a series of behaviours which approximate this final response, for example, visiting the store, browsing, doing a proportion of shopping there, each of which is differentially reinforced and makes the final response the more probable.

Discrimination and generalization

A response which is reinforced in the presence of one stimulus but not another is said to be differentially reinforced. The individual who behaves differently according to the controlling antecedent stimulus is said to have made a discrimination, and this accounts for the situation-specific nature of many actions. Store choice, for example, may be explained in terms of the discriminations which the consumer has learned as a result of differential reinforcement in various shops, or because of different patterns of availability of products or brands. We have noted that reinforcement refers not simply to the strengthening of the precise operant of which it is a consequence: reinforcement of one response may strengthen other responses which belong to the same class as the original operant. The circumstances in which the other responses are emitted will generally resemble (i.e. contain the same discriminative stimuli as) those in which the original response was reinforced. Thus, an individual's purchasing one food product in a given store may, if reinforced, be followed by his buying a range of similar products there.

This process is response generalization. Another example is the trial purchase of a product marketed under the same brand name (the controlling stimulus) as previously purchased items whose purchase has been positively reinforced. The consumer's behaviour in each case amounts to performing a similar operant in the context of a given setting which marks the availability of contingent reinforcement and can be explained in terms of the controlling discriminative stimulus. A response which has been reinforced in one situation may generalize to other similar (but not identical) situations – a process known as stimulus generalization – as when a consumer buys a brand in a given store and subsequently purchases it from similar outlets. Hence it is unlikely that the reinforcement of purchasing a given brand or visiting a specific store will lead to 100 per cent loyalty toward either.

Antecedent and consequent stimuli ought not, on this analysis, to engender or maintain so narrow a loyalty. Rather, on the assumption that generalization of stimuli and responses will normally occur, similar brands and stores are likely to be tried by most consumers and, if the consequences of such trial are positive, some degree of repeat buying/frequenting is probable. In fact, this prediction is borne out by empirical research for most products, whose customers practise multi-brand purchasing and multi-store shopping (Ehrenberg and Goodhardt 1989; Keng and Ehrenberg 1984).

Verbal behaviour

The explanation of verbal behaviour, that is, thought, speech, and some physical gestures, is of critical importance to radical behaviourism since it is here that the paradigm encounters those phenomena, many of them covert, which receive preeminent attention in cognitive psychology. Radical behaviourism categorizes the social use of language as behaviour, whether this is overt and public (as in conversation) or covert and private (as in thinking): both comprise responses which are under the control of contingencies of reinforcement. Those responses which are private such as feelings and thoughts, are responses none the less, and attract no special significance for taking place 'within the skin'. Skinner (1957) analyses verbal behaviour according to the functions of the responses in question; most important to present purposes among the categories of response so identified are 'tacts' and 'mands'.

A tact is verbal behaviour that describes or labels a situation or the observable environment: 'Here is Macy's' or 'This is expensive'. Tacting is reinforced usually by recognition ('Yes it is') or approval ('How wise!') but tacts soon come under stimulus control as their appropriateness to specific situations is learned. A mand is a request or command: 'Give me three packs, please'. Mands are a prime component of the process in which verbal behaviour is shaped in children by the 'verbal community' (the child's group which shares a common language). The use of mands can often be related to the individual's recent history of deprivation (Hillner 1984:154–6). Manding is a necessary part of socialization for adults too in new task situations where coding and decoding of novel responses (for example, use of an automated cash dispenser) must be learned. It is through the development of a verbal community that the human individual acquires consciousness since that community 'arranges contingencies under which he not only sees an object but sees that he is seeing it' (Skinner 1974: 220). This consciousness is not some inherent subjective capacity of the individual, however, but a product of social interaction developed as the person 'comes to see himself only as others see him, or at least only as others insist that he see himself' (Skinner 1957: 140).

Schedules of reinforcement

Schedules of reinforcement influence the rate at which behaviours are learned and extinguished (Ferster and Skinner 1957). When a response is reinforced every time it occurs (continuous reinforcement), activities are quickly learned, but they also extinguish rapidly when reinforcement ceases. Physical responses such as turning on a switch to obtain light are acquired in this way. Complex responses such as those involved in playing chess are similarly best learned when reinforcement is continuous. Purchase responses are often reinforced similarly on each occasion at least for identical, fast moving consumer goods. Quality control and the maintenance of high levels of customer service are designed to ensure that the buyer's request for a branded product is immediately reinforced by instant availability.

Reinforcement may also be intermittent, being given at fixed or variable intervals of time or in fixed or variable ratio to responses. When reinforcement occurs less than every time the response is emitted, the rate of extinction is very slow. Some manufacturers and distributors do not produce or stock every conceivable version of a product; rather they reduce their productive capacity or inventory costs by maintaining customer service levels that will satisfy a reasonable proportion of customers, notably those who, in a competitive market place, can demand continuous reinforcement (perhaps the largest customer or promptest payers or those who otherwise reinforce such supplier behaviour and would quickly punish lapses). Other items can be supplied intermittently since buyers are willing either to perform an operant response several times between reinforcements (say, returning to re-request the product if it is not initially in stock) or to delay gratification by waiting (Christopher 1985). Gambling and spectator sports are also activities that are maintained on intermittent schedules.

Intermittent schedules depend on time (interval schedules) or the performance of a number of responses (ratio schedules) before reinforcement. Under *fixed interval* (FI) schedules reinforcement is given every time a specific interval of time has elapsed for a response made after that interval. Under *fixed ratio* (FR) schedules, reinforcement is given when a specific number of responses has been performed, regardless of the time taken. A schedule parameter of 100 means that every 100th response is reinforced. *Variable interval* (VI), like FI, schedules make reinforcement dependent upon the performance of a single response after an interval of time but the time that must elapse varies from reinforcement to reinforcement. *Variable ratio* (VR) schedules are such that a different number of responses is required for each succeeding reinforcement. The rate of response under variable schedules is typically steady and continual, and VR schedules tend to result in a higer response rate than VI schedules.

Figure 2.2 portrays the patterns of animal performance associated with interval and ratio schedules. In the case of the FI schedules, the delivery of the reinforcer (usually a food pellet) is a discriminative stimulus signalling that the response will be reinforced again after a period of time has elapsed. The post-reinforcement pause in responding indicated in the figure is typical: as the interval passes, the probability of reinforcement

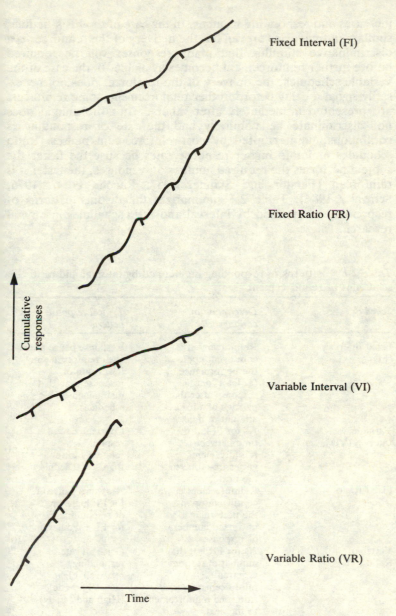

Figure 2.2 Cumulative records of response patterns on interval and ratio schedules of reinforcement
Note: Downward strokes denote presentation of reinforcer.

49

increases and responding resumes. In the case of the FR schedule, similar contingencies prevail but the delivery of the reinforcer is a discriminative stimulus that many responses will be required before further reinforcement becomes available. In the case of the variable schedules, the delivery of the reinforcer does not necessarily signal a delay before further reinforcement: some reinforcers are presented immediately after others. Thus the animal does not discriminate behaviourally and the rate of responding is continuous, uninterrupted by post-reinforcement pauses. Ratio schedules maintain higher response rates because the faster the subject performs the required number of responses, the faster it is reinforced (Ferster and Skinner 1957; Rachlin *et al.* 1976; Schwartz 1984). Table 2.1 summarizes the distinct patterns of responding maintained by interval and ratio schedules in animal research.

Table 2.1 Patterns of responding maintained by interval and ratio schedules of reinforcement

Schedule	Description of contingencies	Typical response pattern
Fixed Interval (FI)	Reinforcement is contingent upon the performance of (at least) one response after the passage of a fixed amount of time.	Response pause after each reinforcement; lower rate of response than that maintained by FR schedules.
Variable Interval (VI)	As for FI but the time between reinforcements varies from one to the next.	Constant rate of responding, relatively lower than VR schedules.
Fixed Ratio (FR)	Reinforcement is contingent upon the performance of a fixed number of responses.	Response pause as for FI; higher rate of responding than for FI schedules.
Variable Ratio (VR)	As for FR but the number of responses required for reinforcement varies from one reinforcement to the next	Constant rate of responding, relatively higher than VI schedules. (High and steady).

Choice and preference

Early operant experimentation presented subjects with the option of responding on a single 'operandum', that part of the apparatus that records a response, for example, a disc which is pecked or a lever which is pressed. 'Choice' is understood non-cognitively by behaviourists (as will be discussed further in Chapter 3), and it has been studied in an operant research framework by observing the way in which animals in experimental chambers divide their responses among operanda that produce reinforcements independently on concurrent schedules. These investigations indicate that when a subject is presented with a reinforcer on each of two independent VI schedules, it matches relative response rates to relative reinforcement rates. This relationship is summarized by the matching law (Herrnstein 1961; 1970) which may be most simply represented in the form:

$$\frac{R_a}{R_a + R_b} = \frac{r_a}{r_a + r_b}$$

where R_a = number of responses on A,
  R_b = number of responses on B,
  r_a = number of reinforcements on A,
  r_b = number of reinforcements on B.

Matching has been found to hold not only for the number of responses but also for the time spent responding on each alternative and for the time delay of reinforcement. Extended accounts can be found in Lea *et al.* (1987) and Rachlin *et al.* (1976); see also Baum and Rachlin (1969).

In another approach to choice and preference, Premack (1965, 1971) proposes than an individual's repertoire of responses can be ordered into a hierarchy of values based on the capacity of a contingent response to reinforce or punish a prior response. The ordering of responses is achieved experimentally by establishing the probabilities of each response available to an individual and by arranging their relationships accordingly. An optimal or natural allocation of responses is displayed by an individual behaving in unrestricted circumstances: a car-owner, for instance, spends some of his or her free time cleaning the vehicle, some time maintaining it, and some time driving it. A probability of occurrence can be attached to each response proportionally to the amount of time the individual spends on its performance relative to the time spent on alternative responses. Moreover, performance of a low probability response may be reinforced by subsequent performance of a high probability response that is contingent upon it.

Reinforcement can, therefore, be defined independently of the circular three-term contingency in terms of the relationships among responses which have been independently established by observation. Assume, for instance, that in the absence of restrictions, an individual allocates far more time to driving than cleaning and maintaining their vehicle; a hierarchy of preferences can be described by reference to the probabilities of each response being emitted (established in terms of the proportion of total time allocated to each). However, if in a particular situation, motoring is made contingent upon having an attractive and reliable vehicle (for example, so that it can be driven in a custom car rally), the individual is likely to increase the amount of time spent maintaining, cleaning, and polishing the car. The contingencies have been so arranged that the less probable response (cleaning, which occupies a lower position in the preference hierarchy) is reinforced by the more probable (driving, which has a higher placing). Driving itself may be reinforced by a still higher behaviour, say talking to other enthusiasts after the event, which is contingent upon it.

In the marketing context, consumption usually reinforces buying, not simply because it occurs subsequently in a chain of related responses, but because it is, given 'free choice' (the absence of aversive consequences), more probable. Naturally, this does not rule out the necessity (for the marketer) of bringing much routine shopping or that which is marked by strong retail competition, under more immediate contingency control, either by presenting reinforcers (such as prompt service or free gifts) that are immediately contiguous upon purchasing or by arranging appropriate discriminative stimuli to signal the benefits and pleasures of eventual consumption.

Skinner's ontological shift: operant versus classical conditioning

Explanation of behaviour in terms of contingencies of reinforcement is distinct from that of the stimulus-response (S-R) psychology (based upon respondent/classical conditioning) which has attracted some attention in consumer research (McSweeney and Bierley 1984; Stuart *et al.* 1987; see also Allen and Madden 1985; Bierley *et al.* 1985; Gorn 1982; Milliman 1982). Classical conditioning consists in basic associative learning in which reinforcement takes place independently of the performance of the response (see, for instance, Marx and Hillix 1979).[3] By contrast, in operant conditioning, as we have seen, the rate of emission of a response is explained in terms of reinforcement contingencies. As Skinner

(1971: 18) summarizes it, 'Behavior is shaped and maintained by its consequences.'

Whilst, within the radical behaviourist framework, behaviour may be described as coming under stimulus control when responses are differentially reinforced in the presence of separate antecedent stimuli, the relationship between a discriminative stimulus and an operant does not involve the automatic elicitation of reflexive behaviour as in classical conditioning. Rather, the discriminative stimulus is described as altering the probability of an individual's emitting the operant. If the reinforcing stimulus is withdrawn, then the response ceases: though there may be a time-lag between withdrawal and cessation when the antecedent stimulus is still presented, the response finally extinguishes, irrespective of that presence. Because operant behaviour is said to be emitted by the individual rather than elicited by a preceding stimulus, it is sometimes said to be 'voluntary'. However, 'voluntary' does not imply that operant behaviour is under 'conscious control'. The radical behaviourist insists that when the other variables which control behaviour – notably succeeding reinforcing stimuli – are identified, that behaviour can be fully explained in terms of environmental factors. Like the 'involuntary' behaviour which is elicited in the course of classical conditioning, operant behaviour is externally controlled: what differs is the sort of control involved (Skinner 1953a: 110–12). In neither case is a cognitively-based consciousness invoked in the explanation of behaviour.

Debate continues, none the less, about the distinctness of operant and classical conditioning in practice and some critics have seen in the first two elements of the three-term contingency the elicitation of a response by a stimulus as described by Pavlov (Hall 1987; Mackintosh 1974; Schwartz and Lacey 1982). Although Skinner's paradigm embraces classical behaviourism, albeit reconceptualized as the reflexive conditioning of respondent behaviour, his definition of the operant distinguishes his system theoretically from S-R psychology in two ways (Foxall 1986a, 1986c, 1987a; Leahey 1987: 383–4).

First, it is worth repeating that, whilst, in classical conditioning, a response is elicited by a prior stimulus, in operant conditioning, the organism emits responses, some of which are reinforced by consequent stimuli. An operant response is never elicited. Antecedent stimuli come to mark the occasion on which the individual discriminates behaviourally (i.e. emits an operant response which has previously been reinforced in the presence of the stimulus). But Skinner's distinction of operant from respondent conditioning derives from his assertion that such discriminative stimuli have no power to elicit responses (Skinner 1938). The reflexive links of S-R psychology are appropriate to the explanation of respondent but not operant behaviour. Note that this reconceptualization has the effect of limiting respondent conditioning to reflex actions, leaving the bulk of behaviour open to operant definition and analysis. Seldom is the extension of an explanatory system ontologically neutral, however: the metatheoretical implications of this reconstruction are significant.

It emerges from the above that Skinner is presenting an alternative paradigm which is distinguished in terms of its explanatory scope from that of classical conditioning. Whilst he retains Pavlov's contribution with respect to the analysis of the reflex, he claims that behaviour in general is not of this kind: it must be explained by reference to its consequences rather than its antecedents. Skinner thereby pursues a subtle ontological redefinition which limits the sphere of applicability of classical conditioning to reflex responses, and offers a quite different explanation of most animal and human behaviours. As a result, much of the consumer behaviour that is currently explained within a classical conditioning framework is open to an operant interpretation in which contingent consequences rather than antecedent eliciting stimuli are the causes of behaviour (Foxall 1985). Skinner's paradigm does not simply complement that which was based upon classical conditioning: it incorporates and supersedes it.

Second, although the behaviour of an individual may, according to Skinner, come under the control of (antecedent, discriminative) variables these factors are never causative. As will be seen in Chapter 4, the insistence that causal stimuli are always found in the environment, even when behaviour is under the control of immediate, internal, verbal discriminative stimuli, is a source of criticism of radical behaviourism. However, it is important to appreciate that radical behaviourism posits that the control of discriminative stimuli is established by their constant pairing with reinforcing stimuli and is maintained by their occasional continued pairing: if the reinforcing stimulus ceases, the operant usually remains for a time under (antecedent) stimulus control but, in the absence of reinforcement, eventually extinguishes (is no longer emitted). The relationship between discriminative stimulus and operant response is not automatic, as is that between eliciting stimulus and respondent behaviour in classical conditioning (Skinner 1953a: 110–12; cf. Blackman 1980).

Chapter three

Radical alternatives

We change the way a person looks at something, as well as what he sees when he looks, by changing the contingencies; we do not change something called perception. We change the relative strengths of responses by differential reinforcement of alternative courses of action; we do not change something called a preference. We change the probability of an act by changing a condition of deprivation or aversive stimulation; we do not change a need. We reinforce behavior in different ways; we do not give a person a purpose or intention. We change behavior toward something, not an attitude toward it. We sample and change verbal behavior, not opinions.

(Skinner 1971: 4)

Critique of 'other realm' theories

By confining enquiry to the observable, radical behaviourism eschews theories that proceed in terms derived from any realm of discourse other than that in which the behaviour to be explained is itself described. It avoids, therefore, 'any explanation of an observed fact which appeals to events taking place somewhere else, at some other level of observation, described in different terms, and measured, if at all, in different dimensions' (Skinner 1950: 193). Its consequent rejection of mental, neural, and conceptual explanations of behaviour rests upon three arguments (Wessels 1981).

First, such theories are *incomplete*: they halt investigation by failing to identify the factors that account for the inner events and processes that are held to be the causes of behaviour. In particular, they ignore the environmental precursors of those inner events (Skinner 1969: 240). Intrapersonal feelings, at best, provide clues to the nature of the contingencies that actually control behaviour, but they are not the causal contingencies themselves, nor can they

replace them. Cognitive and affective theories represent, therefore, an attempt to 'move the environment inside the head'
(Skinner 1977) but, even if this could be done successfully, the
causal attribution of observed behaviour to such theoretical entities as expectations, attitudes, perceptual processes, or encoding
strategies would not constitute a full explanation until those
factors had themselves been related to their antecedent causes
(Wessells 1981: 155).

Second, other-realm theories such as cognitivism are *fictional*:
these explanations merely infer the alleged inner causes of behaviour, for example, attitudes or personality traits, from the very
behaviours they purport to explicate, adding nothing real to
observation but simply redescribing it. They provide ready-made
but inadequate explanations of any observed response: 'It is too
easy to say that someone does something "because he likes to do
it", or that he does one thing rather than another "because he has
made a choice"' (Skinner 1963b: 957). Explanations of behaviour
in terms of intrapersonal activity are frequently a good deal more
complex and formal than this, of course (Mandler 1985), but, as in
these simple examples, they function primarily (according to
behaviourist interpretation) to allay curiosity and end enquiry
(Skinner 1957: 6). The actual causes of behaviour remain external
to the individual: even the control exerted by a discriminative
stimulus depends upon the external contingencies of reinforcement (Skinner 1972a: 325; Wessells 1981). At best, private events
are mediational, never causal (Skinner 1969: 258).

Third, cognitive and similar theories are *unnecessary* because
they can be replaced by simpler, behavioural explanations that
identify the environmental factors that control and predict behaviour without relying on explanatory fictions or circular logic.
Accordingly, Skinner claims that the whole of information processing theory can be reformulated in terms of the stimulus control
of responses (Skinner 1977: 7). This is not simply a matter of
translating terms from one theory to another: behavioural accounts,
based on functional analyses that describe the orderliness and
regularity of behaviour in its controlling settings, are superior
because they offer a more direct route to knowledge, avoiding
both philosophical issues – such as how mental events cause
physical responses – and the wastefulness of more elaborate
interpretations (Skinner 1950: 193–5; see also Ryle 1949).

Radical behaviourism does not, however, reject theorizing
per se: only that approach to theory-building that relies on the
alleged explanatory power of unobservables and the hypothetico-
deductive logic of scientific discovery that generally accompanies

it. Hypothetico-deductivism may be inevitable in the scientific investigation of processes so large (e.g. the solar system) or so small (e.g. subatomic particles) that the observer cannot manipulate them and must guess at their behaviours; in other cases, such as the experimental study of behaviour, hypothesizing is usually trivial and unnecessary. By contrast, the inductive discovery of the lawfulness of nature, leading to parsimonious, empirically-derived functional relationships, hastens the goal of science, the prediction and control of events (Skinner 1969; Zuriff 1985: 89).

These tenets of scientific enquiry are valuable in three ways in a relativistic consumer research. First, they emphasize the need for the critical identification of the unobservables upon which explanation so often rests and for their evaluation in terms of contributing no more than an incomplete and fictional explanation of consumer choice. They thereby raise the possibility that such unobservables may obfuscate explanations based more directly on environmental stimuli. Second, they suggest an alternative explanation of consumer behaviour to that provided by cognitive, affective, and other inner-state theories and are thereby a source of the counter-inductive hypotheses and novel facts upon which relativism depends (Feyerabend 1975). Third, they are the basis of an empirical approach to consumer research, one founded upon experimentation, which has generally been neglected by consumer researchers untrained in behavioural economics or economic psychology. The following account discusses each of these challenges of radical behaviourism and operant conditioning to the orthodox approach to consumer research.

Avoidance of unobservables

In line with Feyerabend's advocacy of the proliferation of tenaciously-held views as an essential component of scientific progress, it has been maintained that a central role of the radical behaviourist paradigm in consumer research is the provision of a critical stance, a counterpoint to the prevailing paradigm's explanatory mode. A radical behaviourist account is thus likely to expose the underlying assumptions of the otherwise taken-for-granted explanation. The following discussion provides an example derived from the use of trait theory in consumer research (for a more general account, see Foxall 1983). It indicates that radical behaviourism can be used to reexamine the hypothetical constructs on which inner-state theories rely in order to suggest alternative directions for research and explanation.

Innate innovativeness

The theory of consumer innovativeness advanced by Midgley and Dowling (1978) makes extensive use of unobservables whilst attempting to avoid the excessive use of simplistic trait-behaviour approaches to the explanation of observed action. These authors argue that the explanation of observed innovative behaviour must take into account the situational, especially social, factors which mediate personal variables and overt action (cf. Mischel 1968). The various measures of consumer innovativeness which have been employed by researchers and their apparent relationships to distinct definitions of this construct (Kohn and Jacoby 1973; Robertson and Myers 1969; Summers 1971) are taken by Midgley and Dowling as indicative of degrees of innovativeness: each extent of innovative behaviour measured requires explanation in terms of successively more abstract constructions of a personality trait, 'innovativeness'.

Thus, at the observational level, innovative behaviour is adequately presented by the idea of the relative time of adoption of a single innovation; this 'actualized innovativeness' is the sole concept and measure of innovative behaviour employed by many researchers (see Rogers 1983: 22). Beyond this, the measurement of innovative behaviour by means of a cross-sectional technique (Robertson and Myers 1969; Robertson 1971) reveals the adoption by some consumers of a multiplicity of discrete innovations within a product category. Midgley and Dowling (1978: 231) comment that, 'In essence, the cross-sectional technique measures a deeper and more abstract construct of innovativeness and one which is closer to some basic expression of an individual's personality.' The measurement of consumer innovation across several product fields by means of an extended cross-sectional methodology (Summers 1971) is interpreted by these authors (Midgley and Dowling 1978: 231) as indicative of 'innovativeness implicitly conceived and measured at a third, yet higher, level of abstraction, namely with respect to all, or at least many, consumer product categories, thus approaching the idea of innovativeness as a generalised personality trait'; this trait is identified as 'innate innovativeness'.

Central to this approach is the belief that observed or reported innovative behaviour can be explained only by the use of 'constructs postulated at a higher (non-observable) level of abstraction which, precisely because they are not tied to specific innovations or specific measurement devices, can explain both individuals' overt behaviour over several innovations and the measurements we obtain with different methodologies' (Midgley and Dowling 1978: 232). The concept of innate innovativeness, a hypothetical construct existing only in the investigator's mind (Bunge 1967), reaches the required level of abstraction in that it is said to account for the differing extents of innovative behaviour exhibited by consumers in diverse situations.

The personality trait, innate innovativeness, is closely linked to cognitive processing in a social context since it is defined as decision-making about novelty in the (relative) absence of interpersonal influence: 'the degree to which an individual makes innovation decisions independently of the communicated experience of others' (Midgley 1977: 49). Midgley and Dowling (1978: 235–6) portray 'decision-making' itself as an unobservable, a prebehavioural procedure not accessible to measurements of overt behaviour. It is a derivative of unspecified personality traits, possessed by all individuals who differ in terms of the amount of information they require from others before making an 'innovation decision'. The extent to which innate innovativeness is actualized as the relatively early purchase of new products is determined by intervening situational factors.

Inherent innovativeness

In a similar representation, Hirschman (1980) posits 'inherent novelty-seeking' as a (conceptual) prebehavioural internal process to account for both actualized novelty-seeking and actualized innovation. She explains actualized innovativeness by reference to two cognitive precursors: inherent and actualized novelty-seeking. Inherent novelty-seeking is a preference for, and desire to seek new and different information. In the consumer domain this becomes inherent innovativeness (equivalent to Midgley and Dowling's innate innovativeness), the capacity and willingness to acquire new information by means of novel product adoption. In order to account for the translation of inherent novelty-seeking into actualized innovativeness, Hirschman introduces the mediating variable, actualized novelty-seeking, which is the overt search for new information as a prelude to the acquisition of an innovation.

Actualized innovativeness may be manifest in three (potentially sequential) ways: vicarious innovativeness (learning about new products not yet acquired); adoptive innovativeness (purchase of new products); and use innovativeness (solving novel consumption problems by adaptive use of an existing product). Whether inherent novelty-seeking leads on to one or other of these forms of actualized innovativeness depends on situational and personal factors: e.g. the consumer's need for new products in order to perform accumulated roles more effectively, or his/her creative capacity to generate new consumption problems intellectually which might be solved by considering, purchasing and/or consuming innovatively. Creativity is necessary in this context both to consumers' understanding and purchasing novel, technically-complex products, and as a prerequisite of consumers' cognitive formulation of consumption problems which may stimulate overt novelty-seeking and innovative behaviour.

Innovative behaviour

By contrast, a radical behaviourist explanation of innovative buying might proceed in terms of the influence of the external antecedents and consequences of that behaviour rather than actual or hypothetical pesonality traits. Innovative behaviour is, within this framework, explicable entirely in terms of the prevailing contingencies of reinforcement; 'innate' or 'inherent' innovativeness would be viewed as no more than explanatory fictions, constructs derived from observations of the behaviour to be explained and which do no more than redescribe responses in terminology derived from another realm. If the term 'decision-making' is employed at all in this context, it refers to a behaviour, the innovative action itself, or a verbal description of the consumer's own future behaviour. As Midgley and Dowling rightly imply, it is necessary to consider innovative buying at a more molar level of analysis than that inherent in simple trait-behaviour models; but the behavioural explanation would not postulate an unobservable 'innate' innovativeness.

How might such explanation proceed? Innovative behaviour does not suddenly appear. It is shaped, as successive approximations to the terminal response of new product purchasing are differentially reinforced. Similarly, the behaviourist interpretation would lead to the hypothesis that a consumer who appears to innovate suddenly by purchasing a full wardrobe of fashionable clothes does not do so spontaneously but as the endpoint in a process in which similar, indeed, increasingly similar, behaviour has been successively reinforced. The investigator would thus look for a pattern of precursor responses (say, the purchase of fashionable shoes, a trend-setting suit, and so on), a pattern of antecedent discriminative stimuli and succeeding reinforcing stimuli, to explain and predict the purchase of new clothes. Managers actively use shaping in order to increase the likelihood of a 'final' response, such as the purchase of their new brands, by such means as the distribution of free samples; if the use of the product is itself reinforced, then the next step, actual purchase of the distributed brand becomes more probable.

Initial purchase of newly-marketed products is also differentially reinforced (compared with the way in which buying existing brands is reinforced) by means of coupons, money-off offers, and other promotional deals; consumer behaviour is thereby shaped, as the terminal response – purchase of the brand at the full retail price – becomes more likely. Complex behaviour, which appears innovative to onlookers who are not familiar with the individual consumer's reinforcement history, may also be explained as the final link in a chain of reinforced responses which culminate in the observed response; the chain is created and maintained as discriminative stimuli come to function as conditioned reinforcers (Skinner 1953a: 91–8, 224).

The endpoint of either shaping or chaining might be the purchase of a single product or several products within a range or across ranges, depending upon the conceptualization of behavioural units employed. The range of buying would be explicable in terms of the extent to which the responses involved come under stimulus control which depends in turn upon the availability of the appropriate discriminative stimuli. In the case of discriminative learning, the range would be small. However, as has been discussed, either stimuli or responses may be generalized so that a given response occurs in multiple situations or a given situation is the setting for the emission of numerous related responses (related in terms of their common elements).

In either case, the behaviours of the individual consumer might be described as 'innovative' by the layman, but they actually involve the learning of a single pattern of behaviour. The ascription of novelty or innovativeness to the observed behaviour is, in some respects, artificial since almost all responses have something in common one with another; as Skinner (1953a: 94) comments, 'We divide behaviour into hard and fast units and are then surprised to find that the organism disregards the boundaries we have set.' The problem might be resolved by making an element of a response the focal unit of behaviour for investigation but there are practical difficulties in isolating elements (Skinner 1953a: 93–4). What is indisputable, however, is that the reinforcement of one response is frequently followed by the strengthening of other responses which are not identical to the first, though both 'old' and 'new' responses usually have some elements in common. Herein lies radical behaviourism's means of conceptualization and explanation – in terms of three-term contingencies – of the generalization of purchase response for new products from item to item within a range and/or across ranges.

Thus, the radical behaviourist analysis of consumer new product purchasing suggests a reevaluation of the concept of innovativeness. If the purchase of recently-launched products within and across product ranges can be explained in terms of the generalization of existing responses, the whole notion of innovative behaviour is called into question. If 'new' patterns of purchasing consist in whole or part of existing behavioural elements, in what sense are they new? Radical behaviourism tends to play down the whole idea of innovation as a sort of spontaneous discontinuity, not because it has no explanation of novel behaviour, but because its explanation stresses continuity, the continuity which is determined by a relatively stable controlling environment, and because it eschews what it designates explanatory fictions such as 'innate innovativeness'.

The innovator is, like the poet, simply a locus, 'a place in which certain genetic and environmental causes come together to have a common effect. ... It is not some prior purpose, intention or act of will which accounts for novel behavior; it is the "contingencies of reinforcement"' (Skinner 1972a: 352, 353). The result is to deny explanation of creativity, novelty, and innovativeness in terms of some autonomous innate or inherent variable, whether mental or conceptual. Instead, 'By analyzing the genetic and individual histories responsible for our behavior, we may learn how to be more original. The task is not to think of new forms of behavior but to create an environment in which they are likely to occur' (Skinner 1972a: 355). This does not mean that operant psychologists avoid genuinely novel behaviour when it occurs. Indeed, there have been attempts to strengthen not only original responses but to increase the frequency with which responses belonging to the class of discontinuous behaviour are emitted. Pryor *et al.* (1969) report experiments with porpoises in which they reinforced only those responses not previously reinforced, and perhaps not within the repertoire of the species. As a result of reinforcing only such responses, they increased the probability of the animals' performing novel types of behaviour. Other work has demonstrated that humans who are reinforced for original behaviour in one situation show a greater propensity to emit original responses in other contexts (Maltzman 1960). The possibility arises that novel behaviour might be a higher order response, though the explanation remains true to the EAB's emphasis upon environmental rather than intrapersonal control.

The purchase of continuous new products (i.e. those, like fluoride toothpaste, which embody incrementally innovative features and are minimally disruptive of consumption behaviour: Robertson 1967) certainly appears, according to this perspective, to require nothing by way of novel concepts: it is entirely explicable in terms of contingencies of reinforcement and the individual's reinforcement history. The continued presentation of discriminative and reinforcing stimuli with respect to recently-launched products within and across product ranges determines the extent of new product purchasing. Given this, the behaviourist would ask what need there is of the ascription to consumers of increasingly abstract conceptual personality traits. What do they purport to add to explanation other than redescription of the observable?

In the case of discontinuous new products (i.e. those, like video recorders, which lead to radically different patterns of consumption) novel responses may be learned accidentally in a process akin to that of the evolutionary development of the species: 'As accidental traits, arising from mutations, are selected by their contribution to survival, so accidental variations in behaviour are selected by their reinforcing consequences' (Skinner 1974: 114). But the radical behaviourist acknowledges little discontinuity in practice. New settings share relevant properties with the old leading to the generalization of responses (Julia 1988: 253–5), and novel instances of behaviour are constantly being emitted, then either selected or abandoned as the outcome of their consequences. Most products permit trial in which the consequences of purchase and consumption become apparent before adoption or rejection occurs; indeed, a comprehensive review of the nature of innovative buying confirms the centrality of this process (Foxall 1984d: 95–105, 128–31). The analysis of new product purchasing in terms of its environmental consequences anchors the researcher's frame of reference more closely to observable behaviour than does that analysis which proceeds in terms of inborn personality traits.

Moreover, the very studies cited by Midgley and Dowling in their search for constructs and terms to describe and 'explain' consumer innovativeness, appear incongruous with the hypothesis that personality variables strongly influence purchase behaviour (Robertson and Myers 1969: 167–8) and draw attention to the need to investigate situational influences (Summers 1971: 316). As has been pointed out, Midgely and Dowling present an elaborate theory of innovativeness which avoids the *naïveté* of some earlier formulations; they take some pains to draw attention to the situational mediation of person and observed behaviour. Given their apparent sophistication, therefore, their insistence on explaining observed behaviour by reference to an inborn personality trait, vaguely defined as 'a function of a number of (yet to be specified) dimensions of the human personality' appears somewhat inconsistent (Midgley and Dowling 1978: 235).

Redundant unobservables

The radical behaviourist critique of other-realm theorizing applies well to the approach considered here. The 'explanation' of observed new product buying in terms of an abstract innate trait existing somewhere other than where the behaviour is taking place simply creates a new problem for theory – that of explaining the trait itself (cf. Foxall 1988a). To the radical behaviourist, such 'explanation' is actually on a par with long-abandoned explanations which proceed in terms of instincts which, like mental processes, are simply inferred from the behaviour to be explained. Moreover, the behaviourist programme sees this method of explanation as wasteful, diverting attention from the very situational determinants which these authors wish to emphasize.

An important contributor to the full understanding of innovative behaviour is the empirical identification of salient situational factors, the assessment of their effect and the development of explanations which proceed in terms of these environmental determinants. However, as a result of the uncritical acceptance of current modes of explanation, the extent to which consumers' purchases of recently-launched products come under stimulus control, and the circumstances in which discrimination and generalization occur in the trial and adoption of innovations are unknown. They will remain so as long as consumer researchers are content with the explanation of innovative behaviour in abstract terms posited by and solely present in the mind of the investigator. Only the adoption, within a relativistic framework, of an alternative perspective to that of the prevailing cognitive/trait psychology is likely to make the environmental control of purchasing intelligible. It is not the purpose of this discussion, however, to advocate a behaviourist perspective as a replacement for intrapsychic explanations, but as an additional interpretation that provides insights not otherwise available, to stimulate the evaluative contrasting of theories based on alternative assumptions, and thereby to engender paradigm erosion.

The adoption of such an alternative perspective would enable consumer researchers to pose and answer questions that are currently ignored, but are central nevertheless to the understanding of innovative behaviour and its extrapersonal determinants: how many customers buy specific new products from just one store, or when a given person is present? How often does the innovator buy the new product on successive occasions from a range of stores and what elements of the buying situation are common across these outlets? Under what circumstances do consumers who have purchased a new product return to the store to talk about, try on or try out similar new items there? In each case, what are the stimuli that control the operant discriminations and generalizations involved? Only when such questions as these have at least tentative answers can the limitations of both intra-psychic and behaviouristic perspectives be gauged as each becomes a standpoint from which to reconstruct the other.

A source of alternative explanations

The prevailing paradigm for consumer research contains a recognizable philosophical foundation in which observed behaviour is explained as the outcome of intrapersonal cognitive and personality factors under varying degrees of autonomous control; a defined subject matter consisting of experience and consciousness as well as behaviour; and a feasible methodology that rests upon the statistical comparison of the means and proportions of groups of sample subjects (Valentine 1982). The paradigm's extensive use of unobservables in explanation has been discussed and the explication of human choice behaviour by analogy with the quasi-intellectual information processing functions of the digital computer has been noted as a central component of cognitivism generally (Engel *et al.* 1973; cf. Boden 1977; Newell and Simon 1972; Neisser 1967). Judged by radical behaviourist criteria, the explanations offered by this school are redolent with theorization in the unacceptable sense; the radical behaviourist would deal quite differently with the same observable facts, without recourse to internal causes and seeking the causes of behaviour entirely in the environment.

The account of operant conditioning presented in Chapter 2 and illustrated above by reference to consumers' innovative behaviour hints at the alternative form such an explanation might assume. The following discussion takes an operant analysis of consumer behaviour further in three ways: first, by considering a theoretical account of consumer choice which relates the probability of a purchase response to the strength of the net difference between the size of its reinforcing and punishing consequences; second, by developing an analysis of consumer decision-making and marketing management in operant terms; and third, by considering marketing as reciprocal interactions of buyers and sellers shaped and maintained by their consequences.

Consumer behaviour as approach and escape

Alhadeff (1982) represents purchasing as the outcome of the relative strengths of conflicting approach and escape behaviours, each of which is determined by its own reinforcers. Purchase responses (approach behaviours) are reinforced by the acquisition of primary, secondary, and escape/avoidance commodities which makes repeat purchase more probable. But purchase is also punished; its aversive consequences, notably the loss of spending power represented by the surrender of the generalized conditioned reinforcer, money, strengthens escape/avoidance responses (non-purchase) and punishes the operant purchase response if it is emitted. (More accurately, a purchase response is punished by the net opportunity cost so incurred.) Whether a given purchase is made depends, therefore, upon the relative strengths of the approach and escape operants. In general the strength of these behaviours depends upon the consequences which similar actions have had in the past, but the following discussion is concerned more specifically with the current circumstances maintaining response strength.

Determinants of strength of approach behaviour

The strength of approach behaviour for primary commodities is a function of the effectiveness of the reinforcer (which depends upon the buyer's level of deprivation, that is, length of time since the last purchase or, we might add, consumption), the schedule of reinforcement in operation, the delay between the response and the presentation of the reinforcer (the longer the delay has been in the past, the weaker the reinforcer, though once again Alhadeff ignores consumption responses and their frequency/recency), the quantity of the reinforcer presented (the rate of response varies directly with this quantity), and the quality of the reinforcer (presentation of adulterated food, for instance, is followed by a reduction in the rate of responding).

The strength of approach behaviour for a secondary commodity depends principally upon the pattern and frequency of its previous pairing with one or more primary reinforcers and thus upon the unique reinforcement history of the consumer. Its strength depends, moreover, upon the level of deprivation of the primary commodity: the probability of a consumer's purchasing a refrigerator, for instance, is not increased by withholding refrigerators, but by factors that strengthen the need for the primary commodity, fresh food (Alhadeff 1982). However, we might add that when the demand for secondary commodities is controlled by strong social factors such as approval/avoidance of criticism, deprivation of the secondary commodity is also likely to strengthen approach. The nature of the reinforcement schedule in operation is also an important determinant of approach behaviour strength for secondary commodities.

Strength of approach for escape commodities is a function of the strength of the aversive stimulus which is avoided by purchase (or consumption) of such commodities. The presentation of the aversive stimulus is equivalent to a state of deprivation, and the degree of deprivation is directly proportional to the strength of the aversive stimulus. Escape goods are, somewhat paradoxically, positive reinforcers controlled by aversive stimuli (Alhadeff 1982: 32). In addition, response strength with respect to escape goods depends on the prevailing schedule, the delay between response and the reduction or elimination of the aversive stimulus (again complicated by consumption behaviour: it may be easy to purchase corn plasters when in company but not so easy to use them quickly), the 'stimulus-off' time or period when the aversive stimulus remains dormant after the response (for example, the length of time an aspirin quells pain), and the quality of the escape good.

Determinants of strength of escape behaviour

The incidence and strength of a consumer's escape behaviour result from the loss of the money exchanged for the primary, secondary, or escape commodity involved. The surrender of money is aversive because such behaviour has previously been followed by others' expressions of disapproval, impeded or blocked access to other positive reinforcers (given the consumer's time constraint), and the loss of a positive reinforcer. The intensity of this aversive stimulus determines the effectiveness of the reinforcer. The length of delay between response and punishment also affects response strength: the provision of credit is a means of increasing the delay and thereby increases response strength. The quantity and quality of the money surrendered in exchange for the positive reinforcers represented by the product also affect response strength, as do the reinforcement schedules in operation (Alhadeff 1982: 173-4).

Simple conflict model of consumer behaviour

A simple model of response strength and its determinants, in which there is a single commodity and one constraint, income, is shown in Figure 3.1. The model is based on the following assumptions.

First, an equilibrium point, P, at which probability of the purchase response and the corresponding size of reinforcer can be established theoretically at the intersection of two curves representing Approach Behaviour, AB, and Escape Behaviour, EB, as in Figure 3.1. Second, the sole determinant of the strength of

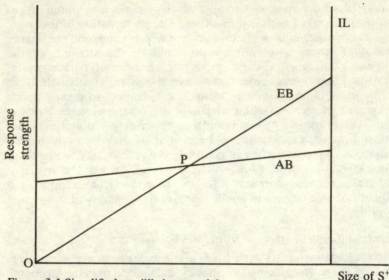

Figure 3.1 Simplified equilibrium model
Source: Alhadeff 1982: 56.

approach behaviour is the size of the positive reinforcer (S^+ in Alhadeff's symbology), while the sole determinant of the strength of escape behaviour is loss of the generalized reinforcer, money (S^-). Third, the relationships between approach/escape response strength and its determinant can be depicted linearly. Fourth, the Income Limit (IL) circumscribes the possibility of emitting escape and approach behaviours; it also influences the intensity of the aversive consequences of yielding up money in return for the positive reinforcer. Fifth, determinants of response strength other than those described above are assumed constant; a change in any of them would shift the respective curve upward or downward. And, finally, based on limited evidence from animal experimentation, the AB and EB curves are as depicted in Figure 3.1, that is, the slope of the EB curve is assumed greater than that of the AB curve (cf. Alhadeff 1982: 55–8; 1986).

Alhadeff's theory presents a logical application of operant principles to the analysis of consumer behaviour but contains a number of shortcomings as an elucidator of consumer choice in the context of marketing. (In fairness, it must be pointed out that increasing the intelligibility of marketing activity was not Alhadeff's intention.) First, the theory is preoccupied with commodities (products and services) and does not embrace a brand level of analysis (Chapter five will return to this). Perhaps as a result of this, the theory cannot consider the impact of non-price marketing mix elements on demand and sales. Second, it is based on the working assumption of the interspecies continuity of operant behaviour; however, as will be discussed at greater length in Chapter four, the implication that humans respond similarly to animals cannot be taken for granted. Third, the analysis is limited largely to purchasing (Alhadeff terms it 'buy-behaviour') rather than consumption, even though the outcomes of consumption have important consequences for repeat buying. Overall, in spite of the merits of the theory, it is severely limited in its relevance to the marketing level of analysis to which we now turn.

Consumer choice as operant response

The process of choice

Whilst Alhadeff's logical analysis of consumer behaviour provides a theoretical basis for behavioural economics, it is of limited value in elucidating observed consumer choice in a marketing context. A more realistic analysis of consumer choice in operant terms, in contrast to the decision process depiction on which cognitive models are based, begins with an external stimulus such as an advertising message or word-of-mouth communication. But the extent to which this stimulus controlled behaviour would depend upon the individual's reinforcement history – whether the purchase/consumption response advocated had come under stimulus control as a result of prior reinforcement of similar responses in the presence of the discriminative stimulus. Advertising and other persuasive messages portray discriminative stimuli in the form of rules, suggestions, norms, promises, prompts, and other verbal and nonverbal descriptions of contingencies.

These discriminative stimuli exert partial control over behaviour, but a radical behaviourist analysis would assume the main source of control to be the contingencies themselves: the individual must have some tendency to behave in the advocated manner before the discriminative stimuli contained in the message can exert control by marking the occasion for reinforcement. The consumer's unique reinforcement history determines whether the message's discriminative stimuli signal reinforcing, punishing, or neutral consequences of behaving; but, important as the stimuli contained in persuasive marketing or ('source-credible') word-of-mouth communications may become, unless the appropriate behavioural discriminations have been learned, advertising and other messages cannot change behaviour (Skinner 1971, p. 93).

At each stage in the 'decision-process', an operant analysis would concentrate upon observable responses and their environmental influences. Cognitive conceptualizations like sensation and perception would be superfluous to describe the way in which consumers learned to discriminate behaviourally as their responses came under the stimulus control of verbal behaviours such as tacts; speech would also be described in terms of symbolic verbal responses under stimulus and reinforcement control; and thinking as a series of covert tacting responses. Affective responses would similarly be described as 'self-descriptive tacting responses under the reinforcement control of the verbal community'. Thus, the presentation of a positive reinforcer leads to responses which are described as 'joyful'; the removal of such a reinforcer, to responses that are 'depressing'. The presentation of a negative reinforcer leads to responses which are called 'fearful'; whilst the removal of such a reinforcer offers 'relief' (Hillner 1984: 159).

In contrast to the cognitive approach, in which the formation of attitudes and intentions is seen as a mechanism of prebehavioural choice (Ajzen and Fishbein 1980; Fishbein and Ajzen 1975), the radical behaviourist finds no place in his explanatory mode for the concept of a 'true' attitude which mediates both statements of attitude and intention, and overt behaviour. Verbal and other classes of behaviour with respect to an object or action are under the control of the various reinforcement contingencies located within the situations in which those behaviours are emitted. Behaviours which belong to different classes (for example, talking about how one will vote and actually voting) will be consistent only when the contingencies of reinforcement applicable to both are functionally equivalent (DeFleur and Westie 1963; Foxall 1984a).

The attempt to predict consumers' brand choices from statements of purchase intent confirms this. Moreover, since contingencies may vary markedly from situation to situation, verbal and non-verbal behaviours with respect to brand choice can be predicted to differ with the elapse of time. This prediction of behavioural analysis is entirely borne out by empirical investigations in the marketing framework (Foxall 1984b; Harrell and Bennett 1974; Ryan and Bonfield 1975, 1980; Wilson *et al.* 1975). At least in the case of low involvement consumer behaviour, there is no need to posit prebehavioural cognitive choice and prior behaviour assumes an increased explanatory significance, supplementing and possibly overshadowing that of cognitive variables such as behavioural intentions (Fredericks and Dossett 1983;

Bentler and Speckart 1981). Interesting empirical evidence relating to a more highly involving purchase, home computers, suggests that a measure of prior behaviour usefully supplements consumers' intentions in the prediction of their subsequent behaviour (McQuarrie 1988.)[1]

In every instance in which the cognitive psychologist speaks of changing behaviour by acting upon the states of mind assumed to prefigure behaviour, the radical behaviourist speaks of changing the probabilities of action through the manipulation of reinforcement contingencies. Feelings of confidence or conviction which are taken by cognitive theorists to be prebehavioural causes of purchase, are, to radical behaviourists, simply effects of those reinforcement contingency responses which also explain operant responses (Skinner 1971: 95–6). Choice is not, therefore, the outcome of internal, mental deliberation, 'psychological decision processes': it is simply a behaviour, the only way of acting in a given set of circumstances defined in terms of controlling contingencies. Alternatively, Herrnstein (1970: 255) conceptualizes choice as 'behavior set into the context of other behavior', with the implication that all behavior is of this nature. Choice is not 'a psychological process or a special kind of behavior in its own right' but nothing more than 'a way of interrelating one's observations of behavior' (ibid., p. 253).

Situations in which individuals report that they have to make choices are those in which several responses are equally probable, that is, in which the contingencies of each response are functionally similar. Such situations are usually aversive and 'any decision-making behavior which strengthens one response and makes the other unlikely is reinforced' (Skinner 1974: 22–3). Freedom is portrayed in this context as the avoidance of aversive consequences, a denial of the existential freedom posited by most cognitive and phenomenological theories of behaviour (Skinner 1971).

The sequence of choice

Such buyer behaviour is usually depicted as a sequential process interpreted in terms of the changing mental processes of an individual consumer during the prepurchase, purchase and post-purchase stages of purchase and consumption (Foxall 1980b). Cast, by contrast, in terms of a behavioural analysis, the sequence of individual consumer behaviour over time still contains three broad stages, understood however in terms of their environmental determinants:

1. The initial presentation of novel discriminative stimuli (typically an advertisement for a new brand within an existing product class) which signals certain reinforcements contingent upon the emission of specified purchase and consumption responses. Not all consumers of the product class will react in the same way to this. Each consumer's unique history of reinforcement determines whether the response is one of immediate rejection, or whether the item is accorded a trial purchase.

2. The second stage involves that subset of current users of the product class who buy the new brand and evaluate its performance in use. Whether trial occurs at all depends on the consequences that have followed buying and using other brands in the product class in the past (and new brands in product classes generally) as well as the reinforcing or punishing consequences of buying and using current product class members. It does not necessarily follow that trial of a novel brand, product or store will occur only if the consumer's recent experiences have had aversive consequences: variety is a powerful primary reinforcer in its own right.

3. The consequences of purchase and of the performance of the brand during the trial phase determine the probability that these behaviours will be maintained or increased. The buyer may include the new brand within his or her repertoire of brands in the product class that are purchased relatively frequently. Trial and repeat buying do not depend upon the consumer reaching a prepurchase conviction of brand/product efficacy, as the final stage in a sequence of mental states through which he or she has been propelled by persuasive marketing communications. Rather, trial and repeat are controlled by the consequences of initial and subsequent purchase and consumption.

These three stages resemble those of the Awareness–Trial–Repeat (ATR) model (Ehrenberg 1974), though the behaviouristic approach attributes causation solely to environmental stimuli and avoids even the minimal causal reference to consumers' perceptions, curiosity, attitudes, and intentions found in the ATR model.

Marketing mix influences

Within this framework, the action of each element of the marketing mix can be understood, not as persuasive influence responsible for the propulsion of the consumer through a hierarchy of psychological functions but by means of the three-term contingency.

Products and services contain numerous elements (attributes or features) each of which is a discriminative stimulus that signals reinforcement conditional upon purchase and consumption responses. As has been noted, after trial and early repeat purchasing, continued purchase and consumption may come under stimulus control, requiring only a logo, brand name, or point-of-sale advertisement to increase the probability of a sale and subsequent consumption. The non-product elements of the mix shape and maintain purchasing, particularly at the first and third stages of the process. Product and brand features, including those displayed on packaging and through other design media, do not act simply as discriminative stimuli. They are also reinforcers in themselves, strengthening customers' attentive behaviours with an immediacy that makes familiarity with similar goods unnecessary (Skinner 1953a: 395). Brand positioning and repositioning would, therefore, entail not a battle for the consumer's mind but the manipulation of the discriminative and reinforcing stimuli represented by the various product and non-product features of the marketing mix.

Marketer-dominated communications, including advertising, portray discriminative stimuli, as noted, in the form of rules, suggestions, norms, promises, prompts, and other verbal and non-verbal descriptions of the contingencies of reinforcement. The messages signal reinforcements (described in terms of the attributes of the advertised brands and their benefits-in-use) and show how they are dependent upon the consumer's performance of specific responses which other elements of the marketing mix facilitate. The implication is that the beneficial consequences depicted can be obtained only when certain procedures which culminate in brand selection are followed and the advertisement may indicate how easily these necessary responses which shape this final choice can be executed: 'Your local shop can ...' 'Our friendly representative will ...' 'Just clip the coupon and. ...'.

It is noteworthy that radical behaviourists claim that, while discriminative stimuli of the kind found in advertising may exert partial control over behaviour, the main source of control is the contingencies themselves, the reinforcements available when particular responses are made. Hence, as already noted, Skinner (1971) claims that the individual must have some tendency to behave in the manner advocated by the commercial before the discriminative stimuli contained in its message can exert control. Important as the stimuli contained in persuasive marketing communications may be, such promotional messages cannot – if

Skinner's assertion is accepted – influence behaviour unless the appropriate behavioural discriminations have already been learned by direct exposure to the contingencies (Skinner 1969). This theoretical assertion, which will be reexamined in Chapter 4, implies that 'contingency-based' behaviour will be more effectively learned, more difficult to extinguish, than 'rule-governed' behaviour which relies simply upon verbal descriptions of the contingencies. If it is accepted, Skinner's claim would suggest that advertising is not the highly powerful medium it is often depicted to be (Driver and Foxall 1984).

Sales promotions are deals which offer the buyer some additional benefit ('Money off' or '20 per cent more' or 'A free gift') which can be obtained by performing specified responses. They may, as in the case of free samples, encourage trial so that the consequences of use will reinforce that response and shape behaviour until the brand is incorporated into the consumer's repertoire of similar brands. They may offer greater value for money which reward the buyer for purchase and use of the promoted brand through the provision of more reinforcers. They can require the performance of a series of responses which involve the repeated purchase of the promoted brand before the additional reinforcer becomes available. Such promotional methods include shaping and chaining as the final response is produced and maintained through a series of individually-reinforced approximations: sampling, coupon redemption, competitions, and collectable items all play a part (Rothschild and Gaidis 1981; Peter and Nord 1982). The effectiveness of sales promotional methods lies in their capacity to offer reinforcements on intermittent (fixed and variable interval and ratio) schedules in addition to those provided by the purchase and use of the brand itself: i.e. promotional deals reinforce every nth purchase or reward only a proportion of purchasers (Nord and Peter 1980).

Distribution strategies also entail the careful management of discriminative stimuli contained in store layouts, store locations, and retail images, all of which are positioned to reduce the time and effort required to make a purchase response. Merchandising techniques aimed at selling particular brands or pack sizes involve the physical presentation of these antecedent stimuli in ways that encourage unplanned or 'impulse' purchasing, the buying of complementary products, and greater overall purchase volume. Retail strategies, particularly merchandising, frequently comprise attempts to encourage stimulus and response generalization, notably by extending the range of discriminative stimuli to which prospective buyers are exposed in order to increase the sales volume of each store visit. Several instore promotional strategies are available for this purpose (Buttle 1984).

(i) *The manipulation of store traffic* ensures that consumers visit as many parts of the store as possible rather than confining their route to the outer perimeter, and to increase the amount of time spent in the shop, both of which are directly related to increased sales. Aisles are, therefore, designed continuously rather than in a grid pattern to ensure that the discriminative stimuli found on packs are brought to consumers' attention. Gondolas are arranged so that merchandise is within easy reach of eye and hand to encourage unplanned purchasing. Response generalization is promoted by the physical location of strongly demanded items, typically perishable products sold as loss leaders, such that exposure to slower moving, more expensive products is encouraged.

(ii) *Shelf positioning* is manipulated to ensure that product class members are adjacent in order to facilitate brand comparisons in which novel discriminative stimuli exert maximal control. This usually requires competing brands to be located vertically above one another, a tactic which allows alternative items (say, new own-label alternatives or expensive alternative product classes) to be located in horizontally adjacent positions. Eye level placings are most conducive to sales (there is no point hiding discriminative stimuli known to control sales) and the rotation of products/brands not only increases exposure to the whole range of stimuli but also provides variety, in itself an important primary reinforcer and often a prerequisite of unplanned buying. Slow-moving brands can be placed next to fast movers for the same reason. Sought-after brands may deviate from these rules, being positioned with less accessibility, to increase consumers' exposure to other merchandise.

(iii) *Point of sale material* ensures that discriminative stimuli featured strongly in advertisements are prominent in the store and that situational cues and rules developed in promotions generalize to the purchasing setting (Branthwaite 1984) and thus promote operant discrimination. Their effectiveness is evident in that signs promoting brand benefits are known to increase sales by between 17 and 27 per cent; those featuring price information, by between 30 and 66 per cent (Buttle 1984).

(iv) *Special displays* promote behavioural generalization by encouraging purchases of related, complementary products (coffee and creamer). Window displays provide discriminative stimuli for store entry, browsing, and buying. Of course, all such stimuli rely on subsequent reinforcement of instore behaviours, especially purchasing, if they are to control consumer responses (Buttle 1984).

Store location strategy is similarly directed towards the physical maximization of traffic flow and sales (Wrigley 1988). Store images comprise a range of discriminative stimuli which show how reinforcements are conditional upon shopping at a given store; these stimuli make up what is usually described as store 'atmosphere' or 'ambience' but can be analysed in terms of quality, price, locale, sales assistants' behaviour, and service (Berry 1969). Other examples include elements of design, for example lighting, colour, style, and materials (Baker *et al.* 1988). Store managers segment their markets on the basis of consumers' learned differential responses to these stimuli and reinforce them accordingly (Kunkel and Berry 1968).

Finally, *price* information is frequently a discriminative stimulus for the aversive consequences of buying: the surrender of a valuable general reinforcer, money. While purchasing is a response which is reinforced by the acquisition of primary and secondary reinforcers, it is simultaneously punished by the forfeit of ability to obtain other reinforcers (Alhadeff 1982). Nevertheless, a segment of many consumer markets employs price within limits as an indicator of quality and/or performance and, within those limits, may prefer to buy at a higher rather than a lower price (Gabor 1988).

Marketing as reciprocal interaction

The contention that marketing comprises exchange processes is uncontroversial, as exchanges of one physical artefact for another in barter, like exchanges of products and services for liquid financial assets in pecuniary markets testify continually. Such exchanges inevitably include symbolic and subjective elements as well as a core of literal and concrete transfers of observable entities such as tangible products or title (Foxall 1981c: 175–9). Intellectual and practical difficulties arise, however, when exchange is attributed entirely metaphorically to social interactions of a totally symbolic nature. The subject matter of marketing has recently accommodated, if somewhat uneasily, 'exchanges' of this kind and the broadened scope of the discipline has been conceptually rationalized by the claim that its subject matter encompasses exchange relationships *per se*, wherever they are encountered, and that it is a science of universal application

(Bagozzi 1974, 1975; Kotler 1972; Kotler and Zaltman 1972; Levy 1978). On this view, the domain of marketing cannot be confined to the so-called 'simple' exchanges involved in barter and pecuniary transactions, but embraces also such 'complex' exchange relationships as occur between marriage partners, the individual and the state, and charities and donors.

Chief among the problems raised by deviations from literal economic exchanges as the domain of marketing are (i) the precise designation of what is exchanged in the social, political, sexual, and altruistic interactions that are held to constitute marketing transactions, since, for at least one party in each case, nothing tangible and measurable passes from one individual or organization to the other, and (ii) the consequent difficulties of determining demand, supply, price, and the efficiency of supply operations (Foxall 1984e).

Nevertheless, to argue that to employ the concept of exchange metaphorically in the marketing context is to drain it of meaning, is not to oppose the extension of the sphere of consumer research. Many who would reserve the term 'marketing' to denote transactions that have some literal and tangible content acknowledge that consumer behaviour is broader than the relationships of businesses and their customers: citizens consume social services and other state provisions, even if many of the decisions that govern the quantity and quality of supply and price are made on their behalf by administrators rather than in markets. The search for a satisfactory generic conceptualization of market and non-market consumer behaviour has not been adequately concluded. A behavioural analysis suggests a resolution.

At the most basic level, the contingencies involved in orthodox marketing exchanges are shown in Figure 3.2 which summarizes the interactions between consumer and marketer in terms of how the outcomes of the responses of one provide stimuli that control the actions of the other. Effective marketing interactions depend upon the synchronicity and physical coordination of the three-term contingencies involved.

The dynamic nature of marketing interactions portrayed in Figure 3.3 derives from the fact that most discriminative and contingent stimuli of one person's behaviour directly or indirectly comprise other people's activities; hence social interaction can be conceptualized as a 'complex lattice of interrelated' $S^D - R - S^R$ chains (Kunkel 1977). Person A is a consumer who enters a store (R_1), an action which is an S^D for another consumer, D, to follow; another S^D, an item in the store window, also signals reinforcement for D's entering (R_2). A's entry is also an S^D for a

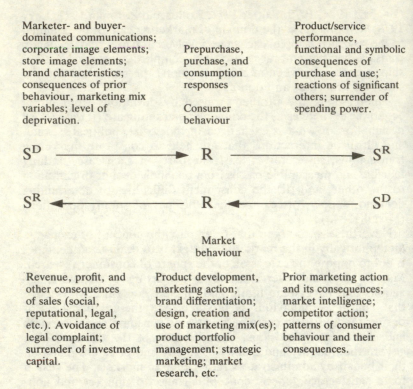

Marketer- and buyer-dominated communications; corporate image elements; store image elements; brand characteristics; consequences of prior behaviour, marketing mix variables; level of deprivation.

Prepurchase, purchase, and consumption responses

Consumer behaviour

Product/service performance, functional and symbolic consequences of purchase and use; reactions of significant others; surrender of spending power.

$$S^D \longrightarrow R \longrightarrow S^R$$

$$S^R \longleftarrow R \longleftarrow S^D$$

Market behaviour

Revenue, profit, and other consequences of sales (social, reputational, legal, etc.). Avoidance of legal complaint; surrender of investment capital.

Product development, marketing action; brand differentiation; design, creation and use of marketing mix(es); product portfolio management; strategic marketing; market research, etc.

Prior marketing action and its consequences; market intelligence; competitor action; patterns of consumer behaviour and their consequences.

Figure 3.2 Marketing as behavioural interaction under contingency control

salesperson, B, to approach and offer assistance (R_3). This action is an S^D for another customer, already in the store, to approach another salesperson (R_5) and request service. And so on.

Several of the actions are reciprocal: each reinforces the other and the term 'exchange theory' has been applied to the analysis of such mutually contingent interactions (Homans 1961/1974). The $S^D - R - S^R$ chains shown in Figure 3.3 describe the pattern of interactions among buyers and sellers and suggest an explanation of the structure of their relatedness in terms of behavioural psychology. The content of the relationships can be summarized in terms derived from operant theory which give rise to five general propositions about human behaviour (Homans 1974: chapter 2 *passim*) which capture the essence of radical behaviourist interpretation in less exacting language and avoid some of the debates that surround them.

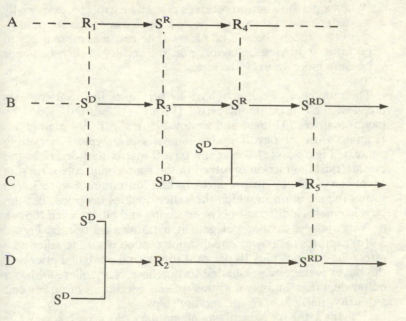

Figure 3.3 Dynamic social interaction in a consumer context
Source: After Kunkel 1977.

The success proposition. 'For all actions taken by persons, the more often a particular action of a person is rewarded, the more likely the person is to perform that action'.

The stimulus proposition. 'If in the past the occurrence of a particular stimulus has been the occasion on which a person's action has been rewarded, then the more similar the present stimuli are to the past ones, the more likely the person is to perform the action, or some similar action, now'.

The value proposition. 'The more valuable to a person is the result of his action, the more likely he is to perform the action'.

The deprivation-satiation proposition. 'The more often in the recent past a person has received a particular reward, the less valuable any further unit of that reward becomes for him'.

The aggression-approval proposition. 'When a person's action does not receive the reward he expected, or receives punishment he did not expect, he will be angry; he becomes more likely to perform aggressive behavior, and the results of such behavior become more valuable to him';
and

'When a person's action receives reward he expected, especially a greater reward than he expected, or does not receive punishment he expects, he will be pleased; he becomes more likely to perform approving behavior, and the results of such behavior become more valuable to him'.

The outcomes of these behaviour principles in social contexts are described in economic terms (Profit = Reward − Cost) by payoff matrices (Thibaut and Kelley 1959). Figure 3.4 exemplifies Homans's use of payoff matrix analysis in a typical marketing context. Figure 3.4(a) shows the payoff matrix that describes the symmetrical interaction involved in the simple mutually-satisfying exchange of money for product/product for money. Figure 3.4(b) shows the situation in which the seller doubles his price, but the buyer remains indifferent between saving and buying even though he will make a smaller net gain if a transaction occurs. Figure 3.4(c) captures the power equalization that occurs if the seller now offers the produce plus 10 per cent for twice the original price and the buyer is thereby persuaded to purchase. The seller still has a better deal than initially and this reflects conditions of power and authority that influence the relationships.

Homans's theory describes 'elementary' forms of social behaviour, that is, behaviour's 'fundamental processes, regardless of the various and complicated ways in which these processes combine to establish and maintain ... social units' (1974: 2; cf. Blau 1964). This is not the place to present either a full exposition of exchange theory or a comprehensive critique (see, for example, Homans 1958; Easton 1972; Hamblin and Kunkel 1977; Gergen *et al*. 1980; Heath 1976; Chadwick-Jones 1986; Blau 1970). However, the theory of social exchange has already found applications in the analysis of marketing interactions (e.g. in professional selling: Tarver and Haring 1988) and the payoff matrix approach suggests an explanatory mechanism not only for much consumer behaviour, but also for the long-term maintenance of the organizational interactions involved in industrial purchasing and marketing.

The description of marketing exchanges by reference to the stable interactions of firms in industrial networks lends itself readily to conceptual underpinning based on exchange theory, even though the latter was developed for individuals rather than organizations. The network approach envisages institutionalized buyer–seller relationships in terms of the exchanges of resources essential to the survival and prosperity of trading partners within networks and of the bonds created through the economically reciprocal interactions inherent in buying and selling but also in

(a) Symmetrical interaction

Seller's Actions	Buyer's actions: b_1 Save	Buyer's actions: b_2 Spend
Store S_1	1 / 1	0 / 1
Sell S_2	1 / 0	2 / 2

(b) Buyer indifference

Seller's Actions	Buyer's actions: b_1 Save	Buyer's actions: b_2 Spend
Store S_1	2 / 1	
Sell S_2		2 / 2

(c) Power equalization

Seller's Actions	Buyer's actions: b_1 Save	Buyer's actions: b_2 Spend
Store S_1	2 / 1	
Sell S_2		3 / 2

Figure 3.4 Pay-off matrices in a marketing context
Source: After Homans 1974.

the transfer of technical expertise, information, personnel, and other resources (e.g. Hakansson 1982; Thorelli 1986; Mattsson 1986). The three basic components of the managerial perspective assumed by this framework – partners' mutual perceptions, their performances of specific instrumental actions one for another, and the particular outcomes of those actions – correspond respectively to the S^D, R and S^R of operant analysis and the relationships it implies.

Although the network approach has been primarily concerned with the long-term management of the continuity of interorganizational relationships, on the assumption that industrial interaction is characterized by co-operation, it is necessary to consider also the possibility of deliberately disruptive actions between firms based on the opportunism of one or other partner to an agreement. This issue, to which transactions cost analysis has been specifically addressed (Williamson 1975), also falls within the purview of an exchange theory approach based on operant performance and its aversive, as well as positive, consequences (Foxall 1988a, 1988b).

A more direct route to knowledge

Research in behavioural economics and economic psychology has proceeded on two broad fronts: operant laboratory studies of economic principles (using, principally, animal subjects) and the study of token economies (using, principally, human subjects). Overall, these experiments indicate the orderly and predictable nature of choice in such contexts. Most of the research in this area has been interdisciplinary and has explored the analogues between demand analysis in neoclassical economics and reinforcement analysis in operant psychology (Kagel 1987). The following account does not attempt to describe comprehensively the techniques commonly available and well-documented (for example, Allison 1983; Lea 1978; Lea *et al.* 1987) but attempts to show how animal research based on the EAB can contribute to the scope of consumer research. It is concerned, moreover, to present an overview of the nature of animals' economic behaviour as a prelude to the discussion in Chapter 4 of the interspecies generalizability of behavioural principles.

Operant laboratory studies of economic principles

Animal experimentation frees consumer research from some of the limitations of direct investigation of human subjects: it makes possible the analysis of responses to substantial risks and payoffs, the (partial or full) elimination of the effects of income or wealth, long-term observation of economic relationships, and the reduction or elimination of the effects of subjects' consciousness of the experimental situation (Castro and Weingarten 1970; Smith 1982).

Animal experiments provide the sole route to knowledge in some spheres, for example, those which would entail ethical problems or which would be inordinately expensive in the case of human subjects; they also allow some investigations to proceed conveniently, for example, studies of price/quantity demanded relationships over broad ranges of price variation (Lea 1981). Animal research also allows direct comparison of the predictive validity of alternative hypotheses (e.g. Battalio *et al.* 1987; cf. Kagel 1987). Animal research is particularly relevant to the investigation of consumer choice in a relativistic framework since it not only provides opportunities to confirm existing knowledge of economic relationships but also to challenge orthodox understandings of market interactions (Lea 1981).

Care must be taken in generalizing from non-human to human behaviour, though it has been argued that, if predictions as precise as those derived from price theory are not substantiated in the case of rats or pigeons in tightly-controlled experimental circumstances offering a very limited range of commodity choices, it is either most unlikely that human demand behaviour will conform to microeconomic laws (as Battalio *et al.* 1987 argue) or improbable that operant psychology alone can account adequately for the observed behaviour. The following discussion is concerned with the extent to which economic behaviour can be considered operant behaviour.

Price elasticity of demand

The central components of microeconomic analysis find analogues in the operant analysis of choice: economic commodities correspond to reinforcers ('they are both classes of things whose contingent presentation will maintain behavior'; Lea 1978: 443); price corresponds to a schedule parameter, since both indicate how much of a limited exchange resource must be given up in order to obtain the reinforcer; and money is equivalent to the number of responses upon which delivery of the reinforcer is contingent. Thus the economist's demand curve, which relates the quantity of a good which is bought to price, is analogous to a function relating the quantity of reinforcements obtained and the number of responses required to obtain them, but only if the experimental analysis of choice occurs in situations where

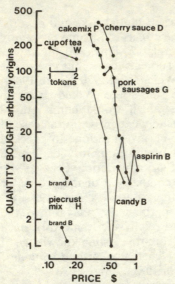

(a) Demand functions from retailing experiments, collected by Lea (1978). The curves are appropriately positioned on the price axis but placed arbitrarily on the quantity axis, with the two curves for piecrust mix in the correct relative positions.

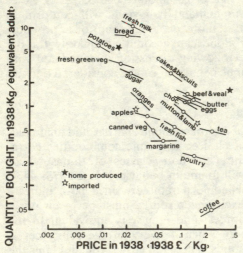

(b) Demand data for several types of food in the United Kingdom between 1920 and 1938, as obtained by Stone (1954). The points show mean price and consumption in 1938, and the lines drawn through them show the elasticity of demand for the whole period. (From Lea 1978.)

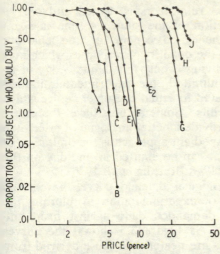

(c) Buy–response curves for ten food commodities, obtained by the method of Gabor and Granger (1966). (From Lea 1978.)

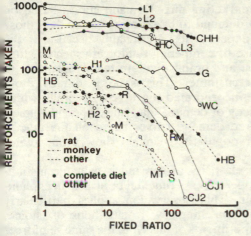

(d) Demand curves from psychological experiments on animals. (Compiled by Lea 1978.)

Figure 3.5 Economic and psychological demand curves and buy–response functions

Source: S.E.G. Lea (1978) 'Economics and psychology of demand', *Psychological Bulletin*, 85: 441–6. Copyright © 1978 by the American Psychological Association. Reprinted by permission of the publishers and author.

extra-experimental access to reinforcers is denied and only a comparatively small proportion of the subject's time is spent responding on the schedule (the 'closed economy' or 'free behaviour situation'). Otherwise, since the quantity of responses which may be expended by an animal living twenty-four hours a day in an experimental chamber is unlimited, the experimental findings could not be realistically related to actual consumer choice which is limited by income constraints.[2] Some authors have, therefore, suggested that time would provide a better analogue of price than responses, though a more expedient approach is the limitation of the number of responses that can be emitted in one day on the schedule (Allison 1983; Lea 1978; Rachlin *et al.* 1976).

Downward-sloping psychological demand curves have been produced by several types of experimentation by plotting the number of reinforcements demanded daily against fixed and variable ratio requirements. As Figure 3.5 shows, the curves obtained in such experiments are neater than those derived from retail experiments, no doubt a reflection of the non-price influences on real world demand, that is, factors such as taste, competition, and availability as well as the strategic use of the non-price elements of the marketing mix. Demand curves based on retail experiments show demand to be far more elastic than those obtained from animal experiments, presumably because of the absence in the latter case of competing reinforcers such as alternative pack sizes, stores, and brands that are readily available to the urban supermarket customer. This is borne out by those experiments which have incorporated concurrent schedules which show greater price elasticity of demand than single-operant studies. Econometrically-estimated demand curves based on the macroeconomic estimation of population demand show even greater variability (Lea 1978).[3]

The concept of price elasticity of demand is valuable in indicating the limitation of operant experimental principles in explaining economic behaviour. This observation applies particularly to the relevance of the matching law to situations of choice. When, as is typical of experiments of this type, the same reinforcer (usually food) is provided for each pattern of operant response, choice is a function of differences in the frequency, amount of delay of reinforcement provided. Each alternative has its own price, therefore, but the same demand curve describes the relationship between price and quantity demanded for each case. In such experiments, the allocation of responses between alternatives is accurately described by the matching law (Hursh 1980).

However, when the alternative reinforcers are distinct commodities, a situation which provides a closer analogue to human consumer choices, the matching law ceases to be an accurate descriptor of the resulting pattern of response allocation. Hursh and Natelson (1981) presented rats with a choice of food or pleasure centre stimulation, initially on FR2 schedules for both and subsequently FR8 schedules for both. In the first situation, electrical brain stimulation was preferred to food by a factor of nine, but when the schedule parameter was increased, food demand remained at its previous level while the amount of brain stimulation obtained dropped dramatically. In other words, demand for the necessity, food, is inelastic, whilst that for the luxury, brain stimulation, is highly elastic.

Cross-elasticity of demand

Cross-elasticities of demand reflect the extent to which the quantity demanded of one commodity is a function of the price of other commodities. In behavioural psychology, the effect of the availability of reinforcement on one schedule upon the rate of responding on another is expressed in terms of behavioural contrast or induction. In the case of concurrent schedules, a reduction in the rate of responding on one schedule when the other is made less severe is known as *simultaneous behavioural contrast*. If the schedules are successively available the result is known as *successive behavioural contrast*. *Behavioural induction* refers to an increase in rate (Lea 1978; Rachlin and Baum 1972). Both economic and psychological reasoning leads to the expectation that cross-price elasticities will be positive; the prediction is, therefore, that contrast will be found more frequently than induction and that in studies employing concurrent schedules and multi-operant designs, there will be more contrast, the closer the alternative reinforcements are mutual substitutes. Indeed, studies of the matching law confirm that when the same reinforcer is employed simultaneous contrast is the norm and induction is rare.

There are similarities in actual consumer behaviour. Detailed descriptions of market dynamics (Ehrenberg 1972), as was noted in Chapter one, page 16, indicate that in mature, steady-state markets (which are the norm for most established product classes), very few users of the product are 100 per cent brand loyal; in the case of ready-to-eat breakfast cereals, for instance, the proportion of such buyers as a percentage of all buyers of the product class is, in a three-month period, about 15 per cent and, in a year, about 6 per cent. Most consumers practise multi-brand buying, selecting from a small repertoire of tried and tested, usually nationally advertised, brands that are considered close or exact substitutes. In physical formulation, these brands are often identical or almost so: they differ by virtue of branding and other distinctions produced by the manipulation of the marketing mix and instore merchandising which provide discriminative stimuli for repeat buying. New brands within a product class are usually tried by current product users but few engender the discriminative learning necessary to be elevated to 'repertoire status'. Up to 90 per cent of new brands fail in the marketplace (Foxall 1984d).

In behavioural science terms, there is limited discrimination (each customer's purchases are confined to the repertoire rather than extending over the whole range of brands available) accompanied by a degree of stimulus generalization insofar as the repertoire brands are selected apparently randomly (though, at the aggregate market level, some brands attain a larger share of the market than others). These observations are also consistent with the expectation of large, positive cross-price elasticities of demand for the close substitutes involved and the consequent prediction of behavioural contrast rather than behavioural induction. Similar effects are found in consumers' store choices and TV viewing selections (Keng and Ehrenberg 1984; Goodhardt *et al.* 1987).

Income elasticity of demand

Understandably, when the possible number of responses that can be emitted is unrestricted in animal experimentation, the effect of demand on choice is minimized since the subject can simply increase its rate of responding as the price increases. When, as is usual, experimental conditions have not restricted responses, neither of the alternative reinforcers available (for example, food and heroin) has a particularly elastic demand: in spite of the very different nature of these goods, demand would not be affected other than minimally by changes in price (that is, in the fixed ratio parameter). A clearer pattern of differential demand between two commodities emerges from experiments involving limitation of th number of responses permitted each day. In experiments offering the alternatives of food and heroin, as long as both were cheap (that is, the FR parameter was low) each commodity was chosen in approximately equal amounts. As the schedule increased, demand for heroin dropped while that for food remained constant. Food demand is inelastic while that for heroin is highly elastic, but the difference shows up only when income is limited (Elsmore 1979; Rachlin *et al.* 1976).

Token economies and behavioural technology

Token economies are experimental situations which contain a high degree of correspondence to known economic systems. The subjects are usually patients in a total institution such as a mental hospital or students in a classroom setting. The token economy requires a medium of exchange in the form of generalized secondary reinforcers (tokens); back-up reinforcers, usually primary, such as food or leisure, which present the 'consumers' with options; and a set of rules which establish how optimal behaviour is related to the earning of tokens and how tokens are related to the back-up reinforcers (Kazdin 1977). The economy systematically delivers consequences that are contingent upon the performance of responses that are judged prosocial by the organizers of the community (Ayllon and Azrin 1968a, b; Kazdin 1981).

Token economies provide, in practice, sufficient incentive to encourage their members to maintain such behaviours as bed-making or light manual work while the tokens are available, but withdrawal of the tokens is often associated with response extinction (Ayllon and Azrin 1965; Kazdin 1983). Also of interest, for purposes of drawing comparisons and contrasts, are the token and quasi-token exchanges studied by economic anthropologists (e.g. Bohannan and Dalton 1962; Dalton 1967, 1971). In addition to their therapeutic relevance, however, token economies provide a laboratory setting for the testing of economic theories and research indicates that several of the postulates of ordinal utility theory are confirmed in such environments (Battalio *et al.* 1973a; Kagel 1972; Krasner and Krasner 1973; Tarr 1976).

Criticism of these findings has come from economists and others who have argued that not all members of token economies have displayed behaviour consistent with neoclassical microeconomics (Ekelund *et al.* 1972; T. P. Roth 1987). Whilst it is true that a small proportion of token economy consumers fail to respond to the initial contingencies, however, manipulation of the reward system, for example, by varying the size of reinforcements, non-contingent reinforcer sampling, member preselection of back-up reinforcers, and changes in scoring patterns (Kazdin 1983), has been shown to increase prosocial responding (see also Battallio *et al.* 1973b). It is not necessary in any case, that every member of an economy conform to microeconomic 'laws'; as long as at least a sizeable minority do so, the economy is likely to act as though all do so.

Practical applications of token reinforcement systems are readily available (Cone and Hayes 1984; Davey 1981b; Kazdin 1981). The main applications include *energy conservation*: where the provision of small monetary rewards/points backed by privileges and prizes (Seaver and Patterson 1976) and informational feedback and prompts (Palmer *et al.* 1978; cf. Kohlenberg *et al.* 1976) has led to a reduction in the use of domestic energy; the provision of token reinforcements resulted in less frequent use of cars (Foxx and Hake 1977), car pool formation (Jacobs *et al.* 1982), and the use of coupons redeemable at a local store increased the use of public transportation (Everett *et al.* 1974; see also Deslauriers and Everett 1977); *recycling of waste*: where monetary incentives/ tickets with a raffle/redemption value have controlled littering (Chapman and Risley 1974; Finnie 1973; Geller *et al.* 1977; Kohlenberg and Phillips 1973; Powers *et al.* 1973), and the recycling of waste products such as drink bottles, metal cases, and paper (Geller *et al.* 1975); and *health and diet* (Kazdin 1980: 142–8; 225–7; 1981).

Experimentation grounded in behaviour theory is also directly relevant to the analysis of consumer behaviour. Chapter 5 will make extensive use of published studies in this area as a prelude to which the following description of an experiment in consumer choice undertaken by operant psychologists exemplifies the techniques employed.

Experimental analysis of consumer behaviour

Animal experiments are a broad analogue of human consumer purchasing, but allow subjects minimal choice and cannot reproduce the full range of influences on behaviour which confront the human consumer. Useful as such experimentation has proved to some consumer economists and psychologists, it is of restricted relevance to the analysis of real world buyer and consumption behaviours. Animal experiments generally permit limited access to a small number of reinforcers, and control the range of non-product influences on demand for primary reinforcers. Human consumer choice, at least in western-style economies, occurs in the context of an abundance of persuasive messages, purchase and saving opportunities, promotional stimuli, alternative distribution channels and a host of social, ethical, and political considerations which complicate the attempt to unravel the causes and consistencies of purchase and consumption. In marketing-oriented economies, the major focus is upon the competitive production and supply of secondary commodities, upon minor brand differentiations and market segmentation (Foxall 1989a).

Experimentation within this system permits, none the less, the monitoring and analysis of the effects of environmental stimuli upon consumers' purchase behaviour. The following account illustrates how an experimental approach to the analysis of consumer choice avoids unobservables, providing an alternative explanation of behaviour, based upon a more direct route to knowledge.

Operant experiments with animals and humans have basically followed an ABA design, i.e. one in which three sequential behavioural measurements are taken: (i) during the baseline period (A), before intervention takes place; (ii) during the experimental period (B), when changes in the assumed independent variable thought to influence behaviour are made; and (iii) the return-to-baseline (A) period, when the intervention is withdrawn. If the manipulated factor is indeed an independent variable, the behavioural change detected at B should extinguish during this third stage when the intervention ceases. The following discussion reviews an experiment (Greene *et al.* 1984; see also Greene and Neistat 1983) concerned with consumer protection in order to illustrate the methodology of behavioural research.

Retail price monitoring

At a time of steady price inflation for fast-moving consumer products, Greene *et al.* (1984) conducted an experiment to ascertain the impact of publishing food price data for selected grocery outlets on the behaviours of retailers and customers. The research took place within the context of the activities of a university-based consumer action group and was intended to determine whether action to publicize the prices of a standard basket of grocery items had a general effect on food prices.

The investigation comprised a 14-month (baseline) period, from May 1980 to July 1981, when prices were monitored approximately weekly at five target stores in Carbondale, Illinois, and two contrast stores some eight miles away in Murphysboro, Illinois. This was followed by an experimental phase in which price information was provided to customers through a local newspaper in the form of a *Pricewatch* advertisement, that is, an information-based announcement appearing in a local newspaper. During this phase, changes in retail prices were related to the appearance of *Pricewatch* and surveys of customers attempted to establish buyers' perception and use of the information presented. The managers of the stores involved were aware that the experiment was taking place.

All seven stores offered full supermarket service (i.e. complete meat, dairy, produce, and non-food selections). In each store, price data were collected on two separate baskets of goods, the experimental and control baskets, each of which consisted of a range of perishable items (e.g. whole milk), cereals, pasta and baking goods (e.g. Pillsbury flour), canned goods and condiments (e.g. Libby Corn Niblets), and household, pet supplies and tobacco items (e.g. Colgate toothpaste). Table 3.1 summarizes the research design and provides some information about the stores. On five occasions during the experimental phase, the prices of the experimental (but not the control) basket were published for each of the target stores. All five publications occurred relatively early in this phase (the first occurring at the end of July 1981, the other four at two-weekly intervals beginning five weeks after the first) but price monitoring continued until May 1982.

Table 3.1   Design for experimental consumer research

	Experimental basket goods prices	Control basket goods prices
Target city stores		
IGA–West (IGA–W)*	p	p
IGA–East (IGA–E)*	p	p
Greg's*	p	p
Kroger (T–Kro)**	p	p
National (Natl)**	p	p
Contrast city stores		
IGA Murphysboro (C–IGA)*	p	p
Kroger (C–Kro)**	p	p

Source: Compiled by the author
Notes: *independently operated store; **member of corporate chain; p price monitoring

The results show that during the baseline period prices at the target independent stores were slightly greater than those at the contrast independents and, at both, price showed a steady inflationary trend. During the experimental phase, however, the prices in the former fell perceptibly while those at the contrast stores continued to rise. Figure 3.6 illustrates the relationship for two of the matched independent stores. Toward the end of the monitoring activity (during what was in effect the return-to-baseline phase), the prices at the target and contrast independent stores converged. Moreover, similar patterns were found for both baskets. The implications of the research are that publicity was associated with unprecedented price divergence between the target and contrast stores' prices relative to the pattern established during the baseline period: 'Prices climbed 4.65 per cent (mean of the experimental and control baskets) at the contrast store, more

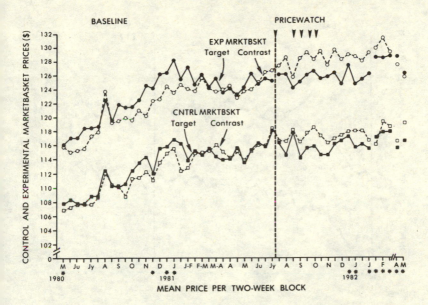

Figure 3.6 Prices at target (IGA–W) and contrast (C–IGA) stores

Note: Prices (in 2-week blocks) of the experimental and control market baskets at the target (IGA–W) and contrast (C–IGA) stores. Arrows indicate publication of *Pricewatch* (which was based on preceding 2 weeks' prices). Asterisks reflect blocks based on a single week's price observation. After the 7th-to-last data points, price checks were made once every other week. After the 3rd-to-last data point, checks were made once per month. Managers' questionnaires were delivered a week prior to the 2nd-to-last point.

Source: B. F. Greene, M. Rouse, R. B. Green, and C. Clay (1984) 'Behaviour analysis in consumer affairs: retail and consumer response to publicizing food price information', *Journal of Applied Behaviour Analysis*, 17: 3–21. Copyright © 1984 by the Society for the Experimental Analysis of Behaviour Inc. Reproduced by permission.

than twice the increase at the independent target stores (2.18 per cent). It would be naïve to regard these differences as "small"' (Greene *et al.* 1984: 19).

The corporate chain stores do not show this pattern (Figure 3.7 shows the pattern for a typical matched pair). The reason may be that corporate stores' managers have little discretion over pricing policy, prices being set centrally; owner–managers of independent

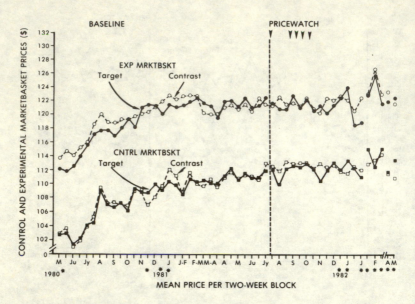

Figure 3.7 Prices at target (T–Kroger) and contrast (C–Kroger) stores

Note: Prices (in 2-week blocks) of the experimental and control market baskets at the target (T–Kro) and contrast (C–Kro) stores. Arrows indicate publication of *Pricewatch* (which was based on preceding 2 weeks' prices). Asterisks reflect blocks based on a single week's price observation. After the 7th-to-last data points, price checks were made once every other week. After the 3rd-to-last data point, checks were made once per month. Managers' questionnaires were delivered a week prior to the 2nd-to-last point.

Source: Greene *et al.* (1984), as for Figure 3.6.

stores would, by contrast, be free to alter their prices during the experimental period.

A sample of customers in the contrast city was made aware of the price information only through the newspaper publication of *Pricewatch*, whereas separate samples of target city consumers were informed either via the paper alone or by the paper plus a delivered flier which publicized the campaign. Table 3.2 shows the result of telephone interviews with the samples. Although the investigators were unable to obtain collaborative evidence on actual consumer behaviour, the figures suggest that the project was visible and useful to those at whom the campaign was aimed

Table 3.2 Postpublication consumer interviews: percentage of affirmative responses among consumers in the contrast, newspaper-only, and newspaper plus flier groups

	After one Pricewatch			After five Pricewatches		
Question	Contrast (n = 41)	Newspaper only (n = 41)	Newspaper + flier (n = 52)	Contrast (n = 41)	Newspaper only (n = 41)	Newspaper + flier (n = 52)
	%	%	%	%	%	%
Saw *Pricewatch*?	22.0	24.4	73.1	46.3	43.9	78.8
Found *Pricewatch* useful?	4.9	9.8	42.3	9.8	24.4	51.9
Shopped at a particular store based on *Pricewatch*?	NA	NA	NA	NA	9.8	23.1
Willing to pay for *Pricewatch*?	NA	NA	NA	NA	4.9	30.8

Note: NA indicates 'not asked'. Data are based on consumers who responded to all three interviews.
Source: Greene *et al.* (1984), as for Figure 3.6.

and that it resulted in some consumers, especially those made abundantly aware of it, switching stores.

Summing up: the promise of operant psychology for consumer research

The prevailing cognitive approach to consumer choice relies extensively upon the use of abstract and unobservable explanatory variables which seldom prove amenable to empirical investigation and evaluation. But consumer research need not involve a high level of abstraction; whatever unobservables are deemed necessary to make observables intelligible should not be treated as immutable but constructed in such a way as to be capable of critical evaluation, rejection, and replacement as progress demands. Unobservables are, in the final analysis, a convenience to researchers and ought not to be used to reify a conceptual world or to confine methodological and explanatory practice within the bounds of a single scientific world view.

The most relevant strength which radical behaviourism offers theoretical development in consumer psychology is the closeness of its explanatory propositions to the observed behaviour it is concerned to explain. It will be argued in the next chapter that its theoretical terms, such as 'reinforcement' and 'generalization', are themselves unobservables; nevertheless, the success of radical behaviourist explanation derives in no small measure from the closeness of its theoretical terms to observed behaviour and their relatively straightforward subjection to empirical test. The promise of radical behaviourism lies in the simplicity of its explanations, their parsimony of expression, and their avoidance of complex 'explanatory fictions' which defy empirical verification and analysis. Hypotheses derived from radical behaviourism are based upon observable controlling factors, which are often ignored or de-emphasized by cognitive research, but which are uniquely amenable to practical investigation and manipulation. As a result, radical behaviourism offers a means by which the unobservables which are often uncritically accepted as a necessary component of cognitive explanation can be subjected to careful comparison with a more parsimonious system founded upon antithetical assumptions about the nature and causation of behaviour.

Unobservables would have greater empirical content if they took the form of extrapolations from observables (consensually agreed) rather than that of constructs posited to exist in some other realm of discourse and requiring – but rarely finding – elaborate rules of correspondence before testing can occur. Such extrapolations are already available in other approaches to social and economic theory: the profit-maximizing firm of neoclassical economic theory is an example of a concept that has no direct empirical correspondent but which is nevertheless recognizable from observations of business organizations and capable of giving rise to testable hypotheses concerning those actual companies. The central assumptions of the theory are not open to empirical test, but the hypotheses which those assumptions make possible are testable and substitutable (e.g. Baumol 1959; Marris 1964; Simon 1959, 1976; Wiseman 1983). Microeconomics has evolved both a structure of theory and a process of theorization which are open to progress in ways which are less obviously available in contemporary consumer psychology. Part of the successful progress made by microeconomics results from the closeness of its unobservables to observation and the willingness of its practitioners to embrace a variety of testable explanatory approaches.

The opportunity for theory-based experimentation provided by operant psychology overcomes some of the problems by which instore experiments have been marked (Doyle and Gidengil 1977; Lea *et al.* 1987: 190–6). Animal experimentation is limited by its capacity to elucidate the influence of only one independent variable, price, neglecting the non-price elements of the marketing mix. There is no inherent reason, however, why consumer researchers should leave this kind of investigation to behavioural economists and economic psychologists. But the use of operant techniques in instore experimentation with human consumers offers a valuable stimulus to the development and testing of more basic models of consumer choice.

In spite of limitations, the EAB provides an essential critical contribution to the active interplay of tenaciously held views, which is vital to scientific progress. To the extent that consumer researchers explain choice in terms of highly-abstracted non-observables, a countervailing theoretical stance is a necessity. It is in this context that the EAB can make a central contribution to the critical analysis of psychological explanations of consumer behaviour. However, like all paradigms, the promise of the EAB is necessarily confined by its scope – a theme taken up in Chapter four.

Chapter four

Human operant behaviour

Hamlet said of man, 'How like a god!' (Act II, Scene ii). Pavlov said of him, 'How like a dog!'. Skinner says, 'That was a step forward. For like a dog, man is within the range of a scientific analysis'.

(Dilman 1988: 3)

Apart from the early stages of development, human behaviour involves active transformation of the environment, and thus requires a description involving contingencies produced by the individual. In that sense, Skinner's (1957) claim that human behaviour is behaviour transforming the environment is correct. Nevertheless, to claim that human behaviour includes processes related to contingencies such as those involved in operant situations, does not necessarily mean that it is governed by those sorts of contingencies alone.

(Ribes 1985: 129)

Verbal control in experimental settings

The question of the interspecies generalizability of the principles established in operant experimentation is central to the issue of how far human behaviour can be explained by reference to environmental stimuli rather than intrapersonal events and processes. Whilst there is increasing interest in human operant learning experiments (Buskist and Miller 1982) and there seems to be no fundamental operational impediment to such research (Baron and Perone 1982; Buskist *et al.* 1983), animal investigation continues to predominate. Treatments of behavioural conditioning in marketing journals, consumer behaviour texts, and the experimental economics literature generally infer that basic operant principles derived from animal research can be directly applied to complex human behaviours involved in purchasing and consumption.

Most psychologists also have assumed a considerable degree of continuity between human and non-human subjects; only a relatively small group has consistently argued that there exists a fundamental discontinuity. But the view that operant techniques and analysis used in the study of non-human behaviour inevitably produce similar results for humans (Miller 1962; Morse 1966; Skinner 1969; Whaley and Malott 1971) has been increasingly subjected to criticism and re-evaluation as empirical data concerning human performance on reinforcement schedules have become available (e.g. Lowe 1979; cf. Perone *et al.* 1988).

Animal and human responses

Based on observed differences in patterns of human operant learning which conflict with straightforward extrapolations from the animal laboratory and which reflect human capacities to verbalize reinforcement contingencies, Lowe and Horne (1985) argue for a dialectical approach: whilst acknowledging the biological and physiological similarities between human and non-human species, their dialecticism takes account of important qualitative differences which are apparent from studies of the schedule performances of human subjects in operant laboratories.

Human subjects display rather different patterns of behaviour from animals on both FI and FR schedules. As has been noted, animals exhibit a scalloped pattern in which rate of responding increases gently over time; the most obvious feature of such behaviour is the post-reinforcement pause. The behaviour of human subjects under experimental conditions based on these contingencies shows no such scalloping but conforms to one or other of two distinct patterns: either (a) a high and continuous rate of responding between reinforcements, or (b) a very low rate of responding, one or two responses being performed just before reinforcement is presented (see Figure 4.1). Animal subjects are, moreover, highly sensitive to changes in schedule parameters, varying their response rates and the length of the post-reinforcement pauses as they adjust their behaviour to obtain reinforcers as 'economically' as possible. By contrast, the high rate of responding shown by humans does not alter when the FI schedule is modified (Lowe 1979, 1983; Harzem *et al.* 1978; Lowe *et al.* 1978). Lowe (1983: 75) summarizes the emerging pattern of human performance as 'an unpredictable and uncontrolled subject matter and certainly one which differs greatly from other animal subjects' (see also Catania *et al.* 1982; Matthews *et al.* 1985).

Animal responses on FR schedules are usually emitted at a high

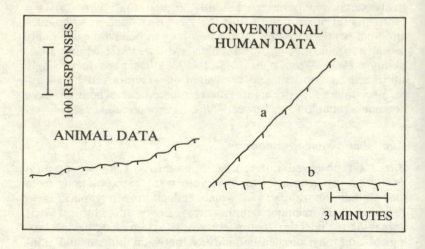

Figure 4.1 Cumulative records of typical animal and human performance of FI schedules

Source: C. F. Lowe, 'Determinants of human operant behaviour', in M. D. Zeiler and P. Harzem (eds) *Advances in Analysis of Behaviour*, vol. 1, 1979: 162. Copyright ©, 1979 J. Wiley and Sons Ltd. Reprinted by permission of John Wiley and Sons Ltd.

and constant rate with pauses after each reinforcer; as the FR value increases (requiring more responses for each reinforcer), so response rates decrease and pauses lengthen. Human performance is, however, insensitive to changes in the schedule ratio and uninterrupted by post-reinforcement rests. Humans also show a tendency towards rigidity in response rate which is not apparent in animals, maintaining the same rate of behavioural output as experimental conditions alter from FR to FI schedules. Such rigidity of performance in the face of considerable modification of the reinforcement contingencies is often economically inefficient in that subjects fail to minimize the response effort required to obtain reinforcement. Such economic 'irrationality' is absent from animal performance (Lowe and Horne 1985).

Studies of choice in animals which have incorporated concurrent VI schedules have led to the formulation of the matching law,

encountered in Chapter two, which states that in such circumstances a subject will emit alternative responses with frequencies
in direct proportion to the frequency of reinforcement available
for each response. Some studies have produced evidence for a
similar pattern of matching in human subjects (Pierce and Epling
1983) but there is mounting evidence that human choice often
deviates substantially from it. Lowe (1983) summarizes the results
of his extensive experimentation with human subjects thus: 'Under
various conditions, the majority of subjects performing on multiple
concurrent variable-interval schedules showed gross departure from
the matching relationship with forms of responding not previously
encountered in animal studies of concurrent performance.'[1]

Verbal control

Lowe (1979) discusses but discounts possible explanations of these
human behaviour patterns in terms of response cost and reinforcement history. He considers the role of verbal instructions in the
form of rules set by the experimenter and concludes that changes
in these might have important effects on rate of responding even
though the contingencies remain constant. Verbal self-instructions
appear also to exert a determinative effect on human subjects'
ability to formulate the task set by the experimenter; if the subject
deduces that the schedule is FR, the tendency is to work out how
many responses are needed to produce the reinforcer and to
respond at a high and steady rate. If the 'rules' are formulated in
terms of an FI schedule, the subjects show the low rate pattern of
responding (Lowe 1979: 169–70).

Furthermore, changing the schedules may not change subjects'
formulations of them; schedule change, therefore, may have no
effect on a rate of emission of behaviour that is no longer optimally
reinforced. The inference drawn is that the experimental behaviour in question must be controlled not by experimental
variables but by self-produced cues which vary from individual to
individual (Lowe *et al.* 1978: 384; Buskist *et al.* 1981). The human
capacity to self-tact, to determine for oneself rules of conduct, is
the obvious explanation of the apparent discrepancy between
human and animal learning (see also Foxall 1987a).

This is of particular interest because Skinner (1969, 1971)
claims emphatically that it is direct exposure to the contingencies
rather than the existence of rules that has the much greater effect
upon learning. The experiments described by Lowe and others
indicate that, in certain circumstances at least, rules exert an
overriding influence on behaviour. Moreover, the explanation of

101

human operant conditioning in terms of rules derives support from studies of the acquisition of verbal behaviour in children. The behaviour of preverbal human infants on FI and FR schedules is indistinguishable from that of animals. Between the ages of two-and-a-half and four years, infants' behaviour contains elements of that of younger children and that of adults; and, once the child has reached the age of five or six, his or her acquisition of verbal skills permits the 'description of reinforcement contingencies expressed in experimental schedules' (Lowe *et al.* 1983). At this stage, the young subjects' behaviour closely resembles that of adults, showing similar response rates and insensitivity to the modification of schedules parameters. In addition, verbal instruction accelerates this development (Lowe and Horne 1985; Bentall and Lowe 1987; Bentall *et al.* 1985; Lowe *et al.* 1983).

It is also clear that in behaviour modification programmes involving token economies and contingency management, much of the participants' behaviour change is under verbal control. Staff in token economy programmes typically provide verbal instructions in order to prompt appropriate prosocial conduct including information on subjects' performance, descriptions of contingencies which are repeated each time new members join the programme, written and posted statements of the contingencies (including notice-board messages like 'Six tokens for making your bed', etc.), and other verbal cues and rewards (Lowe *et al.* 1987). Unclear verbal instructions are, furthermore, likely to be responsible for some subjects' lack of sensitivity to the reinforcing contingencies of which they are part.

'Contingency management' refers to programmes of behaviour modification based on the negotiation and implementation of a contract that specifies the rewards and punishments contingent upon the performance of particular behaviours, for example, avoiding fattening foods or limiting alcohol intake. Once again, contingency contracting includes verbal control which may take precedence over direct exposure to the contingencies; in such therapeutic situations, involving complex social interactions, direct contingency exposure is frequently long delayed and thus ineffective on its own (Lowe *et al.* 1987).

The evidence favours the dialectical approach; human operant behaviour is neither fully continuous nor fully discontinuous with instrumental learning in animals. Whether human behaviour conforms to the laws that describe animal responses appears to depend on the opportunity to reason out the contingencies (accurately or not) and to make rules that govern behaviour. 'Habitual' or low involvement human behaviour may well conform to the matching law, whilst 'reasoned', perhaps high-involvement behaviour of this type deviates from the regularities found in studies of animal choice (Lea 1981).

Theoretical implications of human operant performance

Wearden (1988) goes further in his interpretation of findings such as these, arguing that the term 'reinforcement' may mean different things in animal and human learning. For adult humans, experiments are games and the factors that determine the behaviour of such subjects are likely to differ essentially from those that control the responses of 'food-deprived animals in experimental chambers'. It is improbable that either the points earned by humans in operant experiments or the negligible sums of money for which they are typically exchanged act as reinforcers in the classic sense. Such rewards possess little intrinsic ability to reinforce: in some experiments, subjects threw the small pieces of food produced by their operant behaviour out of the window without even tasting it. Their responses were, moreover, disorderly and variable until graphs were posted showing how many 'reinforcers' each had earned; that their responding became orderly once such information became available attests to their being unmotivated by the food and unreinforced by it in the orthodox sense.

Wearden interprets such results as indicating that the 're-inforcers' are informational rather than hedonic or response-strengthening; they inform subjects of the accuracy of their performance or that it has been otherwise satisfactory. Laboratory studies of human responding on VI schedules indicate highly variable performance from subject to subject and, from session to session, in the same individual. Presumably this is because such schedules provide little systematic information. The provision of further feedback in the form of reinforcement of short inter-response times leads to more accurate and rapid behavioural change rather than the performance rigidity noted by Lowe (1979; Wearden 1988). The categorization of reinforcers suggested by Wearden is important for understanding certain complex social behaviours. For instance, although reinforcers are defined functionally in operant psychology rather than on the basis of any intrinsic property, it is difficult to understand such economic behaviours as saving, giving, and altruism in behavioural terms unless the reinforcers in operation are primarily informational rather than hedonic.

The problem remains of discovering whether instructions (including self-instructions) change behaviour directly (as do the contingencies themselves) or whether they operate indirectly, changing cognitively-based strategies which in turn modify behaviour (Wearden 1988). Wearden concludes that, if experimentation cannot resolve the epiphenomenalism issue inherent in this problem, further theoretical development is necessary. It is surely unsatisfactory to assume that verbal factors are simply discriminative stimuli that set the occasion for non-verbal performance. Whilst contingencies and reinforcement histories certainly play a part in determining human behaviour, even in instructed situations, they may do so only via cognitive mediation, perhaps through the formulation of rules, self-instructions and response strategies. All normal adult behaviour in operant experimentation may be rule-governed rather than contingency-based: conditioning without awareness seems unlikely (Wearden 1988; see also Brewer 1974).[2]

Operant conditioning in complex social situations

Conceptual attenuation

Operant accounts of complex human behaviour in non-laboratory settings have been based primarily on a direct extrapolation of the findings of animal experimentation. The most noteworthy example is the attempt to explain verbal behaviour in terms of an interpretive programme based on operant principles derived from observation of non-verbal organisms (Skinner 1957; see also MacCorquodale 1970). It is here in the realm of 'real world' behaviour that empirical research based on the rigorous model of radical behaviourism as a philosophy of science encounters difficulties, for the precisely-defined elements of the three-term contingency typical of animal experiments are necessarily replaced in programmatic operant psychology by vague surrogates (Schwartz and Lacey 1982).

In his well-known review of Skinner's *Verbal Behavior*, Chomsky (1959) argues that such interpretations of complex behaviours amount to no more than 'analogic guesses . . . formulated in terms of a metaphoric extension of the technical vocabulary of the laboratory.' The scope of the extended account is illusory: terms such as discriminative stimulus, response and reinforcer have quite different meanings in the interpretive account of human verbal behaviour from those carefully assigned in the laboratory. The verbal description of a 'red chair' is claimed by Skinner to be a response under the control of the antecedent stimuli 'redness' and 'chairness' (1957: 110). Chomsky's comment is that the language in which this programmatic explanation occurs is far removed from that used in the objective experimental science of animal behaviour: 'Stimuli are no longer part of the outside physical world; they are driven back into the organism ... [T]he talk of stimulus control simply disguises a complete retreat to mentalistic psychology' (Chomsky 1959: 30).

Operant responses, like discriminative stimuli, can be extremely difficult to identify in complex situations: the explicatory extrapolation from the world of the laboratory to that of human social behaviour offers no guidance on the precise empirical identification of a unit of operant behaviour, or of the ways in or extent to which responses must be similar in order to comprise examples of the same operant. And, finally, the idea of reinforcement is rendered vague when Skinner states that many verbal responses are automatically reinforced: a child is said to be automatically reinforced by his production of sounds that imitate aeroplanes or the speech of adults. Again, a term which is defined so assiduously in the laboratory is employed elsewhere in a way that strips it of its capacity to explain (Chomsky 1959).

The attribution of the causes of an organism's behaviour, frequent in the operant psychology literature, to its 'history of reinforcement' is pertinent here. When the organism in question is an animal whose behavioural history has been spent within the confines of an operant chamber and which can, therefore, be closely documented in its entirety, the attribution can be based on direct empirical observation. But, when the behaviours of adult humans in relatively complex situations are ascribed without such evidence to their 'reinforcement histories' or, more remote still, the 'contingencies of survival' held to have shaped evolutionary development (Skinner 1984a), the resulting 'explanation' ceases to be based on an objective (actually, intersubjective) approach to a science of behaviour and relies on the extrapolation of explicatory principles from a highly-structured yet simply-organized setting in which rudimentary responses can be manipulated by means that are clearly-definable, unambiguous, and isolatable, to settings in which the environmental influences that affect the rate of emission of responses can be no more than inferred.

Indeed, it appears that the existence and identity of the causal consequences that are alleged to control behaviour in such contexts can only be inferred from the very behaviours they purport to explain! At this point, cognitive and behaviouristic accounts have become equivalent, at least in terms of the abstractedness and remoteness of their explicatory devices from the observational level: even the loosest of 'mentalistic' explanations (He does this because he likes to) can be no more objectionable than the best explanation radical behaviourism can offer (He does it because doing it is reinforced/because of his reinforcement history/because of the contingencies of survival).

These criticisms have particular force in the context of purchasing and consuming where, outside the most confined situation (such as that in a store setting), the accurate identification of discriminative and reinforcing stimuli can be difficult in the extreme if not downright impossible. It is feasible to attribute the strengthening of some consumer behaviour in very general terms to the acquisition and use of primary reinforcers such as food, but the ascription of terms like 'reinforcer' to attributes of specific brands can be far more indeterminate, especially since reinforcers inevitably differ from consumer to consumer on the basis of their distinctive histories. It is also the case in complex situations of human interaction that many aspects of the environment could function as discriminative stimuli – for example, when driving through a town – but it is impossible to isolate any as exerting specific control over behaviour. The closest we can get to an operant explanation is to say, rather imprecisely, that combinations of stimuli must act to control action (the lights are green, no pedestrians are crossing, cars at the intersection have stopped, etc.). Many purchase and consumption situations are like this: store logos, familiar merchandise, physical store arrangements and so on could act singly or in one of a large number of possible combinations as controlling stimuli. Such situations are a long way from the operant laboratory where the factors that shape and control behaviour and act as predictors of future actions can be isolated.

Superstitious behaviour

The problem is further complicated by the strong probability that much consumer behaviour is 'superstitious'. When an animal in an experimental chamber receives rewards randomly, the behaviour it happens to be emitting at the time is adventitiously strengthened. Ultimately, there is no contingency between response and reinforcer: they are related only by their temporary contiguity. Such behaviour, said to be 'superstitious' (Skinner 1948a; see, however, Staddon and Simmelhag 1971), is far from trivial in its implications for the operant analysis of complex choice. Superstitious behaviour, necessarily learned by exposure to intermittent reinforcement, usually extinguishes only very slowly after reinforcement is withdrawn. The human capacity to verbalize contingencies and to reason out the causes of behaviour means that adults are likely to attribute their everyday actions to adventitious consequences.

The social environment of the grocery store and the theme-park, as well as dozens of other complex buying and consumption contexts, are likely to promote the superstitious ascription of behaviour to consequences that are not under systematic contingency control but subject nevertheless to spurious rule-making. Despite the 'inaccurate' description of the prevailing contingencies this involves, subsequent action is thereby shaped. Consumer behaviour in non-pecuniary contexts such as state health services is even less amenable to straightforward operant analysis: not only are the putative influences on behaviour prolific; there is also a human incapacity to identify the genuine reinforcers for specific behaviours. Furthermore, the human tendency to rationalize behaviour may itself lead to irrational behaviour (Maital 1982).

Social learning

More problematic still for behaviour theory are instances in which learning occurs in the absence of elements of the three-term contingency. Bandura (1977) argues that most human behaviour occurs as a result of vicarious learning, that is, through observation of the behaviour of others and its consequences for them rather than via direct exposure to the contingencies. This is in sharp contrast to the cardinal principle of operant conditioning that reinforcement must immediately follow a response in order for that response to be maintained. When an individual observes someone else's action and its outcome, he may have to wait some time before an opportunity to perform the action himself arises. When there is an opportunity, however, the observer often replicates the behaviour, having – according to Bandura's social learning theory – learned it by representing it consciously in thought and imagination without direct experience of the consequences of so behaving. Such action will subsequently be maintained only if it is reinforced, though even here the principal function of reinforcement, it is argued, is informational, providing the motivation to repeat the action in order to receive the expected consequences.

Whilst social learning theorists (such as Rotter 1954; Staats 1975; and Bandura 1971a) argue alongside radical behaviourists against the naïve attribution of the causes of behaviour to inner drives and motives, they maintain that the analysis of human behaviour cannot be confined to the operant conditioning model, either. Thus Bandura (1977) contends that the high level of cognitive ability found in humans gives individuals insight into the nature of reinforcement contingencies and thereby permits them to anticipate and determine to some degree the consequences of their actions. They are thus in a position to regulate their own behaviour to an extent which the radical behaviourist denies.

Learning may also take place when neither the observer nor the model is reinforced: in such cases, neither the response nor the discriminative stimulus components of the three-term contingency are available to the observer during the period when the new behaviour is learned. Moreover, the novel behaviour may be performed in a setting which does not resemble that in which it has been observed: the discriminative stimulus is also absent from the initial performance of the action (Bandura 1977: 36). Although they admit that reinforcement has an important role in the maintenance of learned behaviours, social learning theorists argue that the learning of novel behaviours depends upon the cognitive synthesis of observed examples and their creative interpretation.

Such theoretical assertion is far-removed from the naïve use of cognitive variables inferred directly from behaviour in order to provide ready-made explanations of what is seen. Neither the social learning theory of Bandura (1971a, 1971b, 1971c) nor the social behaviourism of Staats (1975; Staats and Staats 1963) invests cognitive events and processes with the autonomy ascribed to them by cognitive psychology. Rather, cognitive events and processes are themselves under stimulus and reinforcer control (Bandura 1977: 187–90; Homans 1974: 24). Staats (1983: 159–60) argues, furthermore, that the capacity to imitate comprises skills learned through conditioning. Nevertheless, both of these authors differ essentially from radical behaviourism in their belief that covert actions such as thoughts and emotions are not mere effects but potential and actual causes of behaviour, albeit themselves caused by aspects of the external environment. In Bandura's phrase, person and environment are reciprocally determinative: radical behaviourism is not so much wrong as incomplete. The concept of reciprocal determination also overcomes the tendency of operant behaviourism to present an impression of a somewhat static environment. The environment is in continual change, as a result both of the modifying effects of the social and physical contexts in which behaviour occurs and of the effects that behaviour has upon the environment. At the same time, the individual's subjective interpretation of the environmental contingencies alters with the unfolding of their personal reinforcement history and their verbalizations of the current situation. (Skinner's (1971, 1986, 1987) strong advocacy of the design and creation of a culture, based upon the behavioural technology he believes operant psychology provides, flies in the face of the usual emphasis of radical behaviourism which posits a somewhat passive humanity whose behaviour is not selected by autonomous actors, but by the environment.)

Open and closed settings

The nature of complex, social situations, described by Schwartz and Lacey (1982, 1988) in terms of deviations in the structure of such situations from that found in operant laboratory settings, is relevant here. They argue that radical behaviourism (and other forms of behaviour theory such as those based on Pavlovian conditioning) are incomplete: to say that behaviour can be controlled by reinforcement contingencies is, they argue, a far cry from saying that it always is so controlled. Even if the continuity principle holds for experimentally-based observations of animal and human operant responses, the EAB may still not be a comprehensive paradigm. They contend that behaviour theory principles are clearly effective only in 'situations from which other potential sources of influence have been eliminated' (Schwartz and Lacey 1988: 38). Such 'closed settings' are those in which:

> Only a few reinforcers are available, and usually, only one has special salience; the experimenter (behavior modifier) has control over conditions of deprivation and access to reinforcers; there is only one, or at most a few, available means to the reinforcers; the performance of clearly-defined, specific tasks is reinforced; different tasks are effectively interchangeable for the one that is reinforced; the contingencies of reinforcement are imposed and varied by agents not themselves being subjected to the contingencies; there are no effective alternatives to being in the situation.
>
> (Schwartz and Lacey 1988: 40)

Schwartz *et al.* (1978) suggest that the circumstances under which operant principles control behaviour can be found in some modern human organizations, the factory workplace, for example, where other influences on behaviour have been suppressed. The modern factory, in which employee behaviour is frequently shaped by principles of 'scientific management' is a relatively closed setting: monetary reinforcement predominates, tasks are interchangeable, and work behaviour is externally controlled by managers who are not subject to the contingencies they impose, and so on. But not all situations in which human behaviour takes place resemble such settings. Indeed, many working environments deviate substantially from this pattern: a wealth of findings in organizational sociology and psychology indicate that, depending upon the external environment of the firm, notably the competitiveness of the labour and product markets in which it operates, internal workplace behaviour varies considerably in terms of the capacity of managers to impose controlling contingencies (e.g. Burns and Stalker 1961).

Lacey and Schwartz (1987) contend that most human behaviour takes place in relatively open settings and is explicable by nonoperant psychologies. The further the sphere of observation deviates from closed settings, the less easily discernible are the elements required for a behavioural explanation (Lacey and Schwartz 1987: 170). Most complex social behaviour involving humans occurs in open settings in which few if any of these requirements obtain (or, if they do, it is impossible to identify the elements of the environment which control behaviour). Even in animal experimental settings that lack one or more of these requirements, Schwartz and Lacey maintain that it may not be possible to demonstrate simple classical or operant conditioning. Their argument is strongly supported by those empirical studies of human operant conditioning under internal verbal control which indicate that, although the environment exerts a degree of control over overt action, it does not embody the causes of behaviour in their entirety. The individual's construal of the effects of the environment, his or her rule making, exert some, perhaps a dominant, influence on subsequent behaviour.

Schwartz and Lacey's (1982, 1988) advocacy of a common-sense teleology is not entirely convincing but, in the absence of empirically-based evidence for an operant explanation of behaviour in open settings, it is inevitable that social scientists will fall back to some degree on cognitive accounts if only to fill the gap left by an incomplete behaviourism. Nor does this of itself imply acceptance of Cartesian dualism since many cognitive psychologists (e.g. Fodor and Chomsky) are as much materialists as Skinner. Beyond this, the idea of a continuum of settings, from the relatively closed to the relatively open, provides a means of classifying and explaining human consumer choice, which will be explored in Chapter 5.

The loci of causation

This discussion of the verbal control of behaviour and the ambiguity inherent in complex settings raises the more specific question of where the causes of behaviour are to be found. Although

Anderson (1986) claims that the issue of whether mind causes behaviour is at the centre of social science, the key question is whether behaviour is entirely caused by the external environment or whether it can be attributed, in part at least, to internal factors, mental or material. The radical behaviourist stance, as should be clear by now, is to confine the search for the factors that cause (influence the rate of emission of) behaviour to elements of the environment. In line with the findings on human operant performance discussed above, the following discussion maintains that (a) the conceptualization of causes as intrapersonal follows from and can be accommodated within a modified operant theory, and (b) operant conditioning provides a necessary but insufficient account of complex human behaviour including consumer behaviour.

If dogma is avoided, there is no legitimate reason, even within operant psychology, for refusing to ascribe causal significance to discriminative stimuli, even when they are intrapersonal rather than elements of the external environment. As Skinner (1974) points out, the skin is an arbitrary barrier. His analysis of verbal behaviour (1957) lays considerable stress on inner thoughts and feelings acting as discriminative stimuli for the performance of both verbal and non-verbal behaviours. Burton (1984: 127) notes that in his early work Skinner (e.g. 1945) 'is far from denying that private events play an important part in the determination of behaviour. To the contrary, the whole analysis is concerned with verbal behaviour under the *control* of private stimuli.' In his later works, which were intended for a lay audience, Burton claims that Skinner (e.g. 1971, 1974) places less stress on the limitations imposed on verbal behaviour by the 'defective' contingencies governing the verbal community's capacity to reinforce, and that, in his crusading against mentalism, Skinner treats the control exercised by private events in a superficial and cavalier manner. Thus he has written that 'Covert responses are not the causes of overt, both are products of common variables' (Skinner 1969: 258) and, of inner states, that 'at best they are mediators ... the ultimate causes of behavior must be found *outside* the organism' (Skinner 1972a: 325).

In his philosophical writings, however, and when pushed by his critics, Skinner (e.g. 1988: 486) admits that 'private events may be causes but not initiating causes', but even this guarded admission hardly receives emphasis in his work. It raises, nevertheless, the questions of what form a non-initiating cause might take, and how it might be definitively distinguished from an initiating cause. This statement appears more a device to maintain the superiority of external contingencies than to clarify their relationship to internal events. The claimed difference between initiating and non-initiating causes is a nice distinction in the context of human problem solving in which, as we have seen, verbalizations of the contingencies of reinforcement may qualitatively alter their effects (Lowe 1988), after which behaviour comes under the control of the verbal representation of the contingencies rather than the contingencies themselves. Which is then the initiator? As Burton points out, it seems reasonable within an operationist framework to conclude that 'if a private event controls a response then it must count as an important determinant ("cause") of behavior' (Burton 1984: 132).

We can go beyond this, however, to argue that not only discriminative stimuli but all the elements of the three-term contingency may be found within-the-skin as well as externally and that reinforcers and punishers, the independent variables which indisputably control responses in a radical behaviourist analysis, can be found within as well as without the skin (see also Zuriff 1979). The elements of the three-term contingency are interchangeable in so far as the same behaviour can function at one and the same time as a discriminative stimulus, a response and a consequential stimulus: one person's wave of the hand is a response that can simultaneously reinforce another's greeting and act as a setting cue to a third person, signalling reinforcement contingent upon his approach.

If a publicly-available event such as a wave can comprise all three elements, there is no reason why a private event cannot also be classified in three ways: what an individual describes as his 'good digestion' is a response in itself (he is feeling the behaviour of his body), a reinforcer of a previous response (eating slowly) and a discriminative stimulus (for further eating or taking exercise). Once the logical sequence of the three-term contingency is interpreted in this way, there is no reason other than dogma to conclude that an internal event must be a collateral response, i.e. an effect; it can equally be a reinforcing stimulus (a cause of behaviour). Whilst this reduces the apparent precision of the operant paradigm, it may nevertheless, even within a behaviouristic analysis, be a more accurate depiction of the nature of the factors that influence the rate of complex behaviours.

Proximate and remote causes

A more complete and reasonable position, given the evidence on human operant learning, is that the causes of behaviour are to be found both within the individual and in the extrapersonal environment (e.g. Wessells 1981). This view remains a somewhat vague guide to explanation, however, unless the distinction is made between the antecedent variables that are proximate or immediate causes of an observed event and those that are its distal or remote causes (Addison *et al.* 1980). The proximate cause of behaviour, say an internal discriminative stimulus such as a self-instruction (Bem 1968, 1972), can itself be the effect of a more remote cause such as prior exposure to the environmental contingencies. The full explanation of the behaviour would, accordingly, require complete documentation of the nature and influence of the remote as well as the immediate causes and their relatedness.

Adherence to the view that the causes of behaviour are to be found in the environment alone appears to be based on a rigid acceptance of the operant research programme rather than on empirical evidence. Hayes (1986: 361) writes that

> In a behavioral analytic approach, all 'causes' are ultimately restricted to environmental events. ... Behavioral influences are often thought to be important aspects of an overall causal chain, but for philosophical reasons the search is never ended until sources of environmental control are established.

Yet the wilful neglect of the possibility that implicit verbal behaviours may assume a useful role as proximate explicators of overt behaviour appears both dogmatic and a far cry from the more direct route to knowledge promised by radical behaviourism. Perone *et al.* (1988) argue that it is too early to reach strong conclusions about animal/human behavioural discrepancies – an open minded approach given the relatively small amount of experimental research on humans and the technical problems this entails. But they go on to assert that the discrepancies do not nullify the idea of a unitary operant principle which provides interspecies explanation of behaviour, and retain the continuity thesis on the grounds that correlations between verbal and non-verbal behaviours do not indicate that one controls the other (Perone *et al.* 1988: 73).

Similarly, Bradshaw and Szabadi (1988) note the tendency of human subjects to exhibit 'gross undermatching' (i.e. to produce fewer than optimal responses on the 'richer' of two concurrently available schedules) and the considerable variability in perform-ance shown by humans. But they claim confidently that both of these effects can be traced to difficulties in establishing experi-mental control over human subjects (see also Baron and Perone 1982).

There is undoubtedly some ultimate logic in the view that 'All behavior is contingency shaped' and that humans 'follow rules because of reinforcing contingencies' (Skinner 1984b: 577) but, in view of the frequent inability of investigators to establish the remote causes of behaviour in complex settings, their ignoring the proximate causes of behaviour appears unreasonable. Indeed, because the remote causes of behaviour are often incapable of identification or documentation by the consumer researcher there is often no alternative but to place some degree of reliance upon respondents' accounts of the proximate causes of their actions (i.e. consumers' verbalizations of their experience, its consequences, and their evaluation, etc.). Even where proximate and remote causes can be identified, both may be the result of yet more remote influences which may or may not be accessible to a rigorous scientific analysis such as operant behaviourism promises. Where they are accessible, the investigator's purpose must determine the extent to which the causal chain is sequentially probed (Addison *et al.* 1980: 150). In summary, it seems reasonable to assume that neither proximate (verbal) nor remote (environmental) events are sufficient explicators of complex human behaviour, though a good case can usually be made for claiming that each is necessary.

Acknowledgement of private verbal behaviour as a proximate cause of overt motor activity does not imply that attitudes or other internal structures invariably control behaviour or that statements of opinion and overt behaviours are both mediated by underlying structures and ought, therefore, to show consistency across situations. Public statements of belief or opinion are under the control of their own particular contingencies which may or may not be functionally equivalent to those controlling the behaviours to which they refer. The poor empirical evidence for attitudinal-behavioural consistency confirms this (Foxall 1983, 1984a). Consumers' spoken evaluations and intentions are, in the absence of direct experience, poor indicators of what they will do (Foxall 1984b, 1984c). But this does not mean that individuals do not instruct themselves through private verbal stimuli or that what they are thinking or saying immediately before or contemporaneously with their public actions exerts no influence upon nor can be a guide to those actions (Bem 1968, 1972). The verbal behaviour is part of the controlling situation and, like any other discriminative stimulus that has accompanied an operant in the past, its present occurrence is a probabilistic guide to the topography of current behaviour.

Theoretical terms and theory-ladenness

Collateral behaviours or proximate causes?

The radical behaviourist's claim to know that thoughts and feelings are invariably collateral behaviours rather than proximate causes must, therefore, be viewed with suspicion (Ribes 1985, 1986). The evidence on the controlling influence of verbal behaviour in operant experiments and its probable influence beyond the laboratory in complex social milieux is equally supportive of both behaviouristic and cognitive accounts: in both cases, the nature and status of internal events is inferred and may not be empirically demonstrable.

Creel (1974) raises the question of what evidence would be required to refute the radical behaviourist assertion that feelings do not determine behaviour. In order to show that feelings have no important reinforcing effect on the behaviours associated with them, the behaviourist must either 'demonstrate experimentally the independence of reinforcement from feelings *et al.*' or 'show that the reinforcing effect and the feelings *et al.* correlated with it are *simultaneous*' or 'show that the reinforcing effect occurs *before* the feelings'. In fact, it is impossible to show that such behaviour can be reinforced in the absence of the feelings or in the presence of different feelings; and it is experimentally impossible both to punish a subject and demonstrate the 'temporal relations between reinforcers and feelings *et al.*' (Creel 1974: 138).

Another behaviourist, Eysenck (1978), perhaps unintentionally, confirms the impossibility of conducting a crucial experiment to establish the prior status of associated internal and external events, in his rebuttal of Bandura's (1977) self-efficacy theory. Bandura (1977: 194) states that 'efficacy expectations are a major determinant of people's choice of activities, how much effort they will expend, and of how long they will sustain effort in dealing with stressful situations'. Eysenck claims that expectations play 'a mere supporting role as epiphenomena of the underlying physiological change in autonomic and other sectors'. He portrays his own view that 'conditioned autonomic responses are a major determinant of people's efficacy expectations' as well as of their behaviour. Bandura's view, he claims, raises numerous philosophical difficulties but in any case, in the absence of sound evidence for the cognitive theory, parsimony requires a simpler account in which the inessential factors have been removed from the causal chain.

We might argue with similar force that, even if something called 'expectations' consistently precede behaviour, they are presumably maintained by the recurrent consequences of the 'expected' behaviour. A parsimonious explanation might well, therefore, confine itself to the environmental consequences of expected behaviour, omitting the expectations themselves. But this does not mean that expectations do not exist, nor that they cannot be usefully inferred in some theoretical contexts as proximate causes of behaviour, nor yet that they are superfluous to a complete scientific explanation. Parsimony is not, in any case, the sole or ultimate evaluative criterion for scientific explanation; nor does parsimony of explanation necessarily lead to accuracy of prediction and control, especially as one moves from closely delineated experimental situations into complex social settings where mediators can provide useful guides to explicating behaviour. What Eysenck's analysis indicates is the equivalence of a descriptively behaviouristic account and one that recognizes that extra-laboratorial research (even that which is confined to a search for the factors that permit prediction and control) must rely on some understanding of the proximate causes of behaviour, if only because of the current limitations of behavioural technology. It does not provide a watertight philosophical basis for choosing between them, and actually underpins Creel's assertion that radical behaviourism is incapable of demonstrating with finality that feelings are invariably collateral responses, the by-products of overt action rather than its mainspring.

Theory-ladenness revisited

The acceptance of internal factors as causes, albeit proximate, of behaviour does not, of itself, denote a switch in theoretical approach towards the acceptance of unobservables as explanatory devices. Internal discriminative stimuli, feelings, and verbalizations, are recognized by radical behaviourism as observables; indeed, it is the distinctive mark of radical as compared with methodological behaviourism to acknowledge the scientific need to give an account of within-the-skin phenomena (Skinner 1974). Some behaviourist philosophers appear to have gone beyond Skinner in describing internal antecedent and consequential stimuli as causes of behaviour (e.g. Zuriff 1979, 1985), but the understanding is still that such inner causes are themselves under contingency control (of remote causes) rather than the autonomous causes of overt responses assumed by cognitive psychologists (Mandler 1985).

A broader consideration concerns the complete avoidance of

mental, neural, and conceptual terms as explanatory devices (Skinner 1945, 1950). The caution raised by Skinner and others with respect to 'explanatory fictions' can be salutary, as pointed out in the case of notions of innate and inherent innovativeness. The style of explanation that automatically attributes behaviour to conceptual personality constructs that exist 'only in the mind of the investigator' can indeed obviate further investigation of environmental factors that shape and maintain behaviour, creating new theoretical problems of explaining the mediators.

However, logically circular theories may expedite progress at least during the early phases of a research programme (Wessells 1981: 159) and are not avoided so rigorously even in nuclear physics as Skinner proposes they be in psychology (Stevenson 1974; cf. Skinner 1983: 395). Conceptual unobservables assist in the organization of observations and thereby help researchers formulate hypotheses and predictions (Wessells 1981). Although it is important to guard against uncritical use of unobservables that terminate enquiry prematurely, there is no inherent reason to believe that logical circularity is more of a problem when encountered in the context of cognitive theories than when it marks behaviourist explanations. The whole point of *Verbal Behavior* (Skinner 1957) is its programmatic nature, as a result of which it contains 'many instances of circularity which may yet guide investigation' (Wessells 1981: 160). Moreover, like any other explanatory system, radical behaviourism is itself theory-laden. It offers explanation of a particular aspect of a subset of responses, the rate at which whole organisms emit operants. The extrapolations from simple to complex behaviours inherent in the explanation of much human social behaviour, especially in the interpretive accounts of verbal behaviour (Skinner 1957) and of cultural design through behavioural technology (Skinner 1971), requires extensive theoretical assumptions (Broadbent 1961: 182–3). Whilst its analysis depends upon data gathered in the investigation of specific bits of rat and pigeon behaviour, its explanations proceed in terms of the generalized environmental control of all human as well as all animal behaviour (Blackman 1983b: 42).

Exactly like any other social science paradigm, radical behaviourism is a way of seeing (and, therefore, of not seeing) and is inescapably founded upon a partial model of human nature and conduct. Skinner has chosen to concentrate upon the behaviour of the whole organism rather than upon circumscribed physiological processes or supra-individual social action; he is preoccupied with the probability of response emission, defined in terms of rate of behaving, though this is but one conception of probability; he focuses upon the objectively available influence of the environment upon the person, ruling out the possibility that persons initiate actions that modify the environment (Schellenberg 1978: 113–15; Stevenson 1974). Nor can Skinner escape the theory-dependency of his ostensibly descriptive terminology. Terms such as 'schedule of reinforcement' and 'punishment' refer to concepts that are clearly unobservables in that they imply organization of observations and rest upon abstractions of those observations into principles of behaviour devised by researchers. The notion of 'reinforcement history' is, in practice, theoretical in just this sense: an individual's history of reinforcement cannot be completely specified, especially in the case of human adults. Although it may be stated in terms similar to those in which behaviour is described, this concept like that of contingencies of survival acts exactly like the other-realm constructs of cognitivism. Radical behaviourism is not exempt from the logical priority of theoretical perspective over observed fact (Popper 1972, 1980).

The effect of these admissions is to temper the trenchant criticism of cognitivistic and some other 'mentalistic' interpretations of human behaviour. Some descriptive cognitivistic theories are incomplete and rely too much on explanatory fictions but this does not mean that non-behaviouristic theories are inherently flawed. Some cognitivists would accept some criticism of some cognitive theories but Skinner goes too far in rejecting other-realm theories in their entirety. Cognitivists do sometimes err in ignoring the effects of environmental contingencies but there is no inherent reason why they should not accommodate these remote causes into improved cognitive theories. Co-operation between behaviourists and non-behaviourists is not only feasible but has been seriously proposed by authors broadly sympathetic to Skinner's approach as well as others (Bowers 1973; Burton 1984; Mischel 1973; Wessels 1981, 1982).

Evaluation

Radical behaviourism provides an alternative explanation of consumer choice to that of the prevailing cognitivist school. It makes available to researchers who normally take cognitive or conceptual intrapersonal causation for granted a programmatic account of behaviour as a series of responses governed by environmental stimuli. By presenting counter-inductive hypotheses, 'inconsistent with accepted and highly-confirmed theories' as well as with 'well-established facts' (Feyerabend 1975: 30), it can play a part in the development of a relativistic approach to research in marketing based on the interaction of paradigms. In addition to providing an account of consumer choice as operant conditioning rather than information processing, the EAB (experimental analysis of behaviour) draws attention to the possibility that some widely-accepted theories rely too heavily upon explanations couched in terms of hypothetical unobservables that preclude further investigation by obviating the need to examine the precise effects of the consequences of prior behaviour on its current rate of emission. Radical behaviourism acts, therefore, as a corrective to the excesses of cognitivism by suggesting an alternative line of explanation which usefully draws attention to the remote causes of behaviour in the face of a widespread tendency to assume that all overt actions are solely the result of intrapsychic precursors (Berger 1965).

The EAB also provides, via operant conditioning experimentation a theory-grounded approach to empirical research into consumer and marketing behaviour, whether it is the restricted economic choice of laboratory animals or the semi-confined consumption of the human members of token economies. It thereby raises the theoretical possibility that economic (including consumer) behaviour is operant behaviour and suggests a methodology by which the meaning of this proposition can be explored. The effect is to extend the range of consumer research to embrace the choice behaviours of non-humans and to test many of the generative and predictive assumptions of consumer theory. More generally, this paradigm makes available an explanation and operational definition of the situational influences on consumer choice, filling a gap in the psychological literature (Scott *et al.* 1979: 25).

These positive evaluations indicate that the EAB can make a valuable contribution to consumer research, especially within a relativistic programme. But the extent of its probable input to such research can only be gauged through considerations of its limitations. There are several reasons for doubting the completeness of the EAB as a comprehensive paradigm for consumer research. For example, observed operant phenomena generated in experiments with human subjects indicate the considerable extent to which such responses are quantitatively and qualitatively rule-governed rather than contingency-based. Although this has been discussed in the context of formal experimentation that has generally been unrelated to consumption and other economic issues, it is clearly an extensive issue in the analysis of the consumer behaviour of non-infant humans. Saving, for instance, is an action governed almost entirely by bankers' promises (to repay depositors' funds on demand) that cannot be kept in all circumstances (e.g. a run on the bank) but it is nevertheless a 'freely chosen' pattern of repeated behaviour for many consumers. Saving is a behaviour that is explicable not in terms of acceptance of delayed gratification but of proximate (verbal) causes which must, on an operant view, be functionally equivalent to or greater than the contingencies of immediate gratification represented by the purchase and consumption of non-durables.

Moreover, scientific observation of the verbal responses that control human operant behaviour provides data that support non-behaviourist as well as behaviourist explanations. Cognitivists welcome the evidence for human reasoning and calculative decision-making presented to anyone who chooses to interpret it that way by human operant experimentation and the consequent de-emphasising of environmental influences. Social learning theorists and some exchange theorists would also have little difficulty incorporating this evidence into models of reciprocal determinism or self-efficacy or ecological theories of social organization, though they would of course maintain that the mediational structures and processes posited in such approaches were themselves ultimately under contingency control. In the inevitable and inescapable absence of any crucial experiment to establish the 'correct' interpretation, a plurality of competing explanations is to be expected.

Whilst empirical demonstration is not essential to a relativistic programme (Feyerabend 1975, 1987), the contribution of the EAB cannot, because of is internal philosophical requirements of objectivity and empiricalness, be considered a complete paradigm for consumer research unless operant conditioning can be unequivocally demonstrated in non-experimental situations. However, not only does the rule–governance of human operant performance promote non-behavioural as well as behavioural explanations, complex social behaviour is demonstrably not under contingency control in all situations. Although it is reasonable to assume that such behaviour is in some way affected by its consequences (Wearden 1988), this common-sense assumption hardly constitutes a rigorous explanation uniquely based on behaviourist reasoning. Empirical confirmation that such behaviour is governed, even remotely, by discernible environmental stimuli that can be documented and catalogued is frequently lacking as are the specific identification of the alleged controlling variables and replicable evidence of their functional relationship to closely-defined bits of behaviour that the principles of the paradigm require. The radical behaviourist explanation of much consumer behaviour must remain programmatic rather than evidential; as with *Verbal Behavior*, the problem is not that it is programmatic (MacCorquodale 1970) but that it is likely always to be so because empirical demonstration of the contingencies of reinforcement in complex social situations is beyond the capacity of behavioural science. In these circumstances, intrapsychic explanations of such behaviour, be they supplementary or complementary, are inevitable.

It has been argued that the further we move from the operant laboratory, the more difficult it is to provide the convincing evidence for instrumental conditioning by reference to its environmental determinants upon which a scientific behavioural analysis is predicated. Of course, Chomsky (1959) and other critics who concentrate on this point have not disproved human operant conditioning; nor have Schwartz and Lacey (1982, 1988) shown that operant conditioning cannot occur in open situations. But the facts that human operant conditioning is difficult to demonstrate in complex contexts, that operant conditioning cannot be observed in the absence of conscious awareness of the contingencies or rules (Brewer 1974), and that learning may occur in the absence of the discriminative and reinforcing stimuli that define the three-term contingency (Bandura 1977), mean that explanations based on modelling, classical conditioning, and cognitive information processing cannot be ignored except by act of faith.

If interspecies extrapolations should never be made without explicit justification (Lea 1981), nor should extrapolations be made from the operant laboratory to social systems of comparatively immense complexity. In the continuing absence of a means of accurately identifying the elements of the three-term contingency in the complex social contexts in which purchasing and consumption occur, the major contribution of the unreconstructed EAB to consumer research can only derive from radical behaviourism as a metatheory and from operant conditioning in closed (e.g. instore) situations rather than from empirical studies of operant conditioning in open economic contexts. The principal value of an unreconstructed EAB perspective on consumer and marketing research derives from the emphasis it places on the ecology of behaviour, its capacity to redress the tendency of cognitive theory to stress intrapersonal causation at the expense of an adequate acknowledgement of the controlling environment. In welcoming the benefits of this reemphasis, however, it is not advocated that researchers become behaviourists. Not only would this be against the spirit of a relativistic programme; there is no point in denying the presence and sometimes proximate causal influence of internal states and processes.

Still less is it of value to berate those who refuse to deny the explicative usefulness of inner states as 'mentalists'. Several leading cognitivists such as Fodor and Chomsky are materialists; nor does behaviourism depend upon a physicalist interpretation of the universe (Eysenck 1972). Even philosophers such as Ryle (1949) and Ayer (1946) reject the view that all mental events can be translated into statements about behaviour, though they accept the weaker thesis that

a correct account can be given, in behaviouristic terms, of a great deal of what is ordinarily classified as talk about the mind. In a great many instances in which a person is said to satisfy 'mental' predicates, what is being said of him is not only, and perhaps not at all, that he is undergoing some inner process, but rather that he is exhibiting or is disposed to exhibit a certain pattern of behaviour. This can apply to the description of intelligence, of motives and purposes, of voluntary actions, of emotions and moods, and of thoughts when they are overtly expressed.

(Ayer 1982: 167)

Eysenck (1972: 302) also rejects the strong position that all behaviour is determined by heredity and environment, a philosophical stance, he maintains, not supported by scientific evidence. He too accepts a weaker position in which human behaviour is partly determined by inherited characteristics and the structure of the environment; but the extent to which these factors alone account for human behaviour is a matter for empirical investigation, a scientific endeavour from which dogma must be purged.

It is unsatisfactory to conclude that relativistic consumer research requires a paradigm that includes both cognitive and behavioural variables, as the interactionists imply without providing a lead as to how to accomplish the task. Consumer research needs, none the less, a framework of conceptualization and analysis that (1) avoids the pitfalls of an uncritical cognitivism, but (2) acknowledges both the proximate and remote causes of behaviour, whilst (3) coherently relating these sources of causation. The SLT/social behaviourism approaches which admit intrapersonal causation but assume it to be under contingency control make available a tenable version of a behaviouristic theory, one that admits that important (if not ultimate) causes of behaviour lie in the environment, which is sufficiently realistic to take the immediately causal nature of some private events into consideration. As the next chapter indicates, however, a less radically altered EAB can contribute to the understanding of aspects of consumer choice currently neglected by inner-state theories. In order to achieve this, however, the EAB requires theoretical modification sensitive to the critique developed above. Before examining that contribution further, it may be useful to review the main elements of the critique in terms of their implications for consumer research.

Summing up: erosion of the EAB

This chapter has not sought to muster all the philosophical arguments that apply to radical behaviourism. Its purpose has not been to substantiate radical behaviourism in some fundamental sense, nor to refute it as in a history of philosophy whose author disposes of each school of thought in turn before presenting a pet theory.[3] The underlying concern has been, rather, with the progress of consumer research. Specifically, it has sought to comprehend the extent of the explanation which the EAB offers this subdiscipline. The outcome of this discussion is to erode this paradigm by upholding the inevitability of intrapersonal causation of overt motor behaviour. The result, as Chapter five shows, is that the modified EAB provides a perspective on consumer behaviour which is neglected by alternative paradigms. In concluding this critical account of radical behaviourist explanation, it may, therefore, be useful to reiterate the following points at which the model pursued in Chapter five departs from the radical behaviourist orthodoxy.

Human operant performance differs in important ways from that of animals, giving rise to the need to reaffirm that internal verbal behaviours act as discriminative stimuli that control observed external acts. The causes of behaviour are, therefore, found to be proximate as well as remote; a full explanation requires that both be documented, but, if only one source is available to the investigator, even if it is the proximate, it should be taken fully into consideration. Cognitivism and radical behaviourism contain differing ontological emphases, but there is no logical reason to believe that they can never contribute to composite paradigms which subsume both intrapersonal and environmental causation. 'Ontological disjunction' is not inevitable. Nor do these systems differ methodologically as much as might be superficially supposed: each relies on theoretical terms; neither is capable of providing unadorned description of its subject matter. However, in order to maintain the essential contribution of behaviour theory, any synthetic paradigms may need to retain, even if only as a working hypothesis, the principle that internal factors which control behaviour are themselves under contingency control; their causes are ultimately to be found in the environment.

Reinforcers may, for humans, act both hedonically and informationally to control behaviour. Reinforcement of human operant

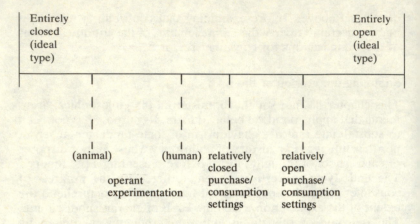

Figure 4.2 Continuum of closed–open behaviour settings

performance may, therefore, play a broader role than is the case for animal responses. In addition, real world situations rarely resemble closely and in detail the closed setting of the operant chamber; a theoretical continuum can be established whose theoretical polar extremes are the entirely closed setting in which behaviour is totally dominated by extrapersonal influences, and the entirely open setting in which behaviour is autonomous. The settings in which purchase and consumption behaviours occur, extending from the relatively closed to the relatively open, can be located within a restricted range of this continuum (see Figure 4.2). The further the setting in question is removed from the closure exemplified by the operant laboratory, and the less obviously behaviour is (or can be shown to be) controlled by environmental factors, the more it must be explained by reference to intrapersonal causes. On such occasions, the investigator has no choice but to take seriously the possibility that consumers' verbal expressions of attitudes, intentions, and opinions may constitute proximate causes of their overt behaviours.

Since, in practice, purchase or consumption settings encountered in consumer research are all relatively open by comparison with that of the animal laboratory, viable explanations of observed consumer choice are likely to involve attributions to internal causes. Without rejecting this possibility, Chapter five is concerned to examine the distinctive contribution of radical behaviourism to consumer research. Hence it builds upon the above critique of operant psychology to construct an alternative model of consumer choice within an extended EAB framework of conceptualization and analysis.

Chapter five

Marketing in behavioural perspective

What really unites operant psychologists is not a blind faith in the ideas of B. F. Skinner, or even the use of the methodology he introduced, but a conviction that an important determinant of behaviour is the environmental consequences it produces. Operant behaviour is instrumental behaviour. And the two most fundamental kinds of economic behaviour, working and buying, are also essentially instrumental.

(Lea 1981: 247)

The behavioural perspective model of purchase and consumption

Although recognition of the theory-dependency of observation and the adoption of a relativistic framework for research involves the investigator in the philosophy of social science, the test of any paradigm's value in this context derives principally from its capacity to elucidate consumer choice phenomena. The preceding discussion of the nature, merits, and demerits of the EAB suggests several contributions which this framework of conceptualization and analysis can make to consumer research, particularly at the neglected marketing level of analysis – that is, that which is defined in terms of brand or store (rather than product, commodity, or channel type) choice and the marketer/non-marketer dominated influences that shape such choice through buyer–seller interactions and social communications.

These contributions involve the critical points raised in the last chapter with respect to the EAB: the issues of (i) the closed vs. open settings which provide the context for behaving; (ii) hedonistic vs. informational reinforcers; and (iii) verbal vs. non-verbal control of behaviour. In line with the theme pursued in the preceding chapters, the extent to which the EAB may contribute to consumer research, it is now appropriate to ask how far an operant psychology which takes account of (is eroded by) these modifications can encompass patterns of consumer choice.

Definition of terms

The purpose of the model described in this chapter is to relate the familiar broad patterns of purchase and consumption behaviour to the nature of the contingency-defined situation in which these actions occur. A situation in this sense consists of: the discriminative stimuli provided in relatively open vs. relatively closed settings, and the nature of the reinforcement consequent upon the performance of purchase/consumption responses (i.e. the relative strengths of the hedonic and informational reinforcers).

Settings

A behavioural setting includes the temporal, physical, and social context within which action occurs. Its bounds are determined by space and time, and also by an entire sequence of associated behaviour. A store which is open daily during specified hours is such a behaviour setting (Barker 1968; Belk 1975). A setting is, therefore, a broader unit of behaviour than a situation as it is usually, somewhat narrowly, defined: the store in question would present numerous such situations during the day as different individuals entered, browsed and made purchases. In the Behavioural Perspective Model, it is the specification of the nature of the hedonic and informational reinforcers available in the setting which completes the definition of the situation of purchase or consumption.

The continuum of available purchase and consumption settings is defined, for the purposes of the Behavioural Perspective Model, in terms derived from but not identical to the open and closed settings posited by Schwartz and Lacey (1982).

Relatively closed settings are defined as those in which the contingencies of reinforcement that shape and maintain behaviour can be closely specified and controlled by either researchers or marketing managers. The fewer salient reinforcers available, the greater control over deprivation and reinforcement exercised by the individuals who manage the circumstances of buying and/or consuming, the fewer the means of obtaining reinforcers and the greater their contingency upon the performance of particular, defined tasks, and the greater external imposition of a reinforcement schedule which controls consumer response, all serve to close the setting.

Relatively open settings are those in which the contingencies cannot be accurately specified through unambiguous identification and manipulation of controlling antecedent (and, perhaps, consequential) stimuli. In particular, the distinction reflects the ease with which behaviour can be brought under stimulus control, or can be unambiguously attributed to the control of discriminative stimuli which can be systematically related to reinforcers and the schedules on which they are presented. In addition, the degree of openness of the setting reflects the extent to which its managers lack the capacity to impose specific reinforcers, prescribe some behaviours and proscribe others, and determine the schedule of reinforcement operating to control the response rate of buying and consuming. Settings are also said to become increasingly open as the isolation and delineation of such determinants becomes progressively more difficult, and as personal control beyond the influence of the consumer intensifies.[1]

Relative conceptions of settings (rather than the absolute definitions proposed by Schwartz and Lacey) are employed because there is no intention here of denying the important environmental determinants of behaviour that exist even in open contexts. (As argued in Chapter four, even the relatively closed settings of purchase and consumption discussed here are comparatively open compared with Schwartz and Lacey's highly restrictive identification of closed settings with the uniquely restrictive nature of the operant chamber.)

Reinforcers

The concept of the relatively open/relatively closed setting subsumes elements of the social and physical contexts of behaviour, the discriminative stimuli that signal reinforcement. However, product and person also influence the nature of purchase and consumption behaviours and are assumed in the Behavioural Perspective Model to be the prime sources of situational influence beyond those imposed by the setting inasmuch as they are the prime sources of reinforcement. Therefore, the model's second independent variable is a qualitative description of the consequences of purchase and/or consumption which indicates the brand/product variables that reinforce or punish these responses, and whose influence is theoretically determined by the reinforcement history of the individual consumer.

Hence the reinforcers which control consumer behaviour in a situation of purchase or consumption are delineated in terms of their informational and hedonic characters; in the theoretical development of the Behavioural Perspective Model, these categories of reinforcer are treated as opposites, independent influences on consumer choice. This does not deny that, in practice, many purchase and consumption operants may be maintained by both types of reinforcement. Both hedonic and informational consequences are, moreover, defined as response-strengthening, though where both occur together they may differ in relative effectiveness. The following analysis, therefore, is founded upon the assumption that both types of reinforcer are found in combination, each of which may be described as 'high', meaning highly response-strengthening by comparison with the other. The analysis also covers instances in which both reinforcers are simultaneously highly response-strengthening, or simultaneously 'low' in this regard.

High versus low hedonic reinforcement refers to the extent to which the consequences of behaviour are pleasant or affective (identified by means of associated behaviours). Those aspects of purchase and consumption which are reinforced by means of fantasies, feelings, fun, amusement, arousal, sensory stimulation, and enjoyment (Holbrook and Hirschman 1982; see also Hirschman and Holbrook 1982; Holbrook and O'Shaughnessy 1984) come into this category. *High versus low informational reinforcement* refers to the extent to which the consequences of behaviour provide data that are powerful in regulating the rate of emission of further members of the operant class.

The assumption that underlies the inclusion of this variable is simply that information produces response reinforcement. As Wearden (1988) notes, the finding that reinforcers may be informational rather than hedonic requires theoretical elaboration within operant psychology. Beyond the bounds of that paradigm, it may be that information produces affective change prior to behaviour modification, or that reinforcers provide information which is cognitively processed with or without the production of accompanying affect. It is also feasible that informational and hedonic reinforcements are respectively related to cognitive and affective functioning. The determination of such mediating effects, if any, lies beyond the scope of the present work, however. In an exploration of the extent to which operant psychology can contribute to the explanation of consumer choice (even one which admits the ultimate necessity of intrapsychic functioning as an additional explanatory element), it is inappropriate to try to specify, without direct evidence, the precise nature of the information processing which may mediate stimulus and response.

Schedules of reinforcement

In a broad sense purchase behaviour may be effectively maintained on continuous reinforcement (CRF) whilst consumption is intermittently reinforced (Alhadeff 1982). But this is to overlook some subtleties that emerge from a closer examination of consumer behaviour over time. An integral part of the analysis is, therefore, to suggest the schedules of reinforcement on which the behaviours typical of the situations defined in terms of the relative openness of purchase and consumption settings and reinforcer quality are maintained. It is rarely possible, however, to relate the maintenance of human behaviour in real world complex social situations definitively to specific schedules of reinforcement, in the way that the response patterns of animals in experimental settings can be authoritatively attributed to known schedules imposed by the investigator. (Inserting coins into a gaming machine, the payout schedule of which has been predetermined, is one of the few examples of behaviour whose maintenance can be ascribed with certainty to a specific schedule; most cannot.)

In the following discussion of the Behavioural Perspective Model, therefore, the schedule(s) closest to those apparently maintaining the illustrative purchase/consumption responses described are suggested as 'typical'. Unlike the laboratory environment, buying and consuming settings lack an experimenter who controls the entire situation; as a result, strictly-enforced scheduling is not usually encountered in the consumer context and the attribution of schedule control is by analogy with the operant laboratory rather than extrapolation from it. Moreover, the appropriate unit of behaviour for analysis in terms of situation type and reinforcer type may not be a discrete act of either purchase or consumption but an entire sequence of prepurchase, purchase and postpurchase responses.

Relationship of settings to reinforcers

A model specifies not only the independent and dependent variables required for explanation but also the relationships among them. The relationships among these components of the Behavioural Perspective Model (i.e. between hedonic/informational reinforcers and behaviour, and between relatively open and relatively closed settings and behaviour) are those derived from the statement and critique of operant psychology in Chapters two and four. The settings, responses, and reinforcers found in each of the Contingency Categories (i.e. situations of purchase and/or consumption) described below correspond respectively to the three-term contingency of antecedent(s), behaviour(s), and consequence(s). The model is concerned to relate the independent variables, defined by the discriminative stimuli embedded in purchase and consumption settings, and the reinforcing stimuli contingent upon

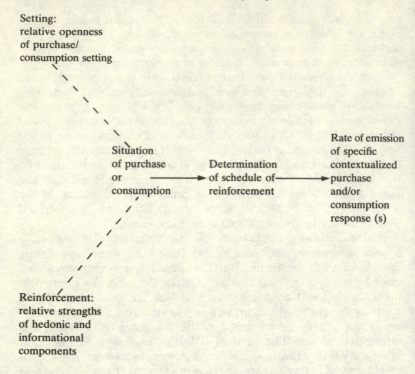

Setting:
relative openness
of purchase/
consumption setting

Situation
of purchase
or ⟶
consumption

Determination
of schedule of⟶
reinforcement

Rate of emission
of specific
contextualized
purchase
and/or
consumption
response (s)

Reinforcement:
relative strengths
of hedonic and
informational
components

Figure 5.1 Behavioural Perspective Model: hypothesized causal sequence

purchasing and consuming, to the basic datum of operant psychology, rate of responding (Figure 5.1).

Contingency Categories and patterns of consumer behaviour

Eight Contingency Categories, that is, situations defined by reference to the relative openness of the setting in which behaviour occurs and the type and strength of reinforcement controlling the rate of response, emerge (Figure 5.2). The following analysis relates each Category to specific purchase and consumption behaviours and the types of schedule on which they are apparently maintained.

1. Open, high hedonic, high informational

This Category includes 'new task' or 'extended problem solving' responses (EPS: described in Chapter one), where interest is evoked and maintained by both types of reinforcer (or, perhaps more accurately, by discriminative stimuli which promise both types of

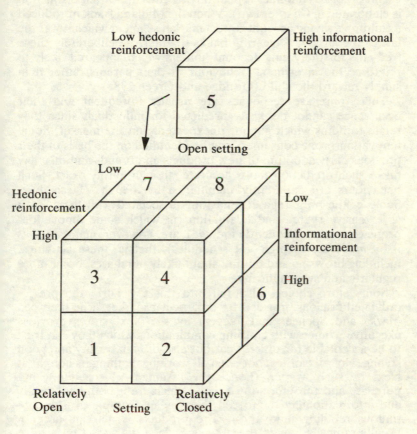

Figure 5.2 Summary of Behavioural Perspective Model of purchase and consumption

reinforcer). The goods involved are generally secondary commodities, highly differentiated by novel function (in the case of innovative product classes) or branding (in the case of luxuries). Purchases of this kind are, for most people, relatively infrequent occurrences.

For innovative brands marketed in established product classes, the marketer usually makes genuine reinforcement (of the response) rather than reward (of the individual) contingent upon purchase or use in order to stimulate repeat buying (this important distinction is elaborated in Chapter two). When the Midland Bank introduced a children's saving account, into a market segment which it was the last of the large UK clearing banks to enter, it deliberately chose free gifts for the young account-holders which appeared likely to reinforce the investment behaviour of their parents rather than simply reward the child (Goudge and Green 1985).

These purchase responses are usually infrequent and their occurrence cannot be easily predicted for individuals since they relate to items which appear unexpectedly on the market. Some innovation-prone consumers can be identified on the basis of their previous early adoption of new products and brands and this may make such prediction more accurate, though hardly exact. Such behaviours are apparently maintained by a high VI schedule. Some of the prepurchase behaviours associated with them, such as extensive search and evaluation (in which some innovation-prone consumers frequently indulge), are, however, maintained as if by moderate to high VR schedules), that is, these activities, including browsing and talking about likely purchases, occur more regularly and systematically.

Some store choices also fall into this Category: the pre-co-ordinated fashions provided for a particular market niche (between Marks and Spencer and Jaeger) by the Next stores provides executive women with clothing combinations which they can trust to be acceptable for office wear but also of high quality and good styling. Not all clothes, not even all working clothing, is bought at Next by such women (hence the assumed VI schedule), but purchase and consumption of those which are is both hedonically and informationally reinforced. Next is an example of a discontinuous retailing innovation. The products it markets are not usually radically new in themselves: indeed, its accent on proven quality probably precludes novelty as such in its range. Furthermore, pre-co-ordination by clothing retailers is a well-established practice. The innovativeness in this case stems from the positioning of this service in price and quality terms for a defined market segment whose purchase and consumption responses were, thereafter, considerably altered.

Product development in these situations is usually fairly discontinuous: the innovations have a considerable modifying effect on consumption behaviours. This is as true of industrial as consumer purchasing: the EMI CAT-scanner, for instance, provided hospitals with the obvious informational reinforcement of more accurate diagnoses and also the hedonic rewards of prestige in owning and operating such powerful equipment.

2. Closed, high hedonic, high informational

This Category describes the consumption of secondary commodities, delivery of which is maintained by a very high (stretched) VR schedule. A typical example is gambling-based entertainment that relies on informational as well as pleasurable feedback, for example, bingo, roulette, poker, etc. Consumption of these services is generally arranged in closed settings such as casinos or special amusement arcades and halls. The provider thereby gains considerable control over the physical context (to the extent of serving free breakfast to punters at gaming tables and supplying opportunities to gamble outside the usual gaming domain, e.g. by sale of Keno cards in restaurants). Social norms and mores also exert control through both direct contingency exposure and rule governance which proscribe quitting when winning/losing etc. (Since the commodities are generally services, purchase and consumption tend to occur coterminously.) The effect is to strengthen approach behaviours whilst avoidance and escape possibilities are punished or extinguished; the more effectively the discriminative stimuli signal these outcomes, the greater is the probability of continued gambling.

Viewing serious TV programmes, attending dramatic performances, theatres and cinemas, and reading literary novels also fall into this Category. In each case, reinforcements are provided on a moderately-high to high VR schedule and prolonged consumption requires specific discriminative stimuli as well as reinforcers. George Steiner claimed recently that 'the end is in sight for the literary novel' precisely because of the scarcity of '"houses of reading", monastic havens from the babble of the electronic media' (Billen 1988). The purchase of literary works, he notes, was once stimulated by the availability in middle class homes of rooms set aside for reading, in which presumably the consumer could await patiently the infrequent but satisfying hedonic and informational reinforcements of reading such 'demanding' books.

Board games such as Trivial Pursuit have replaced more demanding cultural activities for many people, though the consumption of such items is still maintained by relatively closed settings providing antecedent stimuli that control behaviour by indicating social disapproval and through both hedonic and informational reinforcements.

3. Open, high hedonic, low informational

This Category includes the consumption of products and services that are entirely entertainment-based such as watching popular TV game shows, or reading 'cheap' fiction which contains a sensation on every page: the consumer is not expected to be other than a passive recipient of momentary thrills. Personal cassette players, radios, and many TV programmes and films make available frequent and predictable reinforcements which, unlike those governing cultural activities described as typical of Category 2, are not contingent upon long periods of concentrated effort and which thus make more probable the entertainment-based behaviours just mentioned. The portable nature of the technology which provides these services reduces the control exercised by settings. The audience requires frequent reinforcement in order to maintain its presence and attentive behaviour for which a low VR schedule is necessary.

Certain patterns of store selection can also be systematically related to the situational variables which characterize this Contingency Category. Gift shops, amusement arcades, service organizations such as hairdressers and beauticians, spectator sports, bars, popular theatres and cinemas, and so on, all provide predominantly hedonic reinforcement for both purchase and consumption in relatively open settings.

From the marketer's point of view, it is important that many if not most purchase and consumption responses relevant to these products and services are reinforced, though if every response were reinforced, or reinforcement were for some other reason totally predictable, the outcome would be aversive for many consumers who would quickly report boredom.

4. Closed, high hedonic, low informational

This Category includes some 'primary' escape commodity purchasing and consumption: the escape commodities are those which offer relief from acute discomfort, for example, aspirin for the removal of toothache. The routine consumption of commodities at the product level (often primary commodities such as food) also belongs in this Category: 'biological necessity' usually describes aversive situations that are removed or ameliorated by purchase (and, of course, consumption) of such commodities. Physiological processes, therefore, enter into the definition of the setting, closing it rapidly as physical deprivation of primary reinforcers is prolonged.

Behaviour in this Category is maintained by the removal of an aversive stimulus on a low VR or low VI schedule. Although the precise time between using the product and experiencing relief may not be exactly the same on each consumption occasion, and the number of responses required (e.g. the number of times aspirin have to be taken to remove a headache) may also vary from time to time, reinforcement of the purchase response will only be effective when response–reinforcer delay is short.

Some impulse buying falls into this Category: the merchandiser arranges the physical contingencies to maximize the consumer's acquisition of hedonic (usually secondary) reinforcers; some of these are also escape commodities permitting the avoidance of instore boredom.

5. Open, low hedonic, high informational

This Category includes behaviours sometimes described as based on 'limited problem solving' or 'modified rebuys' which are maintained by a low VI or VR schedule. In other words, trials of modified products or services, which solve operating or consumption problems, must be reinforced on virtually every occasion if trials of further items offered on this basis are to continue. An industrial buyer is only likely to change his source of supply if such adaptive behaviour has been quickly and substantially reinforced in the past; to a greater or lesser extent, the purchased item is an escape commodity in that it leads to avoidance of current problems. By definition, the setting is relatively open in that the prospective buyer is already using some means or other of solving his problem.

Consumer behaviour concerning brand selection in a growing (though not mature or saturated) market is also relevant: hedonic benefits of the product class are easily available but information on price, performance, and quality reinforce search and evaluation behaviours. New versions of existing products, such as teletext-equipped TV sets, novel retail concepts such as the introduction of postal shopping by Habitat (Conran), the centralized prepurchase inspection of consumer durables, teleshopping, and home banking, all exemplify the 'dynamically-continuous' (Robertson 1967) innovation which characterizes new product development in this context. Such innovations are moderately disruptive of consumer behaviour, involving usually a technical modification which changes consumption patterns without revolutionizing usage. Electric lawn mowers, and executive briefcases which double as overnight bags are also of this nature.

6. Closed, low hedonic, high informational

Behaviour falling within this Category often includes mandatory purchase and consumption of state-enforced escape commodities such as social worker intervention, taxation, and TV licensing. Often in these circumstances, the consumer avoids punishments by accepting the control of a closed situation. The informational reinforcers provide cues to further behaviours maintained by a FI removal of aversive stimuli usually in the form of threats, but ultimately as financial or physical impositions.

This pattern of consumer behaviour also occurs as a result of private exchange as when the consumer enters an agreement, openly negotiated, to receive products or services in return for regular contractual payments. In these cases, the consumer may accept the closure of the situation as much as the seller imposes it. Clients of book, record, and computer software clubs normally agree to take a prescribed number of items each year of their membership.

The reinforcers sought are primarily informational in these examples: as a rule, the book, record, or software is required for incorporation in an existing fairly intellectual pastime; hedonic reinforcement is not absent from the pastime but it is informational reward which is uppermost in shaping and maintaining the choice of product source. Financial services, such as insurance, are often of this kind: the consumer may not be forced to buy this service but, if he should, payments must usually be made by direct debit from a bank account. Contingent upon their accepting employment, many workers must agree to payment of their salaries into bank or similar accounts, which obliges them to consume the services of financial institutions. Such monopoly retailing is also practised by national postal services which control access to the transmission of information through the mails, as well as some types of cash transfers.

Some instances of this Category of buying are a mixture of state-enforced and privately contracted commitments. Motor insurance, for example, is legally required, though most drivers are free to negotiate with a risk-bearer of their choice. Having done so, however, their payments and other obligations are strictly regulated for the period that the insurance is in force. Escaping from one contract is, moreover, only a prelude to negotiating another.

Reinforcement in each of these instances is not exclusively informational; some hedonic reward is also inevitable, even if relatively small. However, the structure of the setting must, where relevant, be so closed as to ensure that punishment for deviation is probable (compare TV licensing, where aversive consequences are relatively easy to avoid, and taxation, where evasion is more frequently and drastically dealt with). But in very tightly controlled situations, such as token economies in therapeutic institutions, the aim is to reinforce positive behaviours, usually on low FR schedules or by CRF, that is, most if not all responses are reinforced, and the rewards that ensue are closely and predictably related to the performance of the required number of responses.

7. Open, low hedonic, low informational

The behaviour emitted in these circumstances is that described as 'routinized response behaviour' (RRB) involving 'straight rebuys'. (The situations described by Contingency Categories 2 and 3 also produce this pattern to a degree, but its incidence is most obvious here.) Typically, it includes the choice of primary commodities as in regular (say, weekly or monthly) grocery shopping but the chief reinforcers are the brands that are differentiated by marketing activity which take on characteristics of secondary commodities. Neither hedonic nor informational reinforcement is entirely lacking – both pleasure and data are obtained in the course of such purchasing – though each is relatively weak compared with purchasing new products and brands of luxury items.

Behaviour (selection of a specific brand or store) is maintained by low FI or VI schedules, if not by CRF, that is, reinforcement follows most, perhaps all, responses. Regular saving, especially contractual, and investment behaviours, maintained on FI schedules, also fall into this Category.

Elements of the setting assume considerable importance. The setting derives its openness from the large number of alternative brands available to the prospective buyer. His or her failure to find an acceptable brand at one store does not usually pose an insuperable problem since store choice is also considerable. In response to such openness, retailers act to control the purchase context by 'closing' the setting in which purchase may occur. Hence abundant discriminative stimuli are provided; they are generally highly informational, taking the form of brand names, logos, store layouts, and other aspects that permit precise and accurate identification of suitable items.

This is the situation in which multi-brand, multi-store purchasing occurs, relatively few customers showing total loyalty at the brand/store level (Ehrenberg and Goodhardt 1989). Although the primary reinforcer comprises the goods characteristics supplied by all members of the product class, this Category describes the acquisition of a particular form or version of the product (brand selection) via a particular distribution system or delivery method (channel and store choice), though in physical formulation or structural terms, all brands in the established product class tend to be identical one to another, and all competing stores resemble one another in basic outline.

New product development in these circumstances usually takes the form of continuous innovations – items such as fluoride toothpaste, new pack sizes, line extensions, and the like, which hardly affect consumption but provide greater, if generally trivial, variety at the purchase stage. Although such 'new' products rarely provide anything genuinely novel by way of additional reinforcers, they are important to the control of the setting by the competitive provision of discriminative stimuli for customer satisfaction.

8. Closed, low hedonic, low informational

The most obvious behaviours associated with this Contingency Category are the purchase of secondary escape commodities such as pension fund membership, or mortgage-related endowment assurance. Neither hedonic nor informational reinforcement is wholly absent, but the product or service is purchased as a necessary complement of another item which is the principal source of reinforcement. The secondary commodity is purchased only because its consumption is a prerequisite of more strongly reinforced purchase and consumption. It is often the eventual acquisition of the additional product or service and the reinforcements it confers that reinforce purchase of the secondary escape commodity (Premack 1971).

Payment of premia for mortgage-related life insurance may be maintained ultimately by promises of delayed gratification (the cash released on maturity of the policy) but more routinely by removing the threat of punishment (loss of the mortgage loan, for instance).

Continued purchase of such escape commodities is often maintained on a low FI (possibly low VI) schedule: minimal reinforcement, such as entries in an account passbook or on a monthly statement, may follow each payment, and interest or bonuses may be added at known intervals. Yet, for the most part, such behaviours are maintained not by these positive reinforcers but by the avoidance of the aversive consequences of non-compliance.

The patronage of particular stores is often a prerequisite of obtaining specific product- or service-related reinforcers. Often the discriminative and reinforcing stimuli available in stores are so arranged as to maximize consumers' patronage and to shape purchase responses. However, on occasions, use of such retail outlets, in itself, offers little by way of hedonic or informational reinforcement, as when an individual must visit a remote airline terminal to obtain tickets, or an unattractive government office to obtain a passport. If store visits are to be maintained the punishing consequences of locating and making use of the retail outlet must be offset in such circumstances by the positive benefits of buying and using the products and services so obtained.

Such industrial purchase behaviours as the acquisition of such secondary escape commodities as safety equipment and the provision of training seminars also fall into this Category. Although the provision of the appropriate products and services to employees incurs costs, failure to assume these purchase and consumption burdens from time to time would eventually impede the primary activity of the organization. The appropriate managerial behaviours, though they initially attract some aversive outcomes, are reinforced none the less by the removal of potentially more punishing consequences of non-compliance.

Broader patterns of consumer behaviour

The eight Contingency Categories are summarized in Table 5.1, which exemplifies the purchase and/or consumption behaviours typical of each and notes the schedule of reinforcement which most closely describes the factors maintaining the illustrative responses. The above discussion has concentrated on each of the Contingency Categories in turn, but some interesting relationships among the behaviour patterns characteristic of each and the schedules upon which they are apparently maintained emerge from this table. For instance, a general relationship between setting and reinforcing variables is suggested: the implication of the discussion of Contingency Categories and their associated purchase and consumption responses is that the influence of the setting increases as combined reinforcer strength declines. Behaviour is apparently maintained on high variable schedules where both types of reinforcer operate in strength but controlling features of the setting become progressively more important as one descends the list of contingencies in Table 5.1. Several other patterns are also apparent.

Modes of consumer choice

The familiar modes of consumer behaviour – extended problem-solving (EPS), limited problem-solving (LPS), and routine response behaviour (RRB) – are each identified by the above analysis with a peculiar pattern of controlling contingencies. All occur in relatively open settings but each is associated with a distinctive pattern of reinforcer effect (Table 5.2).

In contrast to the cognitive explanation which depicts the progression from EPS through LPS to RRB (see Chapter one) in terms of the gradual growth of brand comprehension and

Table 5.1 Contingency Categories, response patterns, and reinforcement schedules

Contingency Category		Typical resonse pattern	Apparent reinforcement schedule
Setting component	Reinforcement component		
Relatively:			
1. Open	High hedonic,	EPS/new task	High VI/VR
2. Closed	high informational	Gambling	High VR
3. Open	High hedonic,	Popular entertainment	Low VR
4. Closed	low informational	Primary escape	Low VI
5. Open	Low hedonic,	LPS/modified rebuy	Low VI
6. Closed	high informational	Mandatory consumption	FI
7. Open	Low hedonic,	RRB/straight rebuy	Low FI/VI
8. Closed	low informational	Secondary escape	Low FI

Note: EPS = extended problem solving; LPS = limited problem solving; RRB = routine response behaviour.

strengthening of brand attitude as the consumer processes information and acquires experience (Howard and Sheth 1969), the Behavioural Perspective Model stresses the situational factors that are systematically related to such behaviours. In the case of EPS, these are an open setting in which both hedonic and informational reinforcers are available in volume. A range of discriminative stimuli signal these reinforcers contingent upon buying and/or using this or that brand or product. Several means of obtaining the reinforcers are available in the form of differing versions of the product, based on function and styling rather than merely marketing differentiation, which precede the establishment of a generally accepted product design in the case of innovations and the proliferation of benefits presented by luxury goods. There are also many alternatives to being in the situation: other products, services, and venues offer high levels of both types of reinforcer. Marketers strive in these circumstances to manipulate setting and reinforcer variables to control choice, but the innovations and luxuries on offer are secondary commodities, hardly matters of life and death, and consumers enjoy substantial discretion. Their behaviour is unpredictable and occurs in settings that are far from closed.

LPS occurs in less open settings: by this time most brands have

Table 5.2 Selected purchase responses and situational contingencies

Purchase response	Situational contingencies	Typical schedule	Typical NPD pattern

EPS/new task	Setting: open
	Reinforcement:
	  high hedonic
	  high informational
		High variable	Discontinuous innovation

LPS/ modified rebuy	Setting: open
	Reinforcement:
	  low hedonic
	  high informational
		Low variable	Dynamically-continuous innovation

RRB/ straight rebuy	Setting: open
	Reinforcement:
	  low hedonic
	  low informational
		Low fixed	Continuous innovation

been tried and some are bought regularly, even frequently, for the reinforcers they supply. A new version is likely to be considered only if it provides large relative advantages. RRB occurs in settings that are less open still. The range of brands and products, and thus of sources of reinforcement, considered by the customer is typically restricted. Extensive marketer action makes much of the small variations in the primary reinforcers offered by brands, which are usually based on marketing differentiation. Considerable managerial effort is also expended in closing the setting by physical manipulation of store traffic, shelf positioning, and so on. Although it is relatively open compared with that depicted in Category 8, the setting increasingly resembles the closed environment depicted by Schwartz and Lacey as that in which operant conditioning is likely to be effective.

Purchasing and consumption

The discussion of the Behavioural Perspective Model highlights the importance of distinguishing purchasing and consumption behaviours, which are separately controlled and reinforced but which impinge directly upon the rate of emission of one another. Making sense of consumer behaviour as operant response depends on the conceptualization of the scope of the behaviour involved. The molecular unit of a response and its immediate, contiguous consequence, which is appropriate to the observation and recording of animal activity in an experimental chamber, is often insufficient to the understanding of complex human choice. Here, a more molar approach which takes account of the longer-term as well as the short-term consequences of specific behaviour and which considers the correlative rather than contiguous relationship of response and consequence is required (Baum 1973, 1974). The immediate and contiguous consequence of banking up a fire is a colder room; yet the response is reinforced rather than punished (Rachlin 1970). The relationship between the behaviour and its controlling consequence (warmth) is intelligible only as the longer term benefits of adding coal to the fire are considered.[2]

Much consumer behaviour is in the same vein and requires a molar perspective which embraces both buying and consuming. To focus on the former, as does Alhadeff's (1982) theory, is to emphasize the punishment of buy-behaviour, notably by the forfeiture of money, and to assume that the strength of the approach behaviour is at least equal to that of the alternative escape response which it overcomes. This ignores the strength of the buy response which accrues from the positive consequences of prior consumption of the item in question. Refuelling one's car, for instance, incurs the contiguous punishing consequence of giving up spending power; it is positively reinforced only as a stream of consumption benefits is released over a long period of time and involving travelling many miles as well as performing the exacting tasks inherent in prolonged driving. A more molar perspective is required to encompass within a behavioural explanation consumer behaviours such as the purchase of life assurance. Here, the regular payments of premia are maintained – and their contiguous punishing consequences overcome – by a verbal promise from a financial institution of either a lump sum payment on maturity of the policy or benefits for one's dependants in the event of one's prior decease. Only the consequences of previous dealings with finance companies can influence one's acceptance of the former; the latter relies entirely on vicarious reinforcement.

In less dramatic ways, explaining most consumer behaviour in operant terms requires a molar view that encompasses both buying and using if repeat purchase is to be fully comprehended; it also implies the correlational relationship between operant and reinforcer suggested by the matching law. Such reasoning strengthens the argument that the relevant unit of analysis may subsume the whole sequence of consumer behaviour, including pre- and post-purchase activities as well as the act of purchase.

Brands, products and stores

The analysis of Contingency Categories also draws attention to the importance of distinguishing brand and product levels of analysis behaviourally. A product class is defined primarily in terms of a set of reinforcers common to each brand in the class, though appearing in somewhat different combinations from brand to brand; a brand is defined largely in terms of the discriminative stimuli by which marketers seek to differentiate it from competing brands; this is especially so in the case of brands whose conspicuous purchase and consumption are reinforced by outcomes other than those that derive directly from the characteristics of brand or product such as social approval or manifest jealousy (Veblen 1979; see also Mason 1981).

Brand purchase and consumption is largely associated with relatively open situations where primary reinforcer deprivation is not at issue (except in the case of variety) and where brands are physically similar in terms of reinforcer effectiveness, the post-response delay, quantity, quality, and the scheduling of reinforcement each provides. Product purchase and consumption are more likely to occur in relatively closed situations where response strength is more a function of deprivation. Not all of the odd-numbered behaviour patterns in Figure 5.2 (see p. 131) occur in situations of equal openness, however. In the case of Category 7 which includes routine rebuying, discriminative stimuli contained in the physical setting may well be more important than in other open situations, and reinforcer control is, by definition, weaker.

The above discussion and examples of behaviours typical of the situations defined by the eight Contingency Categories also demonstrate the capacity of the model to embrace store choice, something lacking from both animal-based economic psychology/ behavioural economics and the analysis of human buy-behaviour presented by Alhadeff.

A behavioural portrayal of consumer involvement

Consumer involvement is generally conceived to be related to the cognitive and affective processes that mediate consumption-related behaviours. Conceptual complexity marks the rapidly developing analysis of involvement but it is usually defined in terms of the personal relevance of the stimuli provided by advertisements, products, and purchase/consumption situations to the individual consumer. (Among useful reviews and extensions of the concept are Antil 1984; Costley 1988; Park and Mittal 1985; Slama and

Tashchian 1985; Zaichkowski 1986.) Peter and Olson (1987: 126–8) note that all of the many available definitions of involvement stress 'the importance of the product to the consumer' and define involvement as 'the degree of personal relevance, which is a function of the extent to which the product or brand is perceived to help achieve consequences and values of importance to the consumer'. Wilkie (1986: 350) emphasizes the inevitability of an affective as well as cognitive component of involvement, though the relative importance of each varies, defining it in terms of arousal, the directed energy in which motivation consists.

Krugman (1965, 1967) proposed that involvement with advertisements be operationally understood and measured as the quantity of 'bridging experiences' or personal references made by the viewer each minute between the advertisement and his or her life. Zaichkowski (1986) distinguishes two additional types of consumer involvement: involvement with the product, i.e. the perceived relevance of the product class to the consumer, and involvement with purchase decisions, assessed by behavioural criteria such as the amount of time spent or the number of stores visited in prepurchase search.

Involvement is not a property of the individual but a relationship between individual characteristics, such as personal goals and experience of the consequences of buying and consuming, and the stimuli presented by the communication, product, or situation. The dynamic and persisting nature of the relationship is reflected in the distinction between 'enduring involvement', which is influenced by the experiences of the consumer over time, and 'situational involvement', which results from immediate stimuli (Bloch and Richins 1983; Rothschild 1979). The former refers to the overall relevance to the consumer of consumption-related activity and thus to his or her knowledge of the consequences of acquiring, owning, and consuming the product. Over time, such experience changes as the individual develops and as different consumption patterns become salient (e.g. as one acquires new interests, a new job, or progresses through the family life cycle). Hence enduring involvement itself is modified. Situational involvement refers to the immediate consequences of behaviour within a situation of purchase or consumption. It may vary as those consequences become more salient to the individual, for example, as the consumer completes the task of shopping for groceries for the family and begins to buy personal items, and again as personal shopping gives way to gift buying.

The Behavioural Perspective Model suggests a behavioural understanding of consumer involvement. Instead of involvement being conceived primarily in terms of intrapersonal cognitive and affective processing, the behaviourist perspective depicts it in terms of observable behaviours and emphasizes the environmental determinants of the activities associated with high and low involvement. The behavioural conception of involvement views it as instrumental behaviour which is maintained by hedonic and informational reinforcers encountered either during the consumer's reinforcement history or in the immediate situation. What has been termed 'enduring involvement' would, therefore, result from the individual's reinforcement history with the product, the stimulus control and consequences of prepurchase, purchase, and postpurchase responses previously performed. The consumer's reinforcement history would influence situational behaviour by determining the strength of immediately available purchase- and consumption-related stimuli to shape and maintain purchase and/ or consumption.

A behavioural definition of involvement emphasizes what might be called 'actualized involvement', that is, observed activity characterized by sustained attention to consumption-related behaviours and artefacts. Behaviour maintained by high levels of both hedonic and informational reinforcements (characteristic of Categories 1, e.g. EPS, and 2, e.g. gambling) would be that described as most involving. Behaviour maintained principally by situational factors (characteristic of Categories 7, e.g. RRB, and 8, e.g. secondary escape), would be those described as least involving. Those found between these extremes would be described as moderately involving, with greater or lesser involvement being ascribed as informational or hedonic reinforcements became more relevant.

Among the behaviours emitted in the presence of high hedonic and high informational reinforcement (or the antecedent stimuli that signal them) are verbal responses relating to search and evaluation and/or the receipt and handling of information. It is not surprising, therefore, that high involvement has been associated primarily with 'reasoning' behaviour, in contrast with the 'mindlessness' of low involvement routine response (Lea 1981). However, whilst reasoning may be a function of the pattern of reinforcement encountered in high involvement, it is not simply the case that reinforcement can be defined in terms of rational information processing alone. Peter and Olson (1987: 259–65) view the nature and outcome of consumers' problem-solving processes as determined by the interaction of involvement and knowledge. The highly involved consumer who has a high level of knowledge relevant to the product and/or situation (gained presumably as a result of his reinforcement history) may engage in reasoning with the intention of optimizing the satisfaction gained from purchase and/or consumption. But high involvement coupled with a low level of relevant knowledge is likely to lead to confused decision-making and problem-solving: goals poorly defined, choice criteria unclear, and unsatisfactory search. The result is as likely to be limited problem-solving as extensive problem-solving.

Involvement conceived as a behaviour is independent of specific products, decisions, communications, and contexts. It avoids the vague definition of involvement as perceived or felt relevance which may easily become no more than an explanatory fiction: as when a person's involvement is inferred from the actions resulting from his or her sustained attention, with the result that research effort is diverted from any external factors that might be controlling the behaviour. Reasoning is treated on this view as a behaviour in itself which may or may not include rational, goal-directed information processing, and recognizes that reported cognitive activity may amount to *ex post* rationalization of purchases made rather than *ex ante* mental activity which can be consistently related to manifest choice.

Marketer action in behavioural perspective

This analysis also highlights several aspects of a marketing level of analysis, involving the actions of marketing managements in its attempts to shape consumer choice, which have often not received attention in economic psychology and behavioural economics.

The Behaviour Perspective Model recognizes the role of the marketer in attempting, through branding and other forms of differentiation, to redefine (primary) commodities and generic purchase situations as special (repositioning commodities as secondary reinforcers in the form of brands and enhancing store-based experiences) by emphasizing the pertinent informational or hedonic consequences of purchase and consumption. Marketer action also attempts to alter the situation of buying or consuming, perhaps most often by creating closed settings (through the merchandising techniques described in Chapter three). Occasionally, for example, in the attempt to modify the rebuy situation, a seller who does not currently supply the prospect, attempts to broaden the customer's evoked set by suggesting that the requirements of the buyer have altered in ways which only a drastic change of product and supplier can accommodate.

Whether the further behavioural analysis of consumer choice will lead to novel prescriptions for marketing managers remains an open question but an empirical one. Although several authors have cast marketing strategy in operant terms (Peter and Olson 1987; Rothschild and Gaidis 1981), rigorous demonstration, experimental or otherwise, of operant principles applied to marketing management lags behind. Furthermore, the portrayal of marketing mix management in terms of operant conditioning suggests that marketing managers appear to make good use of operant principles already; it is unlikely that a major outcome of the behavioural analysis of marketing will be empirical results that dramatically impact managerial practice even though they lead to a better or alternative understanding of the procedures involved and their efficacy.

It is fruitful, nevertheless, to analyze the activities of marketers on the basis of the EAB-derived model's capacity to elucidate the working of the marketing system as a whole.

Closure of purchase and/or consumption settings

Much marketer action can be interpreted as attempting to close the settings in which purchase and consumption occur in order to increase the probability of certain exchanges. This may be accomplished by modifying the physical and social environment (as in the casino example) to ensure that escape behaviour is punished or even extinguished (i.e. its frequency of occurrence is reduced or it is eliminated). Other purchase settings can be rendered relatively closed once the consumer has shown some interest in buying or has tacitly agreed to a purchase. Hence purchase agreements may be finally negotiated and concluded not in the relatively open store setting where the merchandise has been inspected, sales claims (discriminative stimuli) presented, and consequences of purchase and consumption (hedonic and informational reinforcers) outlined, but in offices or corners of the store, separated by desks or other furniture, where potential interruptions (in the form of alternative discriminative stimuli and reinforcers) cannot obtrude, frivolous or other non-pointed behaviour is discouraged, and escape or avoidance is thus less probable.

Banks and other financial institutions often conclude business in settings that reinforce only the serious behaviour of transacting, and remove stimuli that would impede this. The effect is not to create an entirely closed setting as in Schwartz and Lacey's definition – the operant chamber is not a marketing option! – but to achieve a setting closed within limits for the effective and efficient execution of a temporary purpose (Baker *et al.* 1988). The uses of instore merchandising techniques noted in Chapter three can now be seen as attempts at creating relatively closed settings in which the reinforcers provided and controlled by the seller predominate, other sources of reinforcement being unavailable, and escape/avoidance behaviours being largely or entirely ruled out.

The consumption of some modern personality and social training methods and quasi-religious services takes place in relatively closed settings (as closed as the factory workplace example employed by Schwartz *et al.* 1978) in which the most salient reinforcers and punishers are wielded by the seller (trainer, auditor). Therapeutic seminars such as est (Erhart Seminar Training) require consumers to remain in the training environment (typically a hotel ballroom) for many hours, devoid of timepieces, and having to attend to the trainers who are in full control of the environmental contingencies (Rhinehart 1976). Some modern religious groups base their training on the isolation of individuals from family and friends, which is achieved through voluntary attendance on residential courses. Within these settings, rewards and punishments are manipulated by the leaders who use social approval and disapproval to influence chosen behaviours and who retain control over the performance standards required (Lamont 1986).

Manipulation of reinforcers

When it is not possible to accomplish closure through the manipulation of social and physical settings, the use of hedonic and informational reinforcers may achieve similar effects, by restricting the overall purchase or consumption situation, especially when these reinforcers are clearly linked to appropriate discriminative stimuli. Again, the intention is to strengthen approach and/or reduce escape responses and this may be accomplished by substituting hedonic for informational reinforcement (as in popular entertainment) or by presenting strong hedonic and informational reinforcers in combination.

The five determinants of response strength mentioned by Alhadeff (see Chapter three), are the basis of the marketer's range of techniques for increasing the probability of purchase and/or consumption on the part of customers. Reinforcer effectiveness can be increased by delaying the presentation of the reinforcer, something difficult in an entirely open setting (say, a street market) in which a competitor can step in to satisfy demand, but the more easily accomplished the more closed the setting. Theatre and cinema entertainment is, therefore, often arranged such that the biggest star or most strongly promoted movie appears last on the bill and, as long as discriminative stimuli informing the audience of their eventual appearance are properly designed and presented, the intermediate behaviours of watching preceding acts, short films, or advertisements are likely to come under stimulus control.

The concepts of shaping and chaining, and Premack's concept of a hierarchy of reinforcers (described in Chapter two) are all relevant here: watching the preceding acts or films is eventually reinforced by enjoyment of the main attraction and is therefore more likely to occur on succeeding occasions. The presentation of preceding acts shapes behaviour by reducing the negative influence of response–reinforcer delay. Some reinforcements are not deliberately delayed in this way by marketers but cannot, by their nature, be made available instantly. Vacations may be purchased well in advance of their being taken, but payment and waiting are strengthened by the presentation of intervening reinforcers (e.g. letters of thanks and acknowledgement, receipts and brochures for part payment and instalment credits). The benefits of saving are also necessarily delayed, though prompts and vicarious reinforcement relating to the gaining of interest and the future consumption contingent upon saving are used to strengthen the response.

Marketers also take steps to increase the quantity and quality of the positive reinforcers that strengthen approach and to reduce the quantity and quality of aversive stimuli likely to provoke escape and avoidance. Promotional deals that require repeat brand purchase simultaneously accomplish both. They often involve reinforcers that are qualitatively different from the purchased items, such as prizes or collateral products and, if a prize is contingent upon a sequence of purchases and/or consumption responses, a bigger reinforcement may be forthcoming. They are, moreover, usually hedonic in character or, if instructional (such as trading stamps or collectable tokens) redeemable for hedonic rewards. Products that come in weekly parts (such as the familiar magazines that build into encyclopaedia) may be promoted and delivered such that non-response is punished: missed parts may not be available after a certain time or may cost more. Competitions and deals encouraging repeat brand selection are also an attempt to change the schedule of reinforcement, albeit temporarily, for those consumers not already 100 per cent loyal to the brand.

Mass visual communications are obviously susceptible to the presentation of reinforcers on schedules chosen to gain and keep viewers' attention in the face of strong competition from alternative media and pursuits. A primary function of advertising is the presentation of discriminative stimuli which portray social rules which may be followed through purchase and consumption of the featured brands. They include rules for 'being a good parent', for instance, and show what can be eaten or worn on special occasions

(Branthwaite 1984). The specification of verbal rules for behaviour in complex social situations is consonant with the work described in Chapter four which demonstrates the importance of rule-governed behaviour in the absence of direct exposure to contingencies. But this is not the only function of mass marketing communication: advertisements do not only present discriminative stimuli that signal the availability of the rewards of purchasing and consuming extrinsic products and services, in line with social rules. They themselves provide certain rewards and reinforcers in order to ensure that potential consumers receive their messages. Television advertisements, usually encountered in open settings which offer multiple, immediate rewards for non-viewing activities, generally provide many potentially *reinforcing* informational and hedonic stimuli contingent upon sustained, attentive watching. Competition for the viewer's attention – from alternative reinforcers contingent upon talking, eating, preparing drinks, thinking about something else, and so on – mean that the advertisement must itself reinforce continued viewing. When attention is maintained by strong informational and hedonic reinforcers, the continued viewing is a high involvement activity (defined according to the behavioural portrayal of involvement described above). Postmodern advertising, especially in the United Kingdom, France and Japan, is especially sensitive to this (Grafton-Small and Linstead 1989; Linstead and Grafton-Small 1989).

The constant reduction in consumers' attention spans – American viewers are reported to change TV channels on average every three minutes; others watch two programmes simultaneously using split screen techniques – implies a constant search for informational and hedonic reinforcement. Some TV programmes incorporate the sustained presentation of high levels of informational and hedonic reinforcers. The 'happy talk' news format, in which reports are made as entertaining as possible, feature 'action, pace, [and] an almost dizzy attempt to keep the audience from getting bored' (Tunstall and Walker 1981: 123). In California, where this approach predominated during the 1970s, local news programmes feature a series of sensational and entertaining stories, each of which receives one or two minutes concentrated coverage in a half hour bulletin, interrupted by three two-minute commercial breaks and a five minute weather forecast presented with similar pace and verve (Tunstall and Walker 1981).

Consumer behaviour modification

Empirical testing

Because of the derivative nature of the Behavioural Perspective Model, it cannot be subjected to direct empirical testing to a greater extent than the theoretical base from which it stems. It was argued in Chapter four that operant behaviourist explanations of human behaviour in complex social situations would eventually become programmatic rather than directly empirically verifiable. The difficulty of accurately identifying environmental discriminative and reinforcing stimuli in such situations would ultimately rule out an entirely operant explanation. If this were true of all of the situations to which the Behavioural Perspective Model could be applied, it would still be capable of contributing to the understanding of consumer choice. Its contribution would, however, be wholly hermeneutic: it would suggest an alternative interpretation of complex consumer behaviours which are frequently-observed and well-documented, and it could be subjectively appraised on the extent to which it rendered purchase and consumption more intelligible to researchers with specific and limited purposes. It can be argued that the chief benefit of any theory is of this kind: it is true of interpretivist theories by definition; it follows, by implication, for cognitivism and other inner-state ideas which interpret observed actions by reference to inferential information processing constructs; and it is evident, on the basis of the programmatic character ascribed to radical behaviourist explanation in Chapter four, of even so empirically-based a paradigm as the EAB.

Clearly, the model can perform a useful hermeneutic function, as is indicated by the interpretation of marketer behaviour suggested above. But it does not follow that the model must be confined to the interpretation of complex situations through extrapolation of the results of operant experimentation in closed and confined situations. Whilst the full predictive capacity of the model's independent variables cannot be definitively gauged in the absence of empirical testing of specific hypotheses derived from it, the existing literature on the environmental conditioning of consumer choice in relatively open settings provides valuable evidence of the relevance of its independent variables, contextually-based discriminative stimuli and hedonic and informational reinforcement, to the explanation of consumer behaviour and marketer intervention.

Accordingly, this chapter now reviews studies of attempts to modify consumers' purchase and consumption behaviours in an area where extensive behaviour analytic experimentation has taken place. This research, which is concerned with the reduction of socially and ecologically deleterious effects of consumption, was not conducted with the Behavioural Perspective Model in mind. Nevertheless, the results of the many investigations summarized below indicate the relevance of all three of the model's principal explanatory variables to the analysis of consumer and marketer behaviour.

The management of commons

The following analysis is concerned with a particular facet of marketer action and consumer response: the demarketing of products and services which, in the long term, prove socially or environmentally damaging. The purpose of the discussion is to illustrate further the relevance to an understanding of consumer choice of the independent variables incorporated in the Behavioural Perspective Model and the ways in which they interact to shape consumer behaviours. In addition, it demonstrates the need for researchers to appreciate the separate and combined effects of both proximate and remote causes of consumer behaviour.

The idea of marketing as economic interaction based on the reciprocal reinforcement of market exchange behaviours (developed in Chapter three) is sufficiently flexible to embrace consumer activity outside the usual realm of business marketing. Several social issues involving consumer behaviour fall into this category and can be described by the three-term contingency; in line with the reasoning that has been advanced, the examples considered below involve the use of behavioural analysis and technology to influence literal exchange relationships. The purpose of this discussion is exploratory: to elucidate the causal mechanisms that control consumer choice in the context of social concern. First, the general nature of such issues and the problems they raise is described in behavioural terms. Second, examples are given of the use of behaviour modification methods in the attempt to solve them. Third, a general interpretation of the findings is made in terms of the salient components of the Behavioural Perspective Model.

The 'tragedy of the commons' refers to the depletion or spoliation of public natural resources as a result of the accessibility to individuals whose immediate interests lead to the exploitation of those resources in ways inconsistent with their effective long-term use (Hardin 1968). Even when such resources are already over-exploited, the positive utility enjoyed by any individual user from further consumption is high, almost +1, whilst the negative utility thereby immediately imposed on other users is only a fraction of −1 since the deleterious consequences of over-use are widely shared. Eventually, however, the result is a reduction in the utility available to any user of the common resource and perhaps its total depletion and ruination. In the case of common agricultural land, the benefits to any owner of rights of common from grazing one more sheep are considerable, whilst the deterioration in the quality of the land has only slight immediate implications for other graziers and any additional users (Foxall 1979a). Once the problems stemming from deterioration of the land are well-progressed, however, the costs of rectifying it are sufficient to deter any individual from attempting singularly to effect improvements which would be generally enjoyed (Foxall 1979b). In Hardin's famous phrase, 'Freedom in a commons brings ruin to all.'

In behavioural terms, the unrestricted acquisition of short-term reinforcements by a limited number of individuals leads to long-term aversive consequences for all users. In some cases involving the ownership and use of the environment, voluntarily-entered, legally-controlled co-operative action − 'mutual coercion mutually agreed upon' (Hardin 1968) − may be feasible to prevent the misuse of commons (Foxall 1979b). But, in the absence of technical and scientific solutions to such problems, and the improbability that persuasive appeals to conscience will change the behaviours in question, political, administrative, or market interventions have been prescribed (Hardin and Baden 1977).

Behavioural demarketing

Consumer behaviour modification has frequently been pursued with the intention of reducing demand for products or services with socially- or environmentally-deleterious effects; such action is akin to 'social demarketing'. The resource-exploitive behaviours which environmental behaviour modification programmes have addressed occur in relatively open settings and are strengthened by primarily hedonic reinforcers. Draconian changes which have the effect of closing settings in some degree can effectively produce behavioural change, for example, the bottle laws initiated in 1971 in Oregon, and since then replicated in several other states, that outlawed no-deposit drinks containers led to a significant reduction in litter (up to 65 per cent) from this source (J. H. Skinner 1977). However, such dramatic changes in purchase and consumption settings are generally either politically or economically not viable as well as difficult to monitor and police. Behaviour modification programmes have, therefore, as a rule employed specific, behaviour-related antecedent and consequent stimuli in order to alter situations. The chief antecedent interventions have been in the form of prompts – discriminative stimuli such as warnings, reasoned argument and fact, threats, pleas, and so on relating to the demerits of continued environmental exploitation (e.g. as a result of pollution).

Consequential interventions are of two types: feedback and incentives. Feedback comprises information provided to individuals or groups relating to the actual implications of their pre-specified actions, for example, the amount of electricity consumed by a household in a recent period, or the cost of recent car trips. In the terminology developed earlier, feedback is principally informational reinforcement, though in so far as they indicate savings or social approbation, these reinforcers also have a hedonic content. Incentives consist of rewards, usually financial though sometimes in the form of social approval or praise, that are contingent upon the performance of specified prosocial behaviours such as car pooling, reducing domestic energy consumption, or riding the bus rather than travelling by private car. Incentives are, therefore, primarily hedonic reinforcers, though they also inform to some degree, and usually take the form of generalized secondary reinforcers such as money or tokens redeemable at selected local retail outlets.

Summary of empirical research

Litter reduction

Several experiments have monitored the effects of changing situations directly. Burgess *et al.* (1971) provided children in theatres with bags in which they were to place litter: the effect was slight. When, in addition to the bags, the children received an announcement about the disadvantages of littering, during an intermission, the effect was moderate. Only when a small reward (one dime) was provided for a bag of litter was there any appreciable effect on littering; indeed, a massive improvement ensued. All of these improvements reduced to the initial baseline level during the final return-to-baseline phase of the research. Another form of hedonic reward, the provision of a ticket for a movie, had a similarly substantial effect on littering (Burgess *et al.* 1971; Cone and Hayes 1984). Exhortations, lectures, and relevant general education were ineffective, however.

Similar effects have been found for litter reduction in streets, around buildings and within buildings (Cone and Hayes 1984). The depositing of rubbish in waste bins may be brought under stimulus control simply by increasing the availability of suitable containers and reinforcing their use. The provision at football games of refuse containers that resembled fans' hats, displayed the word 'Push' on the flap, and revealed the word 'Thanks' to their users, had precisely this effect (O'Neill *et al.* 1980). In general, however, whilst the availability of trash cans, their attractiveness and the initial cleanliness of the environment all reduce the rate of littering in these contexts, only positive reinforcements in the form of payments has any dramatic effect on behaviour; prompts such as verbal appeals are ineffective, especially when used alone. One difficulty is that such prompts rely on promises of punishment: getting away with littering is, therefore, reinforced by the failure of punishment to materialize.

Recycling of waste materials

As has been noted, a dramatic change in the situation that includes effective legally-enforced punishments (e.g. the bottle laws) is most effective in modifying behaviour. But this is not always practicable. Attempts to increase sales of returnable bottles based on prompts informing customers of the savings inherent in such behaviour and that they would be fighting pollution by adopting such containers have had mixed results. In a small convenience store, customers for returnables increased 32 per cent over base-line, their numbers being reduced during the return-to-baseline phase. However, this effect was not noted in the relatively open setting provided by supermarkets (Geller *et al.* 1971). Although prompts have some effect within the relatively closed context of the convenience store, it is short-lived (Geller *et al.* 1973, 1977). The provision of small financial rewards for customers' re-use of egg cartons, milk containers and grocery bags has been shown to result in small increases in custom, though factors that slightly close the setting, for example, instore prompts and enthusiastic behaviour on the part of salespersons, are also helpful (Green 1977).

Bottle laws place considerable costs of transactions, inventory space and time on retailers which are subsequently passed on to consumers (Guerts 1986). Both parties are penalized for their participation in the waste reduction campaign and, although legal sanctions may force compliance on the part of the distributors, there is no reason to believe, on the basis of behaviour theory, that customers will in general voluntarily incur discomforts involved in prepayments of deposits and returning glass bottles. Research in this area shows few successes, partly because the 'prosocial' behaviours encouraged are themselves punished by the customers' having to pay out deposits on returnable containers and carry empty cartons back to the store. In absolute terms, such punishments may be small, but given the slight hedonic and informational reinforcers available for the target behaviours, they are probably sufficient to deter compliance.

Experimental attempts to encourage the recovery of waste materials such as paper which can be recycled show, in similar vein, that prompts alone have minimal effect and only the provision of reinforcers, preferably hedonic, changes behaviour significantly. Students offered prizes in contests and raffles are more likely to reduce wastage than those exposed only to educational promptings. The clear implication is that consequential reinforcements rather than antecedent education change behaviour (Cone and Hayes 1984; Couch *et al.* 1978; Geller *et al.* 1975; Ingram and Geller 1975; Witmer and Geller 1976). Closing the setting by providing convenient containers for the collection of recyclable waste also has a significant effect over prompting on performance of the desired behaviours (e.g. Reid *et al.* 1976). Again, the results indicate the importance of moderately high consequential rewards to overcome the moderate punishments involved in recycling.

Prompts and manipulation of the physical environment may, however, have synergystic interactions. Whilst Jacobs *et al.* (1984) found prompting alone to be ineffective in encouraging recycling, prompting coupled with the provision to households of containers into which recyclable rubbish could be sorted had the required effect on householders' behaviour.

Transportation

The aims of behaviour modification programmes in this area have been to reduce fuel consumption, urban congestion and pollution by discouraging the unilateral use of private cars and promoting travel by public transportation (Cone and Hayes 1984). The most prevalent and successful interventions have provided direct financial incentives, for example, paying commuters to travel by bus. Several ABA-design studies have shown that when individuals are given such incentives as they board the bus (typically 25c for a 10c fare) or 5c/10c tokens redeemable for merchandise at a neighbourhood store, the number of users of the public transport system increased by between 50 and 180 per cent (Everett 1973; Everett *et al.* 1974; Deslauriers and Everett 1977; Everett *et al.* 1978). Once the incentive is removed, bus travel usually drops to the baseline level or below. The provision of free-ride tokens also significantly affects the rate of bus travel, something which usefully induces trial of this service, but which is a long-term behaviour modification strategy.

The main difficulty with such programmes is their cost: paying riders two to three times their fare is obviously uneconomical, though rewarding only every third passenger can be just as effective as rewarding all. Bus riding is often punished by inconvenience and discomfort and the hedonic rewards of using one's car are considerable – comfort, speed, control, privacy, choice, etc. The fact that most of the induced passengers, 80 per cent, would otherwise have walked, bears this out. Another strategy is the encouragement of alternative car use. Studies have been conducted in which students were rewarded for reducing their daily car mileage; between $5 and $25 were given to those who reduced mileage by between 10 and 50 per cent of the baseline mean. Though the large experimental period effects were short-lived, the mileage levels during return-to-baseline were slightly lower than during the initial baseline period (Foxx and Hake 1977; Hake and Foxx 1978), an example of the over-justification effect mentioned in Chapter four. Simply providing feedback (informational reinforcement) is less effective: data on operating costs, depreciation, mileage travelled, social costs, singly and in combination, had no effect in terms of mileage reduction (Hayward and Everett 1976). Once again, hedonic reinforcement emerges as the most effective means of changing behaviour (Foxx and Schaeffer 1981).

Research conducted with commercial truck fleets indicates that hedonic reinforcement need not be financial, and that hedonic and informational reinforcements combined can be most effective. Drivers were provided with informational feedback on fuel consumption and mileage, and teams of drivers were entered in competitive prize draws for economy. Information on current performance was publicly posted where all drivers and teams could see it and supervisory staff also provided informal praise for successful performance. Small but commercially significant reductions in fuel use per mile driven resulted (Runnion *et al.* 1978).

Domestic energy conservation

Attempts to reduce the peak consumption of energy by households have involved the antecedent use of information, and consequential feedback and incentives, both separately and in combination. Information alone – for example, relating generally to such environmental effects of peak consumption of electricity as the building of unattractive and waste-producing power stations to cope with maximal demand – had no effect at all on peak energy usage. Feedback – specific information on current energy use gained through consumers' self-monitoring – was effective, however, reducing peaking by about 30 per cent of baseline mean. (Such feedback is not entirely informative: its signalling financial savings gives it a hedonic content, too.) Combined feedback and monetary incentives reduced peaking by about 65 per cent of baseline, another indication of the joint effectiveness of strong informational and hedonic reinforcers (Cone and Hayes 1984).

Experiments designed to effect reductions in overall energy consumption have produced a similar pattern of results. Information-based appeals appear to be ineffective even at times of steep energy price increases such as occurred in the mid-1970s (Heberlin 1975), though feedback can be effective in reducing consumption below baseline levels, especially when combined with prompts (Palmer *et al.* 1978). Daily feedback on usage, especially when combined with group feedback and mild social commendation also works; weekly or monthly feedback (the latter was particularly economical in coinciding with normal electricity billing), is especially effective (Cone and Hayes 1984; Hayes and Cone 1981).

Information and feedback coupled with incentives (such as payments of up to $5 per week for the reduction of gas/electricity consumption by 20 per cent or more of baseline mean) is more effective still (Kohlenberg *et al.* 1976). Separately, information, even if gained by close monitoring, impacts very weakly on consumption, and feedback is moderately effective, whilst incentives are very powerful indeed in modifying consumption (Hayes and Cone 1977). Direct experimental comparisons bear this out. In a study contrasting four conditions – information (e.g. the positive benefits of conservation) alone; information and feedback; information and feedback plus small incentives; and information and feedback plus large incentives (up to 240 per cent of energy bills) – only the last condition was effective in reducing consumption (Winett *et al.* 1977, 1979; Seaver and Patterson 1976; Hayes and Cone 1981). Other studies indicate that prompting may strengthen 'specific, low cost energy-conservation behaviours' like turning out lights in unoccupied rooms (Winett 1977); and that contests leading to cash prizes, and other competitions reduce energy consumption and can be more effective than straightforward feedback alone (Newsom and Makranczy 1978; McClelland and Cook 1977).

The delivery of aversive consequences for unnecessary use of energy may have a similar effect to payment for positive conservation responses, at least where an alternative to the punished behaviour is available. Van Hooten *et al.* (1981) report experiments which incorporated the punishment of energy use rather than payment for its reduction. Making an elevator in a university building less convenient by incorporating a 10, 21 or 36 second delay in the time required for the door to close led to a reduction in power consumption of one-third, and was far more effective than providing feedback on the amount of power consumed by the lift machinery. Posters which contained prompts were also ineffective. There have also been experiments employing the modelling techniques of social learning theory in order to discourage energy consumption. However, whilst vicarious reinforcement of home energy consumption, achieved through a specially-made cable TV programme, appears effective in quickly producing energy savings of up to 10 per cent, maintenance of such behaviour modification is yet to be demonstrated (Winett *et al.* 1982, 1985; cf. Ollendick *et al.* 1983.)

Evaluation

The settings in which attempts at environmental behaviour modification or social marketing usually take place are relatively open. In such contexts, depending upon one's preference for explanation, either the individual is said to have a 'free choice' or his or her behaviour is acknowledged to be difficult to predict simply from a knowledge of the topography of the physical and social context. The behaviours occur in complex circumstances and are of interest, therefore, given the chapter's earlier discussion of the types of influence on behaviour in open settings. On the basis of conclusions reached earlier, it is acknowledged that a full explanation of purchase and consumption in these settings may require the input of explanatory systems other than the EAB. The present discussion is confined to the capacity of the EAB to elucidate such behaviour and, on the whole, it is reasonable to expect the nature and relative availability and strength of reinforcement to influence considerably the pattern of emergent behaviour in these settings. The evidence from the environmental behaviour modification programmes reviewed above suggests not only that this expectation is justified but that, at least in the relatively complex situations reviewed, the environmental determinants of behaviour can be identified and their relative effects compared.

Prompt-based discriminative stimuli

It emerges clearly that prompts are of very limited effectiveness in the relatively open settings in question, especially when used alone. What influence they may exert is also temporally limited. This is not surprising on technical grounds alone, since it is obvious that, in the brief duration of the experiments described, the prompts would hardly have had an opportunity to assume the status of discriminative stimuli which control responses: until they have been paired repeatedly with positive reinforcers, they remain no more than neutral antecedent elements of the situation. In view of the theoretical discussion pursued in Chapter four, we would expect them to be most effective in open settings only after having been internalized by the individual, i.e. having become part of his or her private verbal repertoire.[3] Only then are they likely to act as within-the-skin discriminative stimuli, proximate causes of overt behaviour. Such internalization requires long-term, repeated pairing of antecedent and consequent stimuli, after which the locus of behavioural control might shift from the remote environmental contingencies to proximate, internalized verbal cues which echo and are initiated by the external prompts provided by the researcher or administrator. This interpretation (which will not appeal to unreconstructed behaviourists, but which is none the less consistent with the argument of the preceding chapter) is depicted in Figure 5.3.

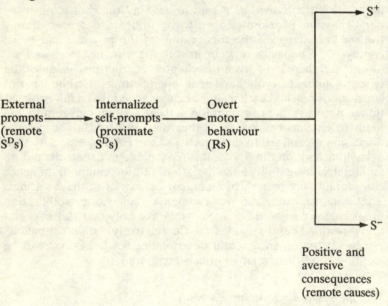

Figure 5.3 Hypothesized sequence of prompts, behaviour, and consequences

160

Other evidence confirms the inefficacy of antecedent stimuli to influence behaviour in the absence of the reinforcers that transform them into discriminative controlling stimuli. From several instances of attempted behaviour change, for example, towards 'healthy eating' or involving road safety, it has emerged that citizens are well aware of the deleterious consequences of, say, consuming excessive amounts of saturated fats, failing to use car seat belts, or driving while under the influence of alcohol. Research indicates further, however, that whilst respondents' verbal behaviour may change accordingly – interviewees provide the 'correct' answers to questions about the 'right' way to eat or drive – their eating and driving behaviours remain under the control of quite different contingencies. Hence food consumers who have recently acquired new beliefs (verbal repertoires) with respect to the content and importance of healthier eating patterns, often continue to cook, serve, and consume traditionally (Foxall and Haskins 1985); moreover, in the absence of changes in the law and close monitoring of seat belt use and alcohol-free driving (i.e. factors that restrict the situation), only the provision of hedonic reinforcers is likely to alter behaviour (Geller *et al*. 1982).

Consumers' beliefs about 'correct' patterns of eating and driving are, like the prompts employed in behaviour modification experiments, highly generalized statements about outcomes; they are only remotely relevant to those consumers' specific behaviours, which are controlled by far more immediate contingencies of reinforcement and discriminative stimuli, the significance of which is derived from long reinforcement histories. Such verbal events can influence the specific behaviours involved in selecting, buying, preparing, perhaps serving, and eating food, and in preparing to drive a car only if (i) they consist of particularized messages indicating that stated consequences will be contingent upon denoted behaviour, and are thus capable of becoming discriminative stimuli; (ii) relevant reinforcers, both positive and aversive, are actually made contingent upon performance/failure to perform the appropriate approach or avoidance behaviours, and follow those responses relatively quickly; and (iii) the antecedent and consequent stimuli are deliberately linked, in order that the proximate causes of behaviour can be established through direct experience of both antecedent events and remote contingencies.

Reinforcement and behavioural change

It also emerges from the studies reviewed that, in straight comparison, hedonic reinforcement is far more effective in changing behaviour than informational reinforcement. In a hierarchy of factors inducing behavioural change, hedonic reinforcement alone is more effective than informational reinforcement alone which is, in turn, more effective than prompting aimed at creating discriminative stimuli alone. Hedonic reinforcement is often prohibitively expensive, however, and if the altered behaviour is to be realistically and economically maintained, informational reinforcers and discriminative stimuli must assume control. Since a combination of the two, backed up by prompts capable of developing into genuine discriminative stimuli appears to be the most effective means of changing and maintaining behaviour, the necessary relationships and associations can be built from the beginning of a campaign.

Nevertheless, the studies reviewed make a vitally important theoretical point which confirms the explicatory relevance of the independent variables of the Behavioural Perspective Model. Although the hedonic reinforcers may be impracticable on a large scale, the results of the experiments identify dramatically the locus of important causes of behaviour: they are to be found ultimately in the environment rather than within the individual, though internal verbal events which, through pairing with the reinforcing consequences of behaviour, acquire the status of discriminative stimuli, may act as environmentally-conditioned proximate causes. To the extent, therefore, that social marketing campaigns are based on attempts to alter cognitive processes in the absence of contingent modification of the environment, they are unlikely to have the desired effect. Attempts to modify environment-impacting behaviour that rely on vague, prompting messages, dissociated from appropriate reinforcers, and poorly designed and delivered, are similarly unlikely to be effective unless reconceptualized and redesigned based on behaviour modification principles (Beales *et al.* 1981; Fox and Kotler 1983; Foxall 1984e; Mazis *et al.* 1981; Winett and Kagel 1984; Winett *et al.* 1982; Winkler and Winett 1982; Wright 1979).

The results and conclusions of the reviewed experiments confirm the usefulness of the Behavioural Perspective Model in another respect. They support the distinction between hedonic and informational reinforcement, indicating not only that these conceptual categories can be made operational, but that both types of reinforcement are required to account fully for complex consumer behaviour. Based on the reasoning developed in the earlier part of the chapter, behavioural change can be expected to be greatest when both hedonic and informational reinforcers are employed simultaneously (assuming, in line with the practical case in 'free market' economies, that closure of the relevant setting is not an option). In instances of behaviour modification where such dual reinforcement ('high hedonic, high informational') occurs, the rate of change of behaviour is indeed high. This effect is apparent from attempts to increase domestic energy conservation by providing almost immediate rewards as well as information relating to recent fuel conservation and the longer-term financial savings that would result. The most probable reinforcement schedules analogous to the rate of presentation of the reinforcers is VI, possibly VR, though the interval and/or number of responses required to effect reinforcement would probably be lower in these circumstances than for the consumption behaviours given as examples of Category 1 responses above. Considerable behavioural change would also be expected where hedonic reinforcement is emphasized and the rate or level of informational feedback is relatively low ('high hedonic, low informational'). Where this obtains – as in the examples provided for the promotion of transportation fuel economy and bus ridership – the effect on behaviour is strong while the reinforcer is present but weak during the return to baseline phase. Reinforcement is probably provided in ways analogous to the low VR/VI schedules suggested for Category 3.

Where informational reinforcement predominates, as in recycling and some domestic energy reduction programmes in which frequent feedback, provided by the investigator or through self-monitoring, is the norm ('high informational, low hedonic'), attempts to influence behaviour have been moderately effective. Reinforcement in such instances is provided (by analogy) on low VI/FI schedules, as for Category 5 behaviours. This is somewhat at variance with Wearden's expectation that informational reinforcement would predominate over hedonic in the analysis of human behaviour; the concept of informational reinforcement is, in some circumstances, an essential component of a behavioural explanation, but its effects are, in general, not as far-reaching as those of hedonic reinforcement. Finally, when neither type of reinforcer is emphasized and the target behaviours are sometimes overtly punished ('low hedonic, low informational'), as in the case of some anti-litter (bottle return) and recycling (bundling and sorting rubbish) programmes, behaviour change has usually been small. Reinforcement in these cases is typically FI or VI, as for Category 7 behaviours.[4]

Relevance to social marketing

Social demarketing campaigns often operate in contexts where strong hedonic reinforcement cannot be provided for the adoption of novel behaviours, and where informational feedback alone has a very limited effect on behaviour change. Anti-smoking campaigns and attempts to promote a low-fat diet, for instance, encounter this problem: the positive reinforcers contingent upon abstinence are usually available only in the remote future whilst consumption results in immediate gratification. The biggest rewards of not smoking or not overeating are in the long-term future and somewhat vague in that increased longevity cannot be incontestably demonstrated to result from avoidance, whereas the hedonically reinforcing consequences of inhaling and gorging are not only immediate but momentary. Their very nature tends to induce a schedule which ensures that the deleterious behaviours recur. In situations of this type, even vicarious reinforcement may be difficult to arrange, and the would-be behaviour modifier must depend upon prompts and informational feedback.

An obvious managerial strategy in those instances in which high hedonic reinforcement cannot be provided is the attempt to close the situation. In publicly supported social demarketing directed towards the reduction of environmentally harmful or wasteful consumption, it may be possible to effect situational closure through legal enforcement of prosocial actions. Campaigns could, accordingly, link prompting discriminative stimuli directly to the consequences of antisocial and prosocial actions. Whilst this can certainly be effective, as bottle laws and legislation enacted to encourage the wearing of seat belts in cars and to curb drink-driving attest, it is often not a practicable option for economic and political reasons, or because a high level of enforcement cannot be achieved. Furthermore, for actions not likely to result in death or injury, legislative intervention is often seen as an unjustifiable infringement of individual liberties. Again, however, the causal relationships suggested by the model are upheld and, in the absence of more socially acceptable means of curbing wasteful behaviour based on an alternative model of human nature, some of the problems to which social demarketing is addressed may remain unresolved.

Conclusion

The aim of this discussion has been to evaluate the relevance of the independent variables comprising the Behavioural Perspective

Model to the analysis of consumer behaviour, and to do so as far as possible on the basis of rigorously designed experimentation providing thoroughly-evaluated empirical evidence (the studies cited all appeared in refereed academic publications) rather than interpretation based on programmatic extrapolation. All-in-all, the review of behaviour modification programmes in social de-marketing contexts confirms the reasoning behind the model and gives confidence that further empirical testing may establish it as a useful means of comprehending consumer behaviour in general. The extent to which this can be achieved by empirical investigation as opposed to a programmatic account is itself an empirical question. However, the incorporation of informational as well as hedonic reinforcers, and open as well as closed settings, within an essentially operant framework implies significant theoretical deviations from Skinner's radical behaviourism. The move reflects paradigm erosion in order to ascertain the extent to which a modified operant model can account for the phenomena of consumer choice in ways neglected by the prevailing information processing perspectives, by relating it systematically to its environment. The analysis presented above indicates that distinct modes of consumer behaviour can be systematically related to the settings in which they occur and the reinforcers consequent upon their emission: each of the eight behaviour patterns depicted has a rate of recurrence which can be related to the relevant configuration of these independent variables.

But the model does not simply attempt a translation of familiar descriptions of consumer behaviour phenomena into the language of a behavioural analysis. Rather, it demonstrates the contribution of the modified EAB, for which the last chapter argued, to understanding and categorizing patterns of consumer choice that would be absent from or deemphasized by a cognitively-based account. This is not, of course, to preclude the future extension of cognitive consumer theory to embrace environmental influences more explicitly (Wessells 1982); nor does it diminish the value of social learning theory as a consumer research paradigm. It simply permits appraisal of the somewhat abstract analysis of the focal paradigm of this book undertaken in Chapter four in the context of the more concrete phenomena of consumer behaviour. Such appraisal, linked to a viable model of consumer behaviour, indicates the necessity of including in a behaviour-based account of consumer choice the very explanatory elements that emerge from a critique of the EAB – relative openness of situation, the dual functions of reinforcement, and the causal nature of internalized discriminative stimuli – and thereby supports

165

the configuration of independent variables incorporated in the Behavioural Perspective Model.

Yet this positive conclusion begs the question of the empirical scope of the model, especially in its application to consumer behaviour in general. It is evident, for instance, that the settings in which social marketing campaigns are conducted are not open to the extent of those encountered in the more familiar contexts of 'commercial' marketing. Within the latter, the structure of the physical, social, and economic setting and the augmented range of hedonic and informational reinforcers employed by competing marketers combine to create a far more complex situation than that which usually encompasses the promotion cf ecologically sound and healthy living. This complexity contains several components which are salient to the extension of the model to cover all consumer behaviour. For example, social marketing proceeds usually at the product or commodity level in that consumers face the blunt choice of altering their consumption habits in response to promises of closely specified contingent gains, or of continued adherence to the status quo, of which the immediate consequences are usually well known. Commercial marketing presents the consumer with a multiplicity of choices, albeit based on configurations of broadly similar reinforcers in the form of brands or stores that share near-identical physical and functional properties. The consumer of such items is faced with more extensive problem-solving, even if it is of a less engaging and more trivial kind, than the citizen who is the target of a social campaign. From one purchase occasion to the next, the brand or store level selections of the individual consumer in a commercial context do not, as a result, lend themselves to accurate prediction. Furthermore, the choices which were the subject of the demarketing studies reviewed above can be assumed to be considerably more involving than those typified by most brand and store selection. Again, the outcomes of social marketing are more precisely identifiable and measurable than those of purchase and consumption in general. On the whole, the campaigner's vision of prosocial behaviour provides the criterion of success and it is taken for granted that the adoption of the advocated conduct increases customer well-being and satisfaction. The benefits gained from individual brand and store choices are often far more ambiguous.

In view of these differences, it cannot be asserted that the appraisal of the Behavioural Perspective Model on the basis of studies of social marketing constitutes a comprehensive empirical evaluation of its relevance to consumer behaviour in general. Although, within its limitations, the appraisal undertaken supports the broad structure and contentions of the model, empirical testing at a more disaggregated level might seem to be a logical next step. Such work would eventually have to investigate brand and store choices in naturalistic, open (rather than laboratorial, closed) settings. Whilst this is unobjectionable in principle, however, it should be noted that the complex situations implied, which evoke low consumer involvement, are those least likely to yield results that demonstrate unequivocally that buyers discriminate behaviourally on the basis of clearly identifiable brand and store based reinforcers. The principal reinforcer associated with the multibrand, multi-store patterns of purchasing typical of buyers in steady-state markets for both consumer and industrial non-durables is apparently variety.

The possibility that empirical tests will demonstrate the differential capacity of brand and store features to reinforce relevant discriminated behaviour must not be pre-empted through speculation. In the cases of infrequently-purchased and innovate items, such responses may indeed occur. Nevertheless, the reasoning developed in Chapter four, on which the model is founded, suggests that the high relative openness of the settings, in which the bulk of purchasing and consumption takes place, may confine the behavioural explanation of consumer choice in typical marketing contexts to a programmatic account based on extrapolative interpretation. As a predictive and controlling device, the EAB apparently performs well in the moderately open settings in which social marketing occurs, but perhaps less so in commercial marketing contexts. (Even the field experiments conducted by Greene *et al.* (1984) and Greene and Neistat (1983) occurred in less open settings than does everyday consumer marketing practice.) It is a moot point whether it performs any worse in the latter situation than do the cognitive and other inner-state approaches. If that is all that can be said, the exercise has still been abundantly worthwhile, for it has doubtless revealed a fundamental characteristic of consumer choice itself. The existence of a behavioural perspective does not exclude others, any more than they preclude it. The marketing level of analysis may yet reveal the limits of the EAB contribution to consumer psychology. If so, it will also mark the bounds of inner-state theories and, perhaps, reveal the way for a viable, comprehensive synthesis.

Chapter six

Summing up

> [T]he received wisdom of today is that behaviorism has been refuted, its methods have failed, and it has little to offer modern psychology. Attacks against behaviorism have reached the frequency and vehemence that marked behaviorism's assaults against its own predecessors. Polemics, intemperate invective, *ad hominem* argument, and caricature pervade discussions of behaviorism by those who seek its demise. Such is the nature of Oedipal conflict. Factors other than effectiveness hold sway, and the search for truth is lost in the battles between movements. Clearly this is not useful to psychology, or to society. What is needed rather is an accurate portrait of behaviorism and an honest search for what is still valuable in it.
>
> (Zuriff 1985: 278)

This book has explored some implications for consumer research of a philosophy of psychology, radical behaviourism, which emphasizes objectivity and empiricalness. It makes no pretension of having contributed to the philosophy of science as a result, though its argument has been firmly grounded in the awareness that theoretical and metatheoretical considerations always accompany, indeed underlie and permeate, any attempt to create, develop or criticize knowledge. The need for such awareness is obvious enough to scholars in many other areas, but has been emphasized only comparatively recently in marketing and economic psychology.

The foregoing argument has supported the emergent relativistic perspective on consumer research, espousing an 'objective epistemic relativism' (Muncy and Fisk 1987) and thus recognizing above all that, whatever the nature of (social) reality may be, our conceptions of it are bound to be multiple and partial, and that the researcher's viewpoint and purposes determine his or her ontological and methodological outlook significantly, if not totally. It has also supported the consistent stance that, where theories are

168

concerned, the more the better – for the scientific community as a whole, if not necessarily for the cognitively constrained individual researcher – and that a decisive element in intellectual progress inheres in the mutual encounter of competing explanations and the outcomes of the 'active interplay' so aroused and stimulated.

Although this prospect recognizes that any intellectual field is likely to contain an influential normal science component as a consequence of the governing paradigm adopted by a substantial portion of its research community, it acknowledges, too, the abiding presence of alternative, potentially subversive paradigms, coexistent though not coeval with that which dominates theory and investigation. The absence of such competitors, or their failure to impinge markedly upon the orthodox wisdom, as well as upon one another, would suggest the stagnation of scientific and intellectual endeavour, the prevalence of dogma over free and vigorous enquiry.

The effects of the dominant position of cognitivism in the consumer research programmes of the last three decades or more must not be exaggerated or dramatized, but the expansion of the vitalizing intervention provided by an array of variously-grounded alternative explanations is, none the less, a current requirement. Fortunately, it is a need that is discerned by some consumer researchers, even if their somewhat selective attention largely confines their ensuing quest to 'post-positivistic' methodological realms. Whilst we might not welcome the demand to consider every myth and fairy tale enjoined upon us by Feyerabend, we should surely be concerned at the omission from our theoretical canon of any major, developed, and empirically-founded approach to the interpretation of behaviour. Indeed, the foregoing analysis has deliberately avoided the fairy-tale utopianism derived from the extension of operant principles to the design of cultures on the basis of 'behavioural technology' (Skinner 1948b, 1971, 1987). Still, our intellectual repertoire is seriously incomplete as a result of our overlooking, to say nothing of our deliberately ignoring, any sophisticated explicative system because it is unfashionable, or because its limitations are apparent, or because its unwarranted extrapolation has produced a social philosophy with which we are at odds.

A comprehensive plurality of paradigms is inescapable if authentic understanding of consumer behaviour is preferable to the doctrinaire parochialism that would follow the domination of consumer research by one ontology and associated methodology, or even by a few contenders for the normal science crown. No one model can capture human nature in its entirety; nor can a handful of theoretical perspectives embrace the scope of human inter-action. No one researcher can embrace all available viewpoints: but a community of researchers can embody many.

Enter the experimental analysis of behaviour. To advocate the EAB, even as no more than a means of establishing a critical standpoint, founded upon antithetical tenets of scientific method and a separate explanatory agenda, from which to overhaul the taken-for-granted assumptions of the prevailing orthodoxy would seem to be a logical enough outcome of these considerations. It would enable consumer researchers to push the idea that be-haviour is fully environmentally determined to its limits, to decide whether so extreme a paradigm provided adequate, feasible, or even usable explanations and, if not, at what point it was necessary to resort to alternative sources of theory. But to do so is to promote the unfashionable (readily mistaken for the outmoded): both the EAB and its proposed, severely limited, use in this sphere are easily misunderstood by inner-state theories and radical be-haviourists alike. To the former, it represents a retrogressive lapse into an antiquated and restrictive physicalism; to the latter, a betrayal of scientific principle, for, as anyone who accurately perceives the nature of the unreconstructed EAB would confirm, its disciples have no truck with beliefs in scientific relativism, or theory-ladenness, or the deductive logic of explanation that under-pins them. Adoption of the relativistic spirit entails tightrope walking, and the advocacy of deliberate paradigm erosion requires the abandonment of the safe ground.

The erosion of the paradigm resulting from the critical analysis conducted in Chapter four removes any claim it might have had to providing an exclusive metatheoretical framework for consumer research. But its philosophical basis, radical epiphenomenalism, is nevertheless an enduring foundation for the assessment of the conventional wisdom (as Chapter three indicates) within a relativistic consumer research. Above all, the 'honest search for what is still valuable' in Skinner's radical behaviourism reveals a central contribution of this philosophy in drawing attention to the un-critical employment of highly abstract unobservables in theory development. It does so not simply on the basis of a common-sense concern with the procedures of theory-building, but on that of a wealth of data derived from rigorous operant experimentation which is the foundation of an alternative and viable interpretation of behaviour in terms of its environmental rather than intra-personal determinants. It is impossible to survey the current state of explanation in consumer research without appreciating the need for a critique of this kind.

At the level of empirical investigation of consumer behaviour, the EAB offers valuable insight, but is ultimately circumscribed. It refers primarily to research in relatively closed situations, both experimental and real world. Animal experimentation itself is a possibility that most consumer researchers in the marketing context have not recognized. It facilitates a hypothetico-deductive approach to the resolution of theoretical issues at the commodity or product level of analysis. But it does not extend to the analysis of brand or store preference; nor can it address the non-price elements of the marketing mix. Nevertheless, operant psychology holds out to instore and other forms of real world experimentation of human market simulation not only an investigative technique, but also a theoretical guide to explanation.

The theoretical limits of the 'pure' radical behaviourism that stems directly from Skinner's insight and work are reached through consideration of the analysis of more complex instances of purchase and consumption. It is evident that the EAB is itself a theory-dependent device which is not (how could it be?) free of theoretical terms that relate to unobservables. In any case, such freedom, were it empirically available, would close off certain routes to the development of knowledge which depend upon speculative theoretical initiative. The necessary, if undervalued, emphasis of operant psychology on the role of the consequences of behaviour in the control of its rate of emission must be tempered by the recognition of the programmatic character of its explication of human choice and action in the complex circumstances of everyday life. In such situations, typified by purchase and consumption, constraints upon the isolation of the very variables by which the EAB account proceeds, that is, the contingencies of reinforcement, with the certainty axiomatic of a theoretical stance that rests four-square upon the criteria of objectiveness and empiricalness, make an eloquent case for the incorporation of complementary, if not supplementary, modes of explanation at this point. The contribution of the EAB to the understanding of human behaviour in complex social situations is ultimately hermeneutic; like other systems, some of which also purport to provide scientific analyses, it offers critical interpretation rather than predictive system.

But the identification of a paradigm's limited sphere of applicability is an essential component of a relativistic perspective which ought not to obscure its positive contribution, especially if, after some erosion of its tenets, the framework in question emerges as a more powerful explicator of observed behaviour. Indeed, the input of operant psychology to consumer research becomes apparent only after the theoretical adjustment of the EAB indicated by the critique conducted in Chapter four which recognized: first, the proximate causative influence of private verbal stimuli and their direct relationship to overt motor behaviour (which does not, of itself, infer a dualistic portrayal of private and public events as, respectively, mental and physical); second, the continuum of closed–open behavioural settings (highlighting the inadequacies of an objective–empirical framework as a means of self-consistent explanation of the latter, and the interpretive essence of the EAB's extrapolative account of complex behaviours); and, third, the dichotomy based on hedonic and informational reinforcement (either or both of which may be required in order to effect behavioural change, for the efficacy of behaviour modification programmes, and, most pertinently here, for the explanation of consumer behaviour).

These represent considerable theoretical deviations from the radical behaviourist orthodoxy. They are, moreover, consistent with explanations based on a synthesis of behavioural and inner-state conceptions (social behaviourism, for instance). But, as developed and applied in Chapters four and five, they retain much of the spirit of the EAB and their incorporation in the Behavioural Perspective Model makes available an operant taxonomy of the established patterns of purchase and consumption as well as their non-cognitive explanation.

The analysis and model which are the subject of Chapter five demonstrate that it is feasible to explain and interpret consumer behaviour in terms of a conceptual and analytical framework derived from, if not entirely faithful to, orthodox operant psychology, and thereby to clarify the nature and role of marketer behaviour, make appropriate policy recommendations, and evaluate policy interventions. Indeed, whilst the comprehensive models merely acknowledge the influence of marketing management upon consumer choice by representing its influence in terms of basic S–R links, the Behavioural Perspective Model explicitly links consumer and marketer aspects of marketing behaviour and provides an understanding of managerial marketing in similar terms to those in which its analysis of consumer behaviour proceeds.

The emergence of a unitary 'coherent theory of human behaviour' is improbable and, almost certainly, undesirable. The experimental analysis of behaviour is, in any event, not such a theory, though its achievement can extensively influence social science in general and consumer research in particular. Failure to incorporate the

EAB in a relativistic consumer research will undoubtedly impede progress in that subdiscipline as surely as would its exclusive and dogmatic adoption as an unchallenged professional paradigm. Nevertheless, those who are reluctant to lose the unique input of operant psychology to consumer research, but who see human beings as more than elements in its subject matter know that we can control our paradigms before they control us.

Appendix

Cognitive behaviour modification: paradigm erosion in practice

Contemporary psychotherapy provides an example of the process of paradigm erosion which is elaborated here because of its closeness to the potentially emergent position in consumer research. Behaviour therapy, which began during the 1950s to rival psychodynamic approaches, is strictly defined as a behaviour modification technology derived from research on classical and operant conditioning. Its practitioners describe their approach as one that concentrates directly upon the behaviour of their patients rather than upon factors such as speech, thought, and emotion that are conceptualized by cognitive and psychoanalytical therapists as causal processes that mediate behaviour (Eysenck 1952; Ledwidge 1978).

Behaviour therapies, on this view, are located at the opposite pole of the therapeutic continuum from the cognitive therapies which rely extensively upon the patient's internal representation of his or her situation (e.g. Beck *et al.* 1979; Ellis 1979). Over the years, however, some behaviour therapists have incorporated cognitions or self-statements into their perspective, sometimes referring to them as behaviours; the resulting 'cognitive behaviour modification' (CBM) therapy consists for these practitioners in changing patients' verbal behaviours in order to modify their maladaptive social behaviours. (This appendix does not attempt to provide a comprehensive description of recent developments in psychotherapy. An historical account of the development of CBM can be found in Dobson and Block 1988.)

Some behaviour therapists, maintaining the traditional definition of their field, have stressed the conceptual incompatibility of behaviour therapies, such as assertiveness training, desensitization, and aversive control procedures, with psychodynamic methods – Freudian, Jungian, Adlerian, etc. – and cognitive techniques, such as rational–emotive therapy, training in cognitive coping skills and self-instruction training (Ledwidge 1978). Franks (1984) claims in addition that the behavioural and psychodynamic approaches are clinically incompatible, so much so that 'Acceptance of the rights of psychoanalytical clinicians and thinkers to pursue and work within their own conceptual and clinical framework should not detract from the behaviour therapist's obligation to avoid condoning that which, in his or her view, is demonstrably not in the public interest' (p. 244). Ledwidge (1978) similarly argues that the distinctiveness of genuine behaviour therapy be maintained; CBM ought, accordingly, to be accurately labelled 'cognitive therapy' to indicate its separate approach, for the efficacy of which, he claims, there is no convincing evidence (cf. Mahoney 1974; Meichenbaum 1978).

Other psychologists, whilst remaining staunchly behaviourist in outlook, admit the therapeutic contribution of CBM. Thus, Lowe and Higson (1981) reaffirm the theoretical imperative that radical, as opposed to methodological behaviourism deals with private events and conclude from their review of the behaviour modification literature that internal self-instructions can, as cognitive therapists argue, control behaviour. However, they interpret private speech as a behaviour under contingency control which influences other behaviour; as long as 'cognition' means no more than such internal behaviour they do not see CBM as something in opposition to radical behaviourism, but if the term refers to some non-physical 'mindstuff' or a conceptual explicator, it must be excluded from a rigorous behavioural analysis.

Davey (1981c) emphasizes that for a therapy to be genuinely behaviouristic: (1) diagnosis must refer to observable behaviours: the therapist is not seeking to identify or treat internal processes such as anxiety unless these can be operationally defined; (2) the causes of behaviour must 'in the last analysis', be found in the environment rather than in mental or cognitive functioning; and (3) treatment manipulates the contingencies that relate behaviour to its antecedent or consequent stimuli on the basis of techniques derived from classical or operant conditioning. Many so-called behaviour therapies, he claims, are based on one of these principles but are not behaviouristic in a pure sense because they do not conform to all three.

Mahoney and Kazdin (1979), despite being behaviourally-oriented psychologists, refuse to accept the limitations of a perspective that is confined to traditionally-defined behaviour therapy. They respond to Ledwidge's attack on CBM by arguing that cognitivism does not imply mentalism: in spite of authors such as Skinner equating the two, most cognitively-orientated therapists do not, they say, believe in a non-physical mind any more than do behaviourists. Moreover, therapies cannot be strictly divided conceptually or practically into cognitive and behavioural: both types of therapy assume that patients think and all therapies are a mixture of cognitive and behavioural. In fact, the irony is that many practitioners of CBM believe that traditional behaviour modification is an essential activator of the cognitive changes required for the patient's readjustment, while behaviour therapists rely on verbal communication in the course of their clinical work. They add that empirical evidence shows that CBM techniques enhance treatment and that it is premature to claim that these methods are not effective when so little evaluative research has been carried out. (From a quantitative analysis of the research evidence available in 1983, Miller and Berman (1983) conclude that cognitive behaviour therapies are as effective as, though no more effective than, other forms of psychotherapy; moreover, those forms of CBM that emphasize behavioural techniques were found to be no more effective than therapies that were primarily cognitive; see also Dush *et al.* 1983.)

Like Mahoney and Kazdin, Locke (1979) argues that a 'pure' behaviour therapy does not exist: the methods employed by behaviour therapists are 'highly cognitive' in that they rely on speech and thought on the part of both therapist and patient as a necessary part of treatment. Further, studies show that cognitive therapy is as efficacious as behaviour therapy, though, because direct behaviour change is impossible and all therapies act on mediating events to alter explicit behaviours, the real distinction between different techniques lies in the degree to which they are cognitive rather than whether they are cognitive or non-cognitive. Clinical practice and observation also lead some behaviourists to accommodate the possibility of non-behaviourist explanations. Hence Rachman (1977) argues that conditioning theory is inadequate to account for the clinical data on agoraphobia which justify the exploration of psychodynamic explanations.

Finally, there are therapists who minimize the role of behaviour therapy as a curative agent in itself, but who, nevertheless, indicate its usefulness and its relationship to other approaches. Hence Seron (1985) argues that behaviour and cognitive therapies have distinct merits but confines the former methodologically as a means of establishing that treatment has produced change in the patient that cannot be attributed to non-therapeutic influences. Cognitive therapies, by contrast, 'seem better able to generate hypotheses about the nature of the neuropsychological disorders, to propose adequate remedial procedures, and to determine the general re-education strategy. In this respect, behaviour modification has lost a great deal of its influence as the ideas underlying the various therapies derive from cognitive neuropsychological investigations' (Seron 1985: 181).

In the midst of paradigm erosion, the extreme positions remain intact: those who claim to adhere to and use only unadulterated behaviour therapy are balanced by those who claim theoretical and clinical integrity with respect to cognitive therapy. In between are those who maintain pragmatically that integration and synthesis not only offer the most complete perspective but also provide the most effective methods of treating patients. Wilson (1982), in a theoretical overview of trends in psychotherapy, concludes that, in spite of the merits of conditioning theory, it is incomplete in so far as it avoids mediational factors, and that therapists and theorists should embrace a broad paradigm such as social learning theory which takes both environmental and personal factors into account.

Notes

Chapter one: The cognitive consumer – and beyond

1 'Inner state' explanation is not derived solely from that branch of cognitivism concerned with information processing. Other actual or conceptual inner events, states, and processes are also frequently adduced as causes of observed behaviour. In particular, personality traits and types fulfil this function. Recourse to personality variables is generally less common now than it was a decade or so ago, largely because of the poor empirical correspondence reported by dozens if not hundreds of investigators between measures of personality and observed consumer choice (Kassarjian 1971; Kassarjian and Sheffet 1981; cf. Foxall and Goldsmith 1988). But they assume on occasion great significance in theoretical accounts of certain aspects of consumer behaviour such as innovativeness (Foxall 1988a, 1989b). Whilst this book is concerned primarily with cognitive explanation, it refers on occasion to the related but independent personality theory, particularly in the light of the increasing association of the two approaches in cognitive personality theory (for example, Ajzen 1988; Cantor and Kihlstrom 1981; Kirton 1989; Loehlin 1968; Messick 1976; Mischel 1973, 1981; Pervin 1984).

2 Organizational buying behaviour has been described in terms of three purchase situations: the new task, the modified rebuy, and the straight rebuy (Robinson *et al*. 1967) which have much in common respectively with EPS, LPS, and RRB. *New task* buying occurs when the purchaser's uncertainty is greatest: because the problem in question has not previously arisen, the decision-maker must draw upon whatever general experience he has. But, because his specific experience is nil, he relies heavily upon information from marketer-dominated sources to compare and evaluate as many feasible solutions as possible. These situations do not occur often, the decision processes they involve are thorough and careful (since not only the firm but the buyer's career may be at risk) and, frequently, the decision outcome plays a decisive part in determining future choices of supplier and make. A typical new task situation would occur when a novel make of capital equipment is introduced into a new product-market at the beginning of the life cycle of an innovative technology; for example, the development of advanced manufacturing

techniques. In this situation, the buying decision requires a number of formal and informal stages (buyphases).

Straight rebuys are, by contrast, recurring purchases which can be dealt with by routine procedures. Previous suppliers are most likely to be considered at this stage and it is most probable that the present supplier will receive the new order. Most industrial/organizational buying decisions fall into this category; there is no need for the buying organization to go through all of the buyphases in order to reorder satisfactory products and the sequence of buyphases is thus severely telescoped. Any seller other than the current supplier is clearly at a disadvantage. His strategy is usually, therefore, to persuade the buyer that some element of the purchase situation has changed: he may offer a major price advantage, new technology, a more extensive system, or other inducement. Buyers faced with such new information normally attempt to obtain the benefits from their existing supplier before considering a switch. Nevertheless, some change has been introduced into their routine buying behaviour if even a modest modification has been made to their decision criteria. If the seller is successful in persuading the buyer that some major facets of his purchasing situation have altered, the task situation becomes a *modified rebuy*.

3 A similar concept to that of a paradigm is employed in an applied social research context by Thelen and Withal (1949: 159) who note that any researcher 'perceives and interprets events by means of a conceptual structure of generalizations or contexts, postulates about what is essential, assumptions about what is valuable, attitudes about what is possible, and ideas about what will work'. Such an ontological and methodological frame of reference, providing the metatheoretical context of research and explanation within a particular scientific community, is referred to in this book as a 'paradigm', though without acceptance of Kuhn's wider philosophy of the nature of scientific advance.

Chapter two: The experimental analysis of behaviour

1 Skinner has not necessarily been consistent, however, over the years in his presentation of radical behaviourism. This chapter attempts to provide a current view of the nature of this philosophy of psychology as presented by Skinner, but draws upon the interpretations of other psychologists and philosophers in order to clarify certain points. See, for instance, Catania and Harnad (1988); Modgil and Modgil (1987); Zuriff (1985). The account of the EAB provided is largely confined to research on operant performance in animals. The interpretations of human behaviour in operant terms are intended to link the formal analysis with the subject of consumer choice; they bear reconsideration in the light of the empirical evidence on human operant performance discussed in Chapter four.

2 An alternative theory of money, in which it is not considered to be a generalized secondary reinforcer, is presented by Lea *et al.* (1987, chapter 12).

3 In classical conditioning, through the pairing of two antecedent stimuli, each on its own comes to elicit a given response (or, more accurately, two responses that resemble each other), where only one had been capable of eliciting the response initially. Specifically, associative learning may be described as follows. A reflex relationship between an unconditional stimulus (UCS), say a piece of food placed in the mouth, and an unconditional response (UCR), salivation, in which the former elicits the latter, is unlearned. The repeated pairing of a neutral stimulus (one, such as the ringing of a bell, which does not initially elicit the UCR) with the presentation of the food, results in the capacity of that stimulus (now termed the condition stimulus, CS) to elicit a similar response (known as the conditioned response, CR) even in the absence of the UCS (i.e. the ringing of the bell elicits salivation though no food is presented).

Chapter three: Radical alternatives

1 Measures of purchase intentions for previously-bought, established brands are, however, often more accurately reflections of past purchasing and usage than of future brand selection on the next purchase occasion (Ehrenberg and Goodhardt 1989; Foxall 1983).
2 If reinforcement by food is available in the periods between experimental sessions, the pattern of responses on either FR or VI schedules is different from that found when extra-experimental availability of food is denied. Most experiments with animals involving food as a reinforcer have been conducted as open economies: in order to ensure a state of deprivation, the animal's body weight is maintained at 80 per cent of its normal body weight throughout the experimental period, a procedure which requires that food be available to the subject between experimental sessions. However, when feeding is made available only during the experimental sessions (i.e. there is a closed economy), quite different results are obtained. In open economy experiments, whether based on FR or VI schedules, there is an initial increase in rate of responding as the schedule parameter increases, but this is followed by a marked decline in response rate as the parameter continues to increase. Demand for food appears elastic. However, in closed economy experiments, the rate of responding goes on increasing as the schedule value increases (again whether it is FR or VI). The demand for food seems inelastic.
3 The buy–response curves shown in Figure 3.5(c) differ from economists' demand curves in that they indicate the proportion of consumers sampled who would be willing to purchase at all at a given price but give no indication of quantity demanded at each price.

Chapter four: Human operant behaviour

1 Another phenomenon, *over-justification*, consists in the tendency of human subjects in ABA-design experiments to emit responses

following the removal of the reinforcer at a rate lower than that established during the baseline period (Lepper and Greene 1978).

Over-justification implies that rewards may provide an incentive in the short term (as long as their presentation follows the performance of the target behaviour) but that their longer-term effect may be to inhibit that very behaviour: extrinsic rewards may actually reduce intrinsic motivation (Deci 1971; Lea *et al.* 1987). This effect is encountered in consumer behaviour when the demand for a promoted brand in an established market falls below the pre-promotional baseline once the deal is withdrawn. The effect is usually temporary, however, and may be due to an inventory effect inasmuch as regular brand users are likely to overstock during the promotion (Ehrenberg and Goodhardt 1989).

2 However, the contention that adult behaviour is essentially rule-governed must not be over-generalized to non-laboratory contexts. Attempts to change behaviour (e.g. with respect to consumption of high cholesterol foods and driving while under the influence of alcohol) often result in the internalization of rules but little or no modification of eating and drink-driving patterns unless the individual's direct exposure to the contingencies is also altered (Foxall and Haskins 1985; Sherman 1988).

3 Other critiques can be found, for instance, in Dilman (1988); Margolis (1984); Modgil and Modgil (1987); Malcolm (1977); Schellenberg (1978); Stevenson (1974) and Zuriff (1985). In addition, a recent issue of *Behavioural and Brain Sciences* (1984b) was devoted to the reprinting of Skinner's key works with critical commentaries by psychologists and responses by Skinner himself, and has been republished in book form (Catania and Harnad 1988).

Chapter five: Marketing in behavioural perspective

1 Theoretically, therefore, the designations 'relatively open setting' and 'relatively closed setting' reflect the character of the discriminative stimuli that indicate the determinants of response strength for approach and escape behaviours. In terms of Alhadeff's (1982) analysis: for approach behaviours, the appropriate discriminative stimuli foreshadow reinforcer effectiveness (reciprocally related to deprivation), response–reinforcer delay, reinforcer quantity and quality, and reinforcement schedule. In the case of escape behaviours, they foreshadow reinforcement effectiveness, response–reinforcer delay, and the quantity and quality (opportunity costs) of the reinforcer to be yielded in the event of an exchange. Thus the behaviours which fall into each of the Contingency Categories, defined in terms of setting-type and reinforcer-type, are the equilibrium outcomes of the probabilities of these two responses.

2 The meaning of 'molar' in this passage reflects an extension of its frequent use in operant psychology. It refers in the latter to a whole sequence of responses and reinforcers rather than to the separate kinds of event which make up the stream. Here and elsewhere in Chapter five, I have reasonably expanded the term, employing it to denote a

series of heterogeneous but related responses (prepurchase–purchase–consumption).

3 One possible means of discovering the rules formulated and followed by consumers is protocol analysis. For recent applications and discussion, see O'Shaughnessy (1987). The use of the technique in the analysis of low commitment consumer behaviour, in which verbalization concurrent with purchasing is usually thought to be minimal in the absence of the attempt to establish and record protocols, remains problematic.

4 Costs of responding must also be borne in mind in predicting rate of response. In spite of the availability of powerful hedonic and informational reinforcers in some cases, and the high variable schedules inferred, the number of responses between reinforcers may be small if (a) the response is punished, e.g. by the surrender of financial assets, or (b) reinforcement of purchase is delayed until consumption occurs. These behaviour patterns, once learned, may extinguish slowly. Where costs of responding are low, however, e.g. in brand selection, purchase and consumption may be fairly frequent, though maintained on FI schedules, and may extinguish more rapidly.

Bibliography

Addison, J. T., Burton, E. J., and Torrance, T. S. (1980) 'On the causation of inflation', *The Manchester School* 48: 140–56.

—— (1984) 'Causation, social science and Sir John Hicks', *Oxford Economic Papers*, 36: 1–12.

Ajzen, I. (1988) *Attitudes, Personality and Behavior*, Milton Keynes: Open University Press.

Ajzen, I. and Fishbein, M. (1980) *Understanding Attitudes and Predicting Social Behavior*, Englewood Cliffs, NJ: Prentice-Hall.

Alhadeff, D. A. (1982) *Microeconomics and Human Behavior: Toward a New Synthesis of Economics and Psychology*, Berkeley, CA: University of California Press.

—— (1986) 'Microeconomics and the experimental analysis of behavior', in A. J. MacFadyen and H. W. MacFadyen (eds) *Economic Psychology – Interactions in Theory and Application*, Amsterdam: North-Holland.

Allen, C. T. and Madden, T. J. (1985) 'A closer look at classical conditioning', *Journal of Consumer Research* 12: 301–15.

Allison, J. (1981) 'Economics and operant conditioning', in P. Harzem and M. D. Zeiler (eds) *Advances in Analysis of Behavior. Vol. 2: Predictability, Correlation and Contiguity*, Chichester: Wiley.

—— (1983) *Behavioral Economics*, New York: Praeger.

—— (1986) 'Economic interpretations of animal experiments', in A. J. MacFadyen and H. W. MacFadyen (eds) *Economic Psychology – Intersections of Theory and Application*, Amsterdam: North-Holland.

Anderson, P. F. (1983) 'Marketing, scientific progress, and scientific method', *Journal of Marketing* 47: 18–31.

—— (1986) 'On method in consumer research: a critical relativist perspective', *Journal of Consumer Research* 13: 155–73.

Antil, J. H. (1984) 'Conceptualization and operationalization of involvement', in T. C. Kinear (ed.) *Advances in Consumer Research* 11: 203–9.

Arndt, J. (1985) 'On making marketing science more scientific: role of orientations, paradigms, metaphors and puzzle solving', *Journal of Marketing* 49: 11–23.

Atkin, C. K. (1984) 'Consumer and social effects of advertising', in B. Dervin and M. J. Voigt (eds) *Progress in Communication Sciences*, Norwood, NJ: Ablex.

Atkinson, R. C. and Wickens, T. D. (1971) 'Human memory and the concept of reinforcement', in R. Glaser (ed.) *The Nature of Reinforcement*, New York: Academic Press.

Ayer, Sir Alfred J. (1946) *Language, Truth and Logic*, 2nd edn, London: Gollancz.

—— (1982) *Philosophy in the Twentieth Century*, London: Weidenfeld and Nicolson.

Ayllon, T. and Azrin, N. H. (1965) 'The measurement and reinforcement of behaviour of psychotics', *Journal of the Experimental Analysis of Behavior* 8: 357–83.

—— (1968a) *The Token Economy: A Motivational System for Theory and Rehabilitation*, New York: Appleton.

—— (1968b) 'Reinforcer sampling: a technique for increasing the behavior of mental patients', *Journal of Applied Behavior Analysis* 1.

Bagozzi, R. P. (1974) 'Marketing as an organized behavioral system of exchange', *Journal of Marketing* 38: 77–81.

—— (1975) 'Marketing as exchange', *Journal of Marketing* 39: 32–9.

—— (1984) 'A prospectus for theory construction in marketing', *Journal of Marketing* 48: 11–29.

Baker, J., Berry, L. L. and Parasuraman, A. (1988) 'The marketing impact of branch facility design', *Journal of Retail Banking* 10, 2: 33–42.

Bandura, A. A. (1971a) 'Vicarious and self-reinforcement processes', in R. Glaser (ed.) *The Nature of Reinforcement*, New York: Academic Press.

—— (1971b) *Psychological Modeling: Conflicting Theories*, Chicago: Aldine Atherton.

—— (1971c) *Social Learning Theory*, Morristown, NJ: General Learning Press.

—— (1977) *Social Learning Theory*, Englewood Cliffs, NJ: Prentice-Hall.

Bannister, D. (1968) 'The myth of physiological psychology', *Bulletin of the British Psychological Society* 21: 229–31.

Barker, R. G. (1968) *Ecological Psychology: Concepts and Methods for Studying the Environment of Human Behavior*, Stanford, CA: Stanford University Press.

Baron, A. and Perone, M. (1982) 'The place of the human subject in the operant laboratory', *The Behavior Analyst* 5: 143–58.

Battalio, R. C., Dwyer, G. P. and Kagel, J. H. (1987) 'Tests of competing theories of consumer choice and the representative consumer hypothesis', *Economic Journal* 97: 842–56.

Battalio, R. C., Kagel, J. H., Winkler, R. C., Fisher, E. B., Basmann, R. L., and Krasner, L. (1973a) 'An experimental investigation of consumer behavior in a controlled environment', *Journal of Consumer Research* 1: 52–60.

—— (1973b) 'A test of consumer demand theory using observations of individual consumer purchases', *Western Economic Journal* 9: 411–28.

Baum, W. M. (1973) 'The correlation-based law of effect', *Journal of the Experimental Analysis of Behavior* 20: 137–53.

—— (1974) 'On two types of deviation from the matching law: bias and undermatching', *Journal of the Experimental Analysis of Behavior* 22: 321–42.

Baum, W. M. and Rachlin, H. C. (1969) 'Choice as time allocation', *Journal of the Experimental Analysis of Behavior* 12: 861–74.

Baumol, W. J. (1959) *Business Behavior, Value and Growth*, New York: Macmillan.

Beales, H., Mazis, M. B., Salop, S. C. and Staelin, R. (1981) 'Consumer search and public policy', *Journal of Consumer Research* 8: 11–22.

Beck, A. T., Rush, A. J., Shaw, B. F., and Emery, G. (1979) *Cognitive Therapy of Depression*, New York: Guilford Press.

Becker, G. S. (1976) *The Economic Approach to Human Behavior*, Chicago: Chicago University Press.

Behavioral and Brain Sciences (1984) 'Canonical papers by B. F. Skinner', Special issue, 7: 473–701.

Belk, R. W. (1974) 'An exploratory assessment of situational effects in buyer behavior', *Journal of Marketing Research* 11: 156–63.

—— (1975) 'Situational variables and consumer behavior', *Journal of Consumer Research* 2: 157–67.

Bell, D. and Kristol, I. (eds) (1981) *The Crisis in Economic Theory*, New York: Basic Books.

Bem, D. J. (1968) 'Attitudes as self-descriptors: another look at the attitude-behavior link', in A. G. Greenwald, T. C. Brock, and T. M. Ostrom (eds), *Psychological Foundations of Attitudes*, New York: Academic Press.

—— (1972) 'Self-perception theory', in L. Berkowitz (ed.) *Advances in Experimental Social Psychology*, Hillsdale, IL: Erlbaum.

Bentall, R. P. and Lowe, C. F. (1987) 'The role of verbal behavior in human learning: III. Instructional effects in children', *Journal of the Experimental Analysis of Behavior* 47: 177–90.

Bentall, R. P., Lowe, C. F., and Beasty, A. (1985) 'The role of verbal behavior in human learning: II. Developmental differences', *Journal of the Experimental Analysis of Behavior* 43: 165–81.

Bentler, P. M. and Speckart, G. (1981) 'Attitudes "cause" behaviors: a structural equation analysis', *Journal of Personality and Social Psychology* 40: 226–38.

Berger, P. L. (1965) 'Toward a sociological understanding of psycho-analysis', *Social Research* 32: 26–41.

—— (1981) *Sociology Reinterpreted*, New York: Anchor/Doubleday.

Berry, L. L. (1969) 'The components of department store image: a theoretical and empirical analysis', *Journal of Retailing* 45: 3–20.

Berry, L. L. and Kunkel, J. H. (1970) 'In pursuit of consumer theory', *Decision Sciences* 1: 25–39.

Bettman, J. R. (1979) *An Information Processing Theory of Consumer Choice*, Reading, MA: Addison-Wesley.

Bierley, C., McSweeney, F. S., and Vannieuwkerk, R. (1985) 'Classical conditioning of preferences for stimuli', *Journal of Consumer Research* 12: 316–23.

Billen, A. (1988) 'End is in sight for the literary book', *The Times*, 15 June.

Blackman, D. E. (1974) *Operant Conditioning: An Experimental Analysis of Behaviour*, London: Methuen.

—— (1980) 'Images of man in contemporary behaviourism', in A. J. Chapman and D. M. Jones (eds) *Models of Man*, Leicester: British Psychological Society.

—— (1981) 'The experimental analysis of behaviour and its relevance to applied psychology', in G. C. L. Davey (ed.) *Applications of Conditioning Theory*, London and New York: Academic Press.

—— (1983a) 'On cognitive theories of animal learning: extrapolation from humans to animals?', in G. C. L. Davey (ed.) *Animal Models of Human Behaviour*, Chichester: Wiley.

—— (1983b) 'Operant conditioning', in J. Nicholson and B. Foss (eds) *Psychology Survey* 4, Leicester: British Psychological Society.

—— (1985) 'Contemporary behaviourism', in C. F. Lowe, M. Richelle, D. E. Blackman and C. M. Bradshaw (eds) *Behavioural Analysis and Contemporary Psychology*, London: Erlbaum.

Blau, P. M. (1964) *Exchange and Power in Social Life*, New York: Wiley.

—— (1970) 'Comment', in R. Borger and F. Cioffi (eds) *Exploration in the Behavioural Sciences, Confrontations*, Cambridge: Cambridge University Press.

Bloch, P. H. and Richins, M. L. (1983) 'A theoretical model for the study of product importance perceptions', *Journal of Marketing* 47: 69–81.

Boden, M. A. (1972) *Purposive Explanation in Psychology*, Cambridge, MA: Harvard University Press.

—— (1977) *Artificial Intelligence and Natural Man*, Brighton: Harvester Press.

Bohannan, P. and Dalton, G. (1962) (eds) *Markets in Africa*, Chicago: Northwestern University Press.

Borger, R. and Cioffi, F. (eds) (1970) *Exploration in the Behavioural Sciences, Confrontation*, Cambridge: Cambridge University Press.

Bowers, K. B. (1973) 'Situationism in psychology: an analysis and a critique', *Psychological Review* 80: 307–36.

Bradshaw, C. M. and Szabadi, E. (1988) 'Quantitative analysis of human operant behavior', in G. C. L. Davey and C. Cullen (eds) *Human Operant Conditioning and Behaviour Modification*, Chichester: Wiley.

Branch, M. and Malagodi, E. (1980) 'Where have all the behaviorists gone?', *The Behavior Analyst* 3: 31–8.

Branthwaite, A. (1984) 'Situations and social actions: applications for marketing of recent theories in social psychology', *Journal of the Market Research Society* 25: 19–38.

Brewer, W. F. (1974) 'There is no convincing evidence for operant or classical conditioning in humans', in W. B. Weimer and D. S. Palermo (eds) *Cognition and the Symbolic Processes*, Hillsdale, NJ: Erlbaum.

Brinberg, D. and Lutz, R. J. (eds) (1986) *Perspectives on Methodology in Consumer Research*, New York: Springer-Verlag.

Broadbent, D. E. (1961) *Behaviour*, London: Eyre and Spottiswood.

Brown, S. W. and Fisk, R. P. (eds) (1984) *Marketing Theory: Distinguished Contributions*, New York: Wiley.

Brownstein, A. J. and Shull, R. L. (1983) 'The analysis of complex cases: a review of Schwartz and Lacey's Behaviorism, Science and Human Nature', *The Behavior Analyst* 6: 77–91.

Bunge, M. (1967) *Scientific Research*, Vols. I and II, Berlin: Springer-Verlag.

Burgess, R. L., Clark, R. N., and Hendee, J. C. (1971) 'An experimental analysis of anti-litter procedures', *Journal of Applied Behavior Analysis* 4: 71–5.

Burns, T. and Stalker, R. M. (1961) *The Management of Innovation*, London: Tavistock.

Burton, R. G. (1984) 'B. F. Skinner's account of private events', *Journal of the Theory of Social Behaviour* 14: 125–40.

Buskist, W. F. and Miller, H. L. (1982) 'The analysis of human operant behavior: a brief census of the literature, 1958–81', *The Behavior Analyst* 5: 137–42.

Buskist, W. F., Bennett, R. H., and Miller, H. L. jnr. (1981) 'Effect of instructional constraints on human fixed-interval performance', *Journal of the Experimental Analysis of Behavior* 35: 217–25.

Buskist, W. F., Morgan, D., and Barry, A. (1983) 'Interspecies generality and human behavior: an addendum to Baron and Perone', *The Behavior Analyst* 6: 107–8.

Buttle, F. (1984) 'Merchandising', *European Journal of Marketing* 18: 4–25.

Calder, B. J. and Tybout, A. M. (1987) 'What consumer research is . . .', *Journal of Consumer Research* 14: 136–40.

Cantor, N. and Kihlstrom, J. F. (1981) *Personality, Cognition and Social Interaction*, Hillsdale, NJ: Erlbaum.

Carrol, J. B. (1971) 'Reinforcement: is it a basic principle, and will it serve in the analysis of verbal behavior?', in R. Glaser (ed.) *The Nature of Reinforcement*, New York: Academic Press.

Castaneda, C. (1972) *A Separate Reality: Further Conversations with Don Juan*, New York: Pocket Books.

Castro, B. and Weingarten, K. (1970) 'Toward experimental economics', *Journal of Political Economy* 78: 598–607.

Catania, A. C. (1971) 'Elicitation, reinforcement, and stimulus control', in R. Glaser (ed.) *The Nature of Reinforcement*, New York: Academic Press.

—— (1984a) *Learning*, 2nd edn, Englewood Cliffs, NJ: Prentice-Hall.

—— (1984b) 'The operant behaviourism of B. F. Skinner', *Behavioural and Brain Sciences* 7: 473–92.

—— (1985) 'Rule-governed behaviour and the origins of language', in C. F. Lowe, M. Richelle, D. E. Blackman, and C. M. Bradshaw (eds) *Behaviour Analysis and Contemporary Psychology*, London: Erlbaum.

Catania, A. C. and Harnad, S. (1988) (eds) *The Selection of Behavior. The Operant Behaviorism of B. F. Skinner: Comments and Consequences*, Cambridge: Cambridge University Press.

Catania, A. C., Matthews, B. A., and Shimoff, E. (1982) 'Instructed versus shaped human verbal behavior: interactions with nonverbal responding', *Journal of the Experimental Analysis of Behavior* 38: 233–48.

Chadwick-Jones, J. K. (1976) *Social Exchange Theory: Its Structure and Influence in Social Psychology*, New York: Academic Press.

—— (1986) 'Social exchange, social psychology and economics', in A. J. MacFadyen and R. W. MacFadyen (eds) *Economic Psychology: Intersections of Theory and Application*, Amsterdam: North-Holland.

Chamberlin, E. (1933) *The Theory of Monopolistic Competition*, Cambridge, MA: Harvard University Press.

Chapman, A. J. and Jones, D. M. (eds) (1980) *Models of Man*, Leicester: British Psychological Society.

Chapman, C. and Risley, T. R. (1974) 'Anti-litter procedures in an urban high-density area', *Journal of Applied Behavior Analysis* 7: 377–84.

Chase, P. N. (1986) 'Three perspectives on verbal learning: associative, cognitive and operant', in P. N. Chase and L. J. Parrott (eds) *Psychological Aspects of Language: The West Virginia Lectures*, Springfield, IL: Charles C. Thomas.

Chomsky, N. (1959) 'Review of B. F. Skinner's *Verbal Behavior*', *Language* 35: 26–58.

Christopher, M. G. (1985) 'The strategy of customer service', in G. R. Foxall (ed.) *Marketing in the Service Industries*, London: Cass.

Colley, R. H. (1961) *Defining Advertising Goals for Measured Advertising Results*, NY: Association of National Advertisers.

Collier, G. H. (1982) 'Determinants of choice', *Nebraska Symposium on Motivation 1981*, Lincoln and London: University of Nebraska Press.

Cone, J. D. and Hayes, S. C. (1984) *Environmental Problems/Behavioral Solutions*, Cambridge: Cambridge University Press.

Cooper, L. G. (1987) 'Do we need critical relativism? Comments on "On method in consumer research"', *Journal of Consumer Research* 14: 126–7.

Costley, C. L. (1988) 'Meta analysis of involvement research', in M. J. Houston (ed.) *Advances in Consumer Research* 15: 554–62.

Couch, J. V., Garber, T., and Karpus, L. (1978) 'Response maintenance and paper recycling', *Journal of Environmental Systems* 8: 127–37.

Creel, R. E. (1974) 'Skinner's Copernican revolution', *Journal of the Theory of Social Behaviour* 4: 131–45.

—— (1980) 'Radical epiphenomenalism: B. F. Skinner's account of private events', *Behaviorism* 8: 31–53.

Dalton, G. (1967) (ed.) *Tribal and Peasant Economies: Readings in Economic Anthropology*, New York: Natural History Press.

—— (1971) *Economic Anthropology and Development: Essays on Tribal and Peasant Economies*, London and New York: Basic Books.

Davey, G. C. L. (1981a) 'Behaviour modification in organizations', in G. C. L. Davey (ed.) *Applications of Conditioning Theory*, London and New York: Methuen.

—— (1981b) 'How Skinner's theories work: behaviour analysis and environmental problems', *Bulletin of the British Psychological Society* 34: 57–60.

—— (1981c) 'Conditioning principles, behaviourism and behaviour therapy', in G. C. L. Davey (ed.) *Applications of Conditioning Theory*, London and New York: Methuen.

—— (1988) 'Trends in human operant theory', in G. C. L. Davey and C. Cullen (eds) *Human Operant Conditioning and Behaviour Modification*, Chichester: Wiley.

Davey, G. C. L. and Cullen, Christopher (eds) (1988) *Human Operant Conditioning and Behaviour Modification*, Chichester: Wiley.

Day, W. F. (1970) 'On certain similarities between the *Philosophical Investigations* of Ludwig Wittgenstein and the operationism of B. F. Skinner', *Journal of the Experimental Analysis of Behavior* 12: 65–131.

—— (1976) 'Contemporary behaviorism and the concept of intention', *Nebraska Symposium on Motivation 1975*, Lincoln and London: University of Nebraska Press.

Deci, E. L. (1971) 'Effects of externally mediated rewards on intrinsic motivation', *Journal of Personality and Social Psychology* 18: 105–15.

DeFleur, M. L. and Westie, F. R. (1963) 'Attitude as a scientific concept', *Social Forces* 15: 17–31.

Dennett, D. C. (1988) *The Intentional Stance*, Cambridge, MA: MIT Press.

Deshpande, R. (1983) '"Paradigms lost": on theory and method in research in marketing', *Journal of Marketing* 47: 101–10.

Deslauriers, B. C. and Everett, P. B. (1977) 'Effects of intermittent and continuous token reinforcement on bus ridership', *Journal of Applied Psychology* 62: 369–75.

Dilman, I. (1988) *Mind, Brain and Behaviour: Discussions of B. F. Skinner and J. R. Searle*, London and New York: Routledge.

Dobson, K. S. and Block, L. (1988) 'The historical and philosophical basis of the cognitive-behavioural therapies', in K. S. Dobson (ed.) *Handbook of Cognitive-Behavioural Therapies*, London: Hutchinson.

Donahoe, J. W. (1971) 'Some observations on descriptive analysis', in R. Glaser (ed.) *The Nature of Reinforcement*, New York: Academic Press.

Doyle, P. and Gidengil, B. Z. (1977) 'A review of in-store experiments', *Journal of Retailing* 53: 47–62.

Driver, J. C. and Foxall, G. R. (1984) *Advertising Policy and Practice*, London: Holt, Rinehart and Winston; New York: St Martin's Press.

—— (1986) 'How scientific is advertising research?' *International Journal of Advertising* 5: 147–60.

Dulaney, D. E. (1974) 'On the support of cognitive theory in opposition to behavior theory: a methodological problem', in W. B. Weimer and D. S. Palermo (eds) *Cognition and the Symbolic Processes*, Hillsdale NJ: Erlbaum.

Dush, D. M., Hirt, M. L. and Schroeder, H. (1983) 'Self-statement modification with adults: a meta-analysis', *Psychological Bulletin* 94: 408–22.

Earl, P. E. (1983) *The Economic Imagination: Toward a Behavioural Analysis of Choice*, Brighton: Wheatsheaf.

Easton, D. (1972) 'Some limits of exchange theory in politics', *Sociological Inquiry* 42: 129–48.

Eelen, P. (1982) 'Conditioning and attribution', in J. Boulougouris (ed.) *Learning Theory Approaches to Psychiatry*, Chichester: Wiley.

Ehrenberg, A. S. C. (1966) 'Laws in marketing: a tail piece', *Applied Statistics* 15: 257–67.

—— (1972) *Repeat Buying: Theory and Applications*, Amsterdam and New York: North Holland. Reprinted 1987, Edinburgh: Griffin.

—— (1974) 'Repetitive advertising and the consumer', *Journal of Advertising Research* 14: 25–34.

Ehrenberg, A. S. C. and Goodhardt, G. J. (with G. R. Foxall) (1989) *Understanding Buyer Behaviour*, in press.

Eiser, J. R. (1981) *Attitudes in Psychology*, Exeter: Exeter University Press.

Ekelund, R. B., Furubotn, E. G., and Gramm, W. P. (1972) *The Evolution of Modern Demand Theory*, Lexington, MA: D. C. Heath and Co.

Ellis, A. (1979) 'The theory of rational–emotive therapy', in A. Ellis and J. M. Whiteley (eds) *Theoretical and Empirical Foundations of Rational–Emotive Therapy*, Monterey, CA: Brooks/Cole.

Elsmore, T. (1979) 'Evaluating the strength of heroin maintained behavior', paper presented at the annual meeting of the Association for Behavior Analysis.

Engel, J. F. and Blackwell, R. D. (1982) *Consumer Behavior*, 4th edn, Hindsdale, IL: Dryden.

Engel, J. F., Blackwell, R. D., and Kollat, D. T. (1978) *Consumer Behavior*, 3rd edn (2nd edn, 1973), Hindsdale, IL: Dryden.

Engel, J. F., Blackwell, R. D., and Miniard, P. W. (1986) *Consumer Behavior*, 5th edn, Hindsdale, IL: Dryden.

Engel, J. F., Kollat, D. T., and Blackwell, R. D. (1968) *Consumer Behavior*, New York: Holt, Rinehart and Winston.

Epling, W. F. and Pierce, W. D. (1983) 'Applied behavior analysis: new directions from the laboratory', *The Behavior Analyst* 6: 27–37.

Ericsson, K. A. and Simon, H. A. (1980) 'Verbal reports as data', *Psychological Review* 87: 215–51.

—— (1984) *Protocol Analysis: Verbal Reports as Data*, Cambridge, MA: MIT Press.

Estes, W. K. (1971) 'Rewards in human learning: theoretical issues and strategic choice points', in R. Glaser (ed.) *The Nature of Reinforcement*, New York: Academic Press.

Everett, P. B. (1973) 'Use of the reinforcement procedure to increase bus ridership', paper presented at the meeting of the American Psychological Association, Montreal, August.

Everett, P. B., Deslauriers, B. C., Newsom, T., and Anderson, V. B. (1978) 'The differential effect of two free ride dissemination procedures on bus ridership', *Transportation Research* 12: 1–6.

Everett, P. B., Hayward, S. C., and Meyers, A. W. (1974) 'The effect of a token reinforcement on bus ridership', *Journal of Applied Behavior Analysis* 7: 1–9.

Eysenck, H. J. (1952) 'The effects of psychotherapy: an evaluation', *Journal of Consulting Psychology* 16: 319–24.

—— (1972) 'Don't shoot the behaviourist; he is doing his best', in *Psychology is About People*, London: Allen Lane.

—— (1978) 'Expectations as control elements in behavioural change', *Advances in Behavior Research and Therapy* 1: 171–5.

—— (1985) *Decline and Fall of the Freudian Empire*, New York: Viking.

Farley, J. U., Howard, J. A., and Ring, L. W. (eds) (1974) *Consumer Behavior: Theory and Applications*, Boston, MA: Allyn and Bacon.

Fennell, G. (1987) 'Is selling marketing? The academic–practitioner gap revisited', in R. W. Belk and G. Zaltman (eds) *Proceedings of the 1987 AMA Winter Educators' Conference*, Chicago: American Marketing Association.

Ferster, C. and Skinner, B. F. (1957) *Schedules of Reinforcement*, New York: Appleton-Century.

Feyerabend, P. (1970) 'Consolations for the specialist', in I. Lakatos and A. Musgrave (eds) *Criticism and the Growth of Knowledge*, Cambridge: Cambridge University Press.

—— (1975) *Against Method*, London: NLB.

—— (1987) *Farewell to Reason*, London: Verso.

Finnie, W. C. (1973) 'Field experiments in litter control', *Environment and Behavior* 5: 123–44.

Fishbein, M. and Ajzen, I. (1975) *Belief, Attitude, Intention and Behavior: An Introduction to Theory and Research*, Reading, MA: Addison-Wesley.

Fodor, Jerry A. (1988) *Psychosemantics: The Problem of Meaning in the Philosophy of Mind*, Cambridge, MA: MIT Press.

Fonagy, P. and Higget, A. (1984) *Personality Theory and Clinical Practice*, London: Methuen.

Fox, K. A. and Kotler, P. (1983) 'The marketing of social causes: the first 10 years', *Journal of Marketing* 44: 24–33.

Foxall, G. R. (1979a) 'On the management of "commons"', *Journal of Agricultural Economics* 30: 55–8.

—— (1979b) 'Agricultural improvement of common land: the relevance of co-operative management', *Journal of Environmental Management* 8: 151–61.

—— (1980a) 'Academic consumer research: problems and prospects', *European Research* 8: 20–3.

—— (1980b) 'Marketing models of buyer behaviour: a critical review', *European Research* 8: 195–206.

—— (1980c) *Consumer Behaviour: A Practical Guide*, London: Routledge; New York: Wiley.

—— (1981a) 'The Treatment of "Attitude" in Consumer Research', Discussion Paper B77, University of Birmingham: Faculty of Commerce and Social Science.

—— (1981b) 'Developments in attitude–behaviour research', in *Marketing Behaviour: Issues in Managerial and Buyer Decision-Making*, Aldershot: Gower.

—— (1981c) *Strategic Marketing Management*, London: Routledge; New York: Wiley.

—— (1983) *Consumer Choice*, London: The Macmillan Press; New York: St Martin's Press.

—— (1984a) 'Evidence for attitudinal–behavioural consistency: implications for consumer research paradigms', *Journal of Economic Psychology* 5: 71–92.

—— (1984b) 'Consumers' intentions and behaviour', *Journal of the Market Research Society* 26: 231–41.

—— (1984c) *Corporate Innovation: Marketing and Strategy*, London: Routledge; New York: St Martin's Press.

—— (1984d) 'Predicting consumer choice in new product development: attitudes, intentions and behaviour revisited', *Marketing Intelligence and Planning* 2, 1: 37–52.

—— (1984e) 'Marketing's domain', *European Journal of Marketing* 18: 25–40. Reprinted 1988 in G. E. Greenley and D. Shipley (eds) *Readings in Marketing Management*, London and New York: McGraw-Hill.

—— (1985) 'Consumer spending on designer jeans: an operant conditioning interpretation', *Journal of Consumer Studies and Home Economics* 9: 147–50.

—— (1986a) 'Consumer theory', *Management Bibliographies and Reviews* 12, 2: 25–52.

—— (1986b) 'Theoretical progress in consumer psychology: the contribution of a behavioral analysis of choice', *Journal of Economic Psychology* 7: 293–314.

—— (1986c) 'The role of radical behaviorism in the explanation of consumer choice', *Advances in Consumer Research* 13: 187–91.

—— (1986d) 'Consumer choice in behavioural perspective', *European Journal of Marketing* 20(3/4): 7–18.

—— (1987a) 'Radical behaviorism and consumer research: theoretical promise and empirical progress', *International Journal of Research in Marketing* 4: 111–29.

—— (1987b) 'Consumer behaviour', in M. J. Baker (ed.) *The Marketing Book*, London: Heinemann.

—— (1988a) 'Consumer innovativeness: novelty-seeking, creativity, and cognitive style', in E. C. Hirschman and J. N. Sheth (eds) *Research in Consumer Behavior* 3: 79–113, Greenwich, CT: JAI Press.

—— (1988b) 'Marketing new technology: markets, hierarchies and user-initiated innovation', *Managerial and Decision Economics* 9: 237–50.

—— (1988c) 'The industrial user as product innovator', *Advances in Consumer Research* 15: 286–91.

—— (1989a) 'Understanding customer behaviour', in M. J. Thomas (ed.) *Marketing Handbook*, Aldershot: Gower, pp. 265–89.

—— (1989b) 'Adaptive and innovative cognitive styles of market initiators', in M. J. Kirton (ed.) *Adaptors and Innovators: Styles of Creativity and Problem-Solving*, London: Routledge.

Foxall, G. R. and Goldsmith, R. E. (1988) 'Personality and consumer research: another look', *Journal of the Market Research Society* 30: 111–25.

Foxall, G. R. and Haskins, C. G. (1985) ' "Naughty but nice": meanings of meat in the 1980s', *Food Marketing* 1, 3: 56–70.

Foxx, R. M. and Hake, D. F. (1977) 'Gasoline conservation: a procedure for measuring and reducing the driving of college students', *Journal of Applied Behaviour Analysis* 10: 61–74.

Foxx, R.M. and Schaeffer, M. H. (1981) 'A company-based lottery to reduce the personal driving of employees', *Journal of Applied Behaviour Analysis* 14: 273–85.

Franks, C. M. (1984) 'On conceptual and technical integrity in psycho-analysis and behavior therapy: two fundamentally incompatible systems', in H. Arkowitz and S. B. Messer (eds) *Psychoanalytic Therapy and Behavior Therapy*, New York: Plenum.

Fredericks, A. J. and Dosset, D. L. (1983) 'Attitude–behavior relations: a comparison of the Fishbein–Ajzen and the Bentler–Speckart models', *Journal of Personality and Social Psychology* 45: 501–12.

Friedman, M. (1953) *Essays in Positive Economics*, Chicago: University of Chicago Press.

Furnham, A. and Lewis, A. (1986) *The Economic Mind*, Brighton: Wheatsheaf.

Gabor, A. (1988) *Pricing: Concepts and Methods for Effective Marketing*, 2nd edn, Aldershot: Gower.

Gabor, A. and Granger, C. W. J. (1966) 'Price as an indicator of quality', *Economica* 33: 43–70.

Gardner, H. (1985) *The Mind's New Science: A History of the Cognitive Revolution*, New York: Harper and Row.

Geller, E.S., Chaffee, J. L., and Ingram, R. E. (1975) 'Prompting paper recycling on a university campus', *Journal of Environmental Systems* 5: 39–57.

Geller, E. S., Farris, J. C., and Post, D. S. (1973) 'Promoting a consumer behavior for pollution control', *Journal of Applied Behavior Analysis* 6: 367–76.

Geller, E. S., Winett, R. A., and Everett, P. B. (1982) *Preserving the Environment: New Strategies for Behavior Change*, Elmsford, New York: Pergamon.

Geller, E. S., Witmer, J. F., and Tuso, M. A. (1977) 'Environmental interventions for litter control', *Journal of Applied Psychology* 63: 344–51.

Geller, E. S., Wylie, R. G., and Farris, J. C. (1971) 'An attempt at applying prompting and reinforcement toward pollution control', *Proceedings of the 79th Annual Convention of the American Psychological Association* 6: 701–2.

Gellner, E. (1985) *The Psychoanalytical Movement*, London: Paladin.

Gergen, K. L., Greenberg, M. S., and Willis, R. H. (1980) *Social Exchange: Advances in Theory and Research*, New York and London: Plenum.

Goodhardt, G. J., Ehrenberg, A. S. C., and Collins, M. (1987) *The Television Audience: Patterns of Viewing*, 2nd edn, Aldershot: Gower.

Goodson, F. E. and Morgan, G. A. (1976) 'Evaluation of theories', in M.

H. Marx and F. E. Hillix (eds) *Theories in Contemporary Psychology*, New York: Macmillan.

Gorn, G. J. (1982) 'The effects of music in advertising on choice behavior: a classical conditioning approach', *Journal of Marketing* 46: 94–101.

Goudge, P. and Green, F. (1985) 'Child's play – developing a savings account for kids', *Marketing Intelligence and Planning* 3, 2: 13–24.

Grafton-Small, R. and Linstead, S. A. (1989) 'Artifact as theory', in P. Gagliardi (ed.) *The Symbolism of Corporate Artifacts*, Berlin and New York: Walter De Gruyter.

Greene, A. K. (1977). 'Bring 'em back, repack, and save', *Proceedings, 1975 Conference on Waste Reduction*, Washington, DC: US Environmental Pollution Agency.

Greene, B. F. and Neistat, M. D. (1983) 'Behavior analysis in consumer affairs: encouraging dental professionals to provide consumers with shielding from unnecessary X-ray exposure', *Journal of Applied Behavior Analysis* 16: 13–27.

Greene, B. F., Rouse, M., Green, R. B. and Clay, C. (1984) 'Behavior analysis in consumer affairs: retail and consumer response to publicizing food price information', *Journal of Applied Behavior Analysis* 17: 3–21.

Guerts, M. D. (1986) 'The "bottle bill" effects on grocery stores' costs', *International Journal of Retailing* 1, 2: 12–17.

Guthrie, E. R. (1935) *The Psychology of Learning*, New York: Harper and Row.

Hakansson, H. (ed.) (1982) *International Marketing and Purchasing of Industrial Goods: An Interaction Approach*, Chichester: Wiley.

Hake, D. F. and Foxx, R. M. (1978) 'Prompting gasoline conservation: the effects of reinforcement schedules, a leader and self-reinforcing', *Behavior Modification* 2: 339–69.

Hall, G. (1987) 'The implications of radical behaviourism: a critique of Skinner's science of behavior and its application', in S. Modgil and C. Modgil (eds) *B. F. Skinner: Consensus and Controversy*, London: Falmer Press.

Hamblin, R. L. and Kunkel, J. H. (eds) (1977) *Behavioral Theory in Sociology: Essays in Honour of George C. Homans*, New Brunswick, NJ: Transaction Books.

Hansen, F. (1976) 'Psychological theories of consumer choice', *Journal of Consumer Research* 3: 117–42.

Hardin, G. (1968) 'The tragedy of the commons', *Science* 162: 1243–8.

Hardin, G. and Baden, J. (eds) (1977) *Managing the Commons*, San Francisco, CA: W. H. Freeman.

Harlow, H. F. (1962) 'The development of learning in the Rhesus monkey', in W. R. Brode (ed.) *Science in Progress*, New Haven, Connecticut: New York University Press, N.Y.

Harlow, H. F. and Zimmerman, R. R. (1959) 'Affectional responses in the infant monkey', *Science*, 30, August 21: 421–32.

Harrell, G. D. and Bennett, P. D. (1974) 'An evaluation of the expectancy value model of attitude measurement for physician prescribing behavior', *Journal of Marketing Research* 11: 269–78.

Harvey, L. (1982) 'The use and abuse of Kuhnian paradigms in the sociology of knowledge', *Sociology* 16: 85–101.

Harzem, P., Lowe, C. F., and Bagshaw, M. (1978) 'Verbal control in human operant behavior', *The Psychological Record* 28: 405–24.

Hayes, S. C. (1986) 'The case of the silent dog: verbal reports and the analysis of rules: a review of Ericsson and Simon's *Protocol Analysis: Verbal Reports as Data*', *Journal of the Experimental Analysis of Behavior* 45: 351–63.

Hayes, S. C. and Cone, J. D. (1977) 'Reducing residential electrical energy use: payments, information, and feedback', *Journal of Applied Behavior Analysis* 10: 425–35.

—— (1981) 'Reduction of residential consumption of electricity through simple monthly feedback', *Journal of Applied Behavior Analysis* 14: 81–97.

Hayward, S. C. and Everett, P. B. (1976) 'A failure of response cost feedback to modify car driving behavior', paper presented at the meeting of the Midwestern Association of Behavior Analysis, Chicago, May.

Heath, A. (1976) *Rational Choice and Social Exchange: A Critique of Exchange Theory*, Cambridge: Cambridge University Press.

Heberlin, T. A. (1975) 'Conservation information: the energy crisis and electricity consumption in an apartment complex', *Energy Systems and Policy* 1: 105–17.

Herrnstein, R. J. (1961) 'Relative and absolute strength of response as a function of frequency of reinforcement', *Journal of the Experimental Analysis of Behavior* 4: 267–72.

—— (1970) 'On the law of effect', *Journal of the Experimental Analysis of Behavior* 13: 243–66.

Herrnstein, R. J. and Vaughan, W. (1981) 'Melioration and behavioral allocation', in J. E. R. Staddon (ed.) *Limits to Action: The Allocation of Individual Behavior*, New York: Academic Press, pp. 143–76.

Hillner, K. P. (1984) *History and Systems of Modern Psychology: A Conceptual Approach*, New York: Gardner Press.

Hinson, J. (1987) 'Skinner and the unit of behaviour', in S. Modgil and C. Modgil (eds) *B. F. Skinner: Consensus and Controversy*, Lewes, Sussex and Philadelphia, PA: Falmer Press.

Hirschman, E. C. (1980) 'Innovativeness, novelty-seeking and consumer creativity', *Journal of Consumer Research* 7: 283–95.

—— (1985a) 'Scientific style and the conduct of consumer research', *Journal of Consumer Research* 12: 225–39.

—— (1985b) 'Cognitive processes in experiential consumer behavior', in J. N. Sheth (ed.) *Research in Consumer Behavior* 1: 67–102, Greenwich, CT: JAI Press.

Hirschman, E. C. and Holbrook, M. B. (1982) 'Hedonic consumption: emerging concepts, methods and propositions', *Journal of Marketing* 46: 92–101.

—— (1986) 'Expanding the ontology and methodology of research on the consumption experience', in D. Brinberg and R. J. Lutz (eds) *Perspectives on Methodology in Consumer Research*, New York: Springer-Verlag.

Holbrook, M. B. (1974) 'A synthesis of the empirical studies', in J. U. Farley, J. A. Howard, and L. W. Ring (eds) *Consumer Behavior: Theory and Applications*, Boston, MA: Allyn and Bacon.

—— (1987) 'What is consumer research?' *Journal of Consumer Research* 14: 128–32.

Holbrook, M. B. and Hirschman, E. C. (1982) 'The experiential aspects of consumption: consumer feelings, fantasies and fun', *Journal of Consumer Research* 9: 132–40.

Holbrook, M. B. and O'Shaughnessy, J. (1984) 'The role of emotion in advertising', *Psychology and Marketing* 1: 45–64.

Homans, G. C. (1958) 'Social behavior as exchange', *American Journal of Sociology* 63: 597–606.

—— (1961/1974) *Social Behavior: Its Elementary Forms*, 1st and 2nd edns, New York: Harcourt Brace Janovich.

Honig, W. K. (ed.) (1966) *Operant Behavior: Areas of Research and Application*, New York: Appleton-Century-Crofts.

Howard, J. A. (1977) *Consumer Behavior: Application of Theory*, New York: McGraw-Hill.

—— (1983) 'Marketing theory of the firm', *Journal of Marketing* 47: 90–100.

Howard, J. A. and Sheth, J. N. (1969) *The Theory of Buyer Behavior*, New York: Wiley.

Hull, C. L. (1951) *Essentials of Behavior*, New Haven, CT: Yale University Press.

—— (1952) *A Behavior System*, New Haven, CT: Yale University Press.

Hulse, S. H., Fowler, H., and Honig, W. K. (1978) *Cognitive Processes in Animal Behavior*, Hillsdale, NJ: Erlbaum.

Hunt, S. D. (1983) 'General theories and the fundamental explananda of marketing', *Journal of Marketing* 47: 9–17.

—— (1984) 'Should marketing adopt relativism?' in P. F. Anderson and M. J. Ryan (eds) *Scientific Method in Marketing*, Chicago: American Marketing Association.

Hursh, S. R. (1980) 'Economic concepts for the analysis of behavior', *Journal of the Experimental Analysis of Behavior* 34: 219–38.

—— (1984) 'Behavioral economics', *Journal of the Experimental Analysis of Behavior* 42: 435–52.

Hursh, S. R. and Natelson, B. H. (1981) 'Electrical brain stimulation and food reinforcement dissociated by demand elasticity', *Physiology and Behavior* 26: 509–15.

Hursh, S. R., Raslear, T. G., Bauman, R., and Black, H. (1987) 'The quantitative analysis of economic behavior with laboratory animals', in *Understanding Economic Behavior*, proceedings of the 12th Annual Colloquium of the International Association for Research in Economic Psychology, Ebeltoft, Denmark: IAREP.

Ingene, C. A. and Hughes, M. A. (1985) 'Risk management by consumers', in J. N. Sheth (ed.) *Research in Consumer Behavior*, 1: 103–58, Greenwich, CT: JAI Press.

Ingram, R. E. and Geller, E. S. (1975) 'A community-integrated, behavior modification approach to facilitating paper recycling', *JAS Catalog of Selected Documents in Psychology* 5, MS no. 1097.

Jacobs, H. E., Bailey, J. S., and Crews, J. I. (1984) 'Development and analysis of a community-based resource recovery program', *Journal of Applied Behavior Analysis* 17: 127–45.

Jacobs, H. E., Fairbanks, D., Poche, C. E., and Bailey, J. S. (1982) 'Multiple incentives in encouraging car pool formation on a university campus', *Journal of Applied Behavior Analysis* 15: 141–9.

Jacoby, J. (1978) 'Consumer research: a state of the art review', *Journal of Marketing* 42: 87–96.

—— (1983) 'Consumer and industrial psychology: prospects for theory corroboration and mutual contribution', in M. D. Dunnette (ed.) *Handbook of Industrial and Organizational Psychology*, New York: Wiley.

Jacoby, J., Chestnut, R. W., and Silberman, W. (1977) 'Consumer use and comprehension of nutrition information', *Journal of Consumer Research*, 4: 119–28.

Jacoby, J., Speller, D. E., and Kohn, C. A. (1974) 'Brand choice as a function of information load', *Journal of Marketing Research* 11: 63–9.

Jary, D. (1988) 'Review of P. Feyerabend', *Farewell to Reason*, Sociology 22: 312–14.

Julia, P. (1988) 'Contingencies, rules and the "problem" of novel behavior', in A. C. Catania and S. Harnad (eds) *The Selection of Behavior. The Operant Behaviorism of B. F. Skinner: Comments and Consequences*, Cambridge: Cambridge University Press.

Kagel, J. H. (1972) 'Token economies and experimental economics', *Journal of Political Economy* 80: 779–85.

—— (1987) 'Economics according to the rats (and pigeons too). What have we learned and what can we hope to learn?' in A. E. Roth (ed.) *Laboratory Experimentation in Economics: Six Points of View*, Cambridge: Cambridge University Press.

Kagel, J. H., Battalio, R. C., Rachlin, H., Basmann, Robert L., Green, L., and Klemm, W. R. (1975) 'Experimental studies of consumer demand behavior using laboratory animals', *Economic Inquiry* 13: 22–38.

Kakkar, P. and Lutz, R. J. (1981) 'Situational influence on consumer behavior: a review', in H. H. Kassarjian and T. S. Robertson (eds) *Perspectives in Consumer Behavior*, Glenview, IL: Scott Foresman.

Kanfer, F. H. (1973) 'Behavior modification: an overview', in C. E. Thoresen (ed.) *Behavior Modification in Education*, Chicago: Chicago University Press.

Kassarjian, H. H. (1971) 'Personality and consumer behavior – a review', *Journal of Marketing Research* 4: 409–18.

—— (1978) 'Anthropomorphism and parsimony, presidential address 1977', *Advances in Consumer Research* 5: xiii–xiv.

—— (1982) 'Consumer psychology', *Annual Review of Psychology* 33: 619–49.

—— (1986) 'Consumer research: some recollections and a commentary', R. J. Lutz (ed.) *Advances in Consumer Research*, 13: 6–8.

Kassarjian, H. H. and Sheffet, M. J. (1981) 'Personality and consumer research: an update', in H. H. Kassarjian and T. S. Robertson (eds) *Perspectives in Consumer Behavior*, Hindsdale, IL: Scott Foresman.

Katona, G. (1975) *Psychological Economics*, New York: Elsevier.

Kazdin, A. E. (1977) *The Token Economy: A Review and Evaluation*, New York: Plenum.

—— (1980) *Behavior Modification in Applied Settings*, Homewood, IL: Dorsey.

—— (1981) 'The token economy', in G. C. L. Davey (ed.) *Applications of Conditioning Theory*, London: Methuen.

—— (1983) 'The token economy: a decade later', *Journal of Applied Behavior Analysis* 15: 431–45.

Keehn, J. D. (1969) 'Consciousness, discrimination and the stimulus control of behaviour', in R. M. Gilbert and N. S. Sutherland (eds) *Animal Discrimination Learning*, London: Academic Press.

Keng, K. A. and Ehrenberg, A. S. C. (1984) 'Patterns of store choice', *Journal of Marketing Research* 21: 399–409.

Kernan, J. B. (1987) 'Chasing the holy grail: reflections on "What is consumer research?"' *Journal of Consumer Research* 14: 133–5.

Kirton, M. J. (ed.) (1989) *Adaptors and Innovators: Styles of Creativity and Problem Solving*, London: Routledge.

Knapp, C. W. (1982) 'The acquisition and maintenance of behavioral skills: a response to Michael', *The Behavior Analyst* 5: 77–93.

Kohlenberg, R. and Phillips, T. (1973) 'Reinforcement and rate of litter depositing', *Journal of Applied Behavior Analysis* 6: 391–6.

Kohlenberg, R., Phillips, T., and Proctor, W. (1976) 'A behavioral analysis of peaking in residential electrical–energy consumers', *Journal of Applied Behavior Analysis* 9: 13–18.

Kohn, C. A. and Jacoby, J. (1973) 'Operationally defining the consumer innovator', *Proceedings*, American Psychological Association, Washington, DC: APA.

Kotler, P. (1972) 'A generic concept of marketing', *Journal of Marketing* 36: 46–54.

Kotler, P. and Zaltman, G. (1972) 'Social marketing', *Journal of Marketing* 35: 3–12.

Krasner, L. and Krasner, M. (1973) 'Token economies and other planned environments', in C. E. Thoresen (ed.) *Behavior Modification in Education*, Chicago: Chicago University Press.

Krugman, H. E. (1965) 'The impact of television advertising: learning without involvement', *Public Opinion Quarterly* 29: 349–56.

—— (1967) 'The measurement of advertising involvement', *Public Opinion Quarterly* 30: 583–96.

Kuhn, T. S. (1963) 'The function of dogma in scientific research', in A. C. Crombie (ed.) *Scientific Change*, London: Heinemann.

—— (1970a) 'Reflections on my critics', in I. Lakatos and A. Musgrave (eds) *Criticism and the Growth of Knowledge*, Cambridge: Cambridge University Press.

—— (1970b) *The Structure of Scientific Revolutions*, Chicago: Chicago University Press.

Kunkel, J. H. (1977) 'The behavioral perspective of social dynamics', in R. L. Hamblin and J. H. Kunkel (eds) *Behavior Theory in Sociology: Essays in Honor of George C. Homans*, New Brunswick, NJ: Transaction Books.

Kunkel, J. H. and Berry, L. L. (1968) 'A behavioral conception of retail image', *Journal of Marketing* 32: 21–7.

Lacey, H. M. (1974) 'The scientific study of linguistic behaviour: a perspective on the Skinner–Chomsky controversy', *Journal of the Theory of Social Behaviour* 4: 17–51.

—— (1979) 'Skinner on the prediction and control of behavior', *Theory and Decision* 10: 353–85.

—— (1980) 'Psychological conflict and human nature: the case of behaviorism and cognition', *Journal of the Theory of Social Behavior* 10: 131–55.

Lacey, H. M. and Schwartz, B. (1987) 'The explanatory power of radical behaviourism', in S. Modgil and C. Modgil (eds) *B. F. Skinner: Consensus and Controversy*, London: Falmer Press.

Lakatos, I. (1970) 'Falsification and the methodology of scientific research programmes', in I. Lakatos and A. Musgrave (eds) *Criticism and the Growth of Knowledge*, Cambridge: Cambridge University Press.

Lakatos, I. and Musgrave A. (eds) (1970) *Criticism and the Growth of Knowledge*, Cambridge: Cambridge University Press.

Lamont, S. (1986) *Religion Inc.*, London: Harrap.

Lastovicka, J. L. and Bonfield, E. H. (1982) 'Do consumers have brand attitudes?' *Journal of Economic Psychology* 2: 57–76.

Lavidge, R. J. and Steiner, G. A. (1961) 'A model for predictive measurements of advertising effectiveness', *Journal of Marketing* 25: 59–62.

Lea, S. E. G. (1978) 'The psychology and economics of demand', *Psychological Bulletin* 85: 441–66.

—— (1981) 'Animal experiments in economic psychology', *Journal of Economic Psychology* 1: 245–71.

Lea, S. E. G., Tarpy, R. M., and Webley, P. (1987) *The Individual in the Economy: A Survey of Economic Psychology*, Cambridge: Cambridge University Press.

Leahey, T. H. (1987) *A History of Psychology: Main Currents in Psychological Thought*, Englewood Cliffs, NJ: Prentice-Hall.

Ledwidge, B. (1978) 'Cognitive behavior modification: a step in the wrong direction?', *Psychological Bulletin* 85: 353–75.

Leigh, J. H. and Martin, C. R. (1981) 'A review of situational influence paradigms and research', in B. E. Enis and K. J. Roering (eds) *Review of Marketing 1981*, Chicago: American Marketing Association.

Le Ny, J.-F. (1985) 'European roots of behaviourism and recent developments', in C. F. Lowe, M. Richelle, D. E. Blackman, and C. M. Bradshaw (eds) *Behaviour Analysis and Contemporary Psychology*, London: Erlbaum.

Leong, S. M. (1985) 'Metatheory and metamethodology in marketing: a Lakatosian reconstruction', *Journal of Marketing* 49: 23–40.

Leontieff, W. (1971) 'Theoretical assumptions and nonobserved facts', *American Economic Review*, 61.

Lepper, M. R. and Greene, D. (1978) *The Hidden Costs of Reward*, Hillsdale, NJ: Erlbaum.

Levy, S. J. (1978) 'Marcology 101 or the domain of marketing', in S. H. Britt and H. W. Boyd (eds) *Marketing Management and Administrative Action*, New York: McGraw-Hill.

Lindblom, C. E. (1959) 'The science of "muddling through"', *Public Administration Review*, 19.

Linstead, S. A. and Grafton-Small, R. (1989) 'Theory as artifact', in P. Gagliardi (ed.) *Symbolism of Corporate Artifacts*, Berlin and New York: Walter De Gruyter.

Locke, E. A. (1979) 'Behavior modification is not cognitive – and other myths: a reply to Ledwidge', *Cognitive Therapy and Research* 3: 119–25.

Loehlin, J. C. (1968) *Computer Models of Personality*, New York: Random House.

Loudon, P. L. and Della Bitta, A. J. (1983) *Consumer Behavior: Concepts and Applications*, New York: McGraw-Hill.

Lowe, C. F. (1979) 'Determinants of human operant behaviour', *Advances in Analysis of Behavior* 1: 159–92.

—— (1983) 'Radical behaviourism and human choice', in G. C. L. Davey (ed.) *Animal Models of Human Behaviour*, Chichester: Wiley.

—— (1988) 'The flight from human behavior', in A. C. Catania and S. Harnad (eds) *The Selection of Behavior. The Operant Behaviorism of B. F. Skinner: Comments and Consequences*, Cambridge: Cambridge University Press.

Lowe, C. F. and Higson, P. J. (1981) 'Self-instructional training and cognitive behaviour modification: a behavioural analysis', in G. C. L. Davey (ed.) *Applications of Conditioning Theory*, London: Methuen.

Lowe, C. F. and Horne, P. J. (1985) 'On the generality of behavioural principles: human choice and the matching law', in C. F. Lowe, M. Richelle, D. E. Blackman and C. M. Bradshaw (eds) *Behaviour Analysis and Contemporary Psychology*, London: Erlbaum.

Lowe, C. F., Beasty, A., and Bentall, R. P. (1983) 'The role of verbal behavior in human learning: infant performance on fixed-interval schedules', *Journal of the Experimental Analysis of Behavior* 39: 157–64.

Lowe, C. F., Harzem, P., and Hughes, S. (1978) 'Determinants of operant behavior in humans: some differences from animals', *Quarterly Journal of Experimental Psychology* 30: 373–86.

Lowe, C. F., Horne, P. J., and Higson, P. J. (1987) 'Operant conditioning: the hiatus between theory and practice in clinical psychology', in *Theoretical Foundations of Behaviour Therapy*, London: Plenum.

Lowe, C. F., Richelle, M., Blackman, D. E., and Bradshaw, C. M. (eds) (1985) *Behaviour Analysis and Contemporary Psychology*, London: Erlbaum.

McClelland, L. and Cook, S. W. (1977) 'Encouraging energy conservation as a social psychological problem', paper presented at the meeting of the American Psychological Association, San Francisco, September.

MacCorquodale, K. (1970) 'B. F. Skinner's *Verbal Behavior*: a retrospective appreciation', *Journal of the Experimental Analysis of Behavior* 12.

MacCorquodale, K. and Meehl, P. E. (1948) 'On a distinction between hypothetical constructs and intervening variables', *Psychological Review* 55: 95–107.

MacFadyen, A. J. and MacFadyen, H. (eds) (1986) *Economic Psychology: Intersections in Theory and Application*, Amsterdam: North-Holland.

McGinn, C. (1983) *The Character of Mind*, New York: Oxford University Press.

McGuire, W. J. (1976a) 'Some internal psychological factors influencing consumer choice', *Journal of Consumer Research* 2: 302–19.

— (1976b) 'An information processing model of advertising effectiveness', in H. L. Davis and A. J. Silk (eds) *Behavioral and Management Sciences in Marketing*, New York: Ronald Press.

Mackenzie, B. D. (1977) *Behaviourism and the Limits of Scientific Method*, London: Routledge and Kegan Paul.

Mackintosh, N. J. (1974) *The Psychology of Animal Learning*, London: Academic Press.

McQuarrie, E. F. (1988) 'An alternative to purchase intentions: the role of prior behaviour in consumer expenditure on computers', *Journal of the Market Research Society* 30: 407–37.

McSweeney, F. K. and Bierley, C. (1984) 'Recent developments in classical conditioning', *Journal of Consumer Research* 11: 619–31.

Mahoney, M. J. (1974) *Cognition and Behavior Modification*, Cambridge, MA: Ballinger.

— (1979) 'Cognitive and noncognitive views in behavior modification', in P. O. Sjoden, S. Bates, and W. S. Dockens (eds) *Trends in Behavior Therapy*, New York: Academic Press.

Mahoney, M. J. and Kazdin, A. E. (1979) 'Cognitive behavior modification: misconceptions and premature evacuation', *Psychological Bulletin* 86: 1044–9.

Maital, S. (1982) *Minds, Markets and Money: Psychological Foundations of Economic Behavior*, New York: Basic Books.

Malcolm, N. (1977) 'Behaviorism as a philosophy of psychology', in *Thought and Knowledge*, Ithaca and London: Cornell University Press. (First published 1964 in T. W. Wann (ed.) *Behaviorism and Phenomenology*, Chicago and London: University of Chicago Press.)

Maltzman, I. (1960) 'On the training of originality', *Psychological Review* 67: 229–42.

Mandler, G. (1985) *Cognitive Psychology: An Essay in Cognitive Science*, Hillsdale, NJ: Erlbaum.

March, J. G. (1978) 'Bounded rationality, ambiguity, and the engineering of choice', *The Bell Journal of Economics* 9: 587–608.

Margolis, J. (1984) *Philosophy of Psychology*, Engelwood Cliffs, NJ: Prentice-Hall.

Marris, R. (1964) *The Economic Theory of 'Managerial' Capitalism*, London: Macmillan.

Marx, M. H. and Hillix, W. A. (1979) *Systems and Theories in Psychology*, 3rd edn, New York: McGraw-Hill.

Mason, R. S. (1981) *Conspicuous Consumption*, Aldershot: Gower Publishing.

Masterman, M. (1970) 'The nature of a paradigm', in I. Lakatos and A. Musgrave (eds) *Criticism and the Growth of Knowledge*, Cambridge: Cambridge University Press.

Matthews, B. A., Catania, A. C., and Shimoff, E. (1985) 'Effects of uninstructed verbal behavior on nonverbal responding: contingency descriptions versus performance descriptions', *Journal of the Experimental Analysis of Behavior* 43: 155–64.

Mattsson, L.-G. (1986) 'An application of a network approach to marketing: defending and changing market positions', in N. Dholakia and J. Arndt (eds) *Changing the Course of Marketing: Alternative Paradigms for Widening Marketing Theory*, Greenwich, CT: JAI Press.

Mazis, M. B., Staelin, R., Beales, H., and Salop, S. C. (1981) 'A framework for evaluating consumer information regulation', *Journal of Marketing* 45: 11–21.

Meehl, P. E. (1950) 'On the circularity of the law of effect', *Psychological Bulletin* 47: 52–75.

Meichenbaum, D. (1978) *Cognitive Behavior Modification: An Integrative Approach*, New York: Plenum.

Messick, S. (1976) *Individuality and Learning*, San Francisco: Jossey-Bass.

Meyer, W. (1982) 'The research program of economics and the relevance of psychology', *British Journal of Social Psychology* 21: 81–91.

Michael, J. (1980) 'Flight from behavior analysis', *The Behavior Analyst* 3: 1–21.

Midgley, D. F. (1977) *Innovation and New Product Marketing*, London: Croom Helm.

— (1984) 'Parsimony or explanation: on the estimation of systems defined by nonlinear differential equations', *Journal of Consumer Research* 10: 445–7.

Midgley, D. F. and Dowling, G. R. (1978) 'Innovativeness: the concept and its measurement', *Journal of Consumer Research* 4: 229–42.

Miller, G. A. (1962) *Psychology: The Science of Mental Life*, London: Penguin Books.

Miller, R. C. and Berman, J. S. (1983) 'The efficacy of cognitive behavior therapies: a quantitative review of the research evidence', *Psychological Bulletin* 94: 39–53.

Milliman, R. E. (1982) 'Using background music to affect the behavior of supermarket shoppers', *Journal of Marketing* 46: 86–91.

Mills, J. A. (1988) 'An assessment of Skinner's theory of animal behaviour', *Journal of the Theory of Social Behaviour*, 18, 197–218.

Mintzberg, H. (1975) 'The manager's job: folklore and fact', *Harvard Business Review* 53, 4.

Mischel, T. (1976) 'Psychological explanations and their vicissitudes', *Nebraska Symposium on Motivation 1975*, Lincoln and London: University of Nebraska Press.

Mischel, W. (1968) *Personality and Assessment*, New York: Wiley.

— (1973) 'Toward a cognitive social learning reconceptualization of personality', *Psychological Review* 80: 252–83.

— (1981) 'A cognitive-social learning approach to assessment', in T. V. Merluzzi, C. R. Glass, and M. Genest (eds) *Cognitive Assessment*, New York: The Guilford Press.

— (1986) *Introduction to Personality: A New Look*, 4th edn, New York: CBS.

Modgil, S. and Modgil, C. (eds) (1987) *B. F. Skinner: Consensus and Controversy*, London: Falmer Press.

Montgomery, D. B. and Ryans, A. B. (1973) 'Stochastic models of consumer choice behavior', in S. Ward and T. S. Robertson (eds) *Consumer Behavior: Theoretical Sources*, Englewood Cliffs, NJ: Prentice-Hall.

Moore, J. (1981) 'On mentalism, methodological behaviorism and radical behaviorism', *Behaviorism* 9: 60–9.

Morris, E. K., Higgins, S. T., and Bickel, W. K. (1982) 'Comments on cognitive science in the experimental analysis of behavior', *The Behavior Analyst* 5: 109–25.

Morse, W. H. (1966) 'Intermittent reinforcement', in *Operant Behaviour: Areas of Research and Application*, New York: Appleton-Century-Crofts.

Muncy, J. A. and Fisk, R. P. (1987) 'Cognitive relativism and the practice of marketing science', *Journal of Marketing* 51: 20–33.

Naylor, T. H. (1972) 'Experimental economics revisited', *Journal of Political Economy* 80: 347–52.

Neisser, U. (1967) *Cognitive Psychology*, New York: Appleton-Century-Crofts.

Newell, A. and Simon, H. A. (1972) *Human Problem Solving*, Englewood Cliffs, NJ: Prentice-Hall.

Newell, A., Shaw, J. C., and Simon, Herbert A. (1958) 'Elements of a theory of human problem solving', *Psychological Review*, 65.

Newsom, T. J. and Makranczy, V. J. (1978) 'Reducing electricity consumption of residents living in mass-metred dormitory complexes', *Journal of Environmental Systems* 1: 215–36.

Nicosia, F. M. (1966) *Consumer Decision Processes*, Englewood-Cliffs, NJ: Prentice-Hall.

Nisbett, R. F. and Wilson, T. D. (1977) 'Telling more than we know: verbal reports and mental processes', *Psychological Review* 84: 231–59.

Nord, W. R. (1969) 'Beyond the teaching machine: the neglected area of operant conditioning in the theory and practice of management', *Organizational Behavior and Human Performance* 4: 375–401.

Nord, W. R. and J. P. Peter (1980) 'A behavior modification perspective on marketing', *Journal of Marketing* 44: 36–47.

Ollendick, T. H., Dailey, D., and Shapiro, E. S. (1983) 'Vicarious reinforcement: expected and unexpected effects', *Journal of Applied Behavior Analysis* 16: 485–91.

Olshavsky, R. W. and Granbois, D. H. (1979) 'Consumer decision making: fact or fiction?' *Journal of Consumer Research* 6: 93–100.

Olson, J. C. (1982) 'Toward a science of consumer behavior. Presidential Address 1981', *Advances in Consumer Research* 11: v-x.

O'Neill, G. W., Nlanck, L. S., and Joyner, M. A. (1980) 'The use of stimulus control over littering in a natural setting', *Journal of Applied Behavior Analysis* 13: 379–81.

O'Shaughnessy, J. (1987) *Why People Buy*, New York: Oxford University Press.

O'Shaughnessy, J. and Holbrook, M. B. (1988) 'Understanding consumer behavior: the linguistic turn in marketing', *Journal of the Market Research Society*, 30, 197–223.

Oxenfeldt, A. R. and Moore, W. L. (1978) 'Customer or competitor: which guideline for marketing?' *Management Review*, August: 43–8.

Palmer, M. H., Loyd, M. E., and Lloyd, K. E. (1978) 'An experimental analysis of electricity conservation procedures', *Journal of Applied Behavior Analysis* 10: 655–71.

Park, C. W. and Mittal, B. (1985) 'A theory of involvement in consumer behavior: problems and issues', in J. N. Sheth (ed.) *Research in Consumer Behavior* 1: 201–32.

Paxton, R. (1976) 'Some criteria for choosing between explanations in psychology', Bulletin of the British Psychological Society 29: 396–9.

Perone, M., Galizio, M., and Baron, A. (1988) 'The relevance of animal-based principles in the laboratory study of human operant conditioning', in G. C. L. Davey and C. Cullen (eds) *Human Operant Conditioning and Behaviour Modification*, Chichester: Wiley.

Pervin, L. A. (1984) *Personality: Theory and Research*, New York: Wiley.

Peter, J. P. and Nord, W. R. (1982) 'A clarification and extension of operant conditioning principles in marketing', *Journal of Marketing* 46: 102–7.

Peter, J. P. and Olson, J. C. (1983) 'Is science marketing?' *Journal of Marketing* 47: 111–25.

Peter, J. P. and Olson, J. C. (1987) *Consumer Behavior: Marketing Strategy Perspectives*, Homewood, IL: Irwin.

Pierce, W. D. and Epling, W. F. (1983) 'Choice, matching and human behavior: a review of the literature', *The Behavior Analyst* 6: 57–76.

Poling, A. (1984) 'Comparing humans to other species: we're animals and they're not infrahumans', *The Behavior Analyst* 7: 211–12.

Poppen, R. (1982) 'The fixed-interval scallop in human affairs', *The Behavior Analyst* 5: 127–36.

Popper, Sir Karl (1972) *Conjectures and Refutations: The Growth of Scientific Knowledge*, 4th edn, London: Routledge and Kegan Paul.

— (1980) *The Logic of Scientific Discovery*, 10th edn, London: Hutchinson.

Postman, L. (1947) 'The history and present status of the law of effect', *Psychological Bulletin* 44: 489–563.

Powers, R. B., Osborne, J. G., and Anderson, E. G (1973) 'Positive reinforcement of litter removal in the natural environment', *Journal of Applied Behavior Analysis* 6: 579–86.

Premack, D. (1965) 'Reinforcement theory', in D. Levine (ed.) *Nebraska Symposium of Motivation*, Lincoln and London: University of Nebraska Press.

— (1971) 'Catching up with common sense or two sides of a generalization: reinforcement and punishment', in R. Glaser (ed.) *The Nature of Reinforcement*, London and New York: Academic Press.

Pryor, K. W., Haag, R., and O'Reilly, J. (1969) 'The creative porpoise: training for novel behavior', *Journal of the Experimental Analysis of Behavior* 12: 653–61.

Rachlin, H. C. (1970) *Introduction to Modern Behaviorism*, San Francisco, CA: W. H. Freeman.

— (1971) 'On the tautology of the matching law', *Journal of the Experimental Analysis of Behavior* 15: 249–51.

— (1976) *Behavior and Learning*, San Francisco: Freeman.

— (1980) 'Economics and behavioral psychology', in J. E. R. Staddon (ed.) *Limits to Action: The Allocation of Individual Behavior*, New York: Academic Press.

— (1982) 'Absolute and relative consumption space', *Nebraska Symposium on Motivation 1981*, Lincoln and London: University of Nebraska Press.

Rachlin, H. C. and Baum, W. M. (1972) 'Effects of alternative reinforcement: does the source matter?' *Journal of the Experimental Analysis of Behavior* 18: 231–41.

Rachlin, H. C., Green, L., Kagel, J. H., and Battalio, R. C. (1976) 'Economic demand theory and psychological studies of choice', *The Psychology of Learning and Motivation* 10: 129–54, New York: Academic Press.

Rachman, S. (1977)'The conditioning theory of fear acquisition: a critical examination', *Behaviour Research and Therapy* 15: 375–87.

Ray, M. L. (1973a) 'Marketing communications and the hierarchy-of-effects', in P. Clarke (ed.) *New Models for Mass Communication Research*, London: Sage.

— (1973b) 'Psychological theories and interpretations of learning', in S. Ward and T. S. Robertson (eds) *Consumer Behavior: Theoretical Sources*, Englewood Cliffs, NJ: Prentice-Hall.

Reid, D. H., Luyben, P. L., Rawers, R. J., and Bailey, J. S. (1976) 'The effects of prompting and proximity of containers on newspaper recycling behavior', *Environment and Behavior* 8: 471–82.

Rhinehart, L. (1976) *The Book of est*, London: Sphere.

Ribes, E. (1985) 'Human behaviour as operant behaviour: an empirical or conceptual issue?' in C. F. Lowe, M. Richelle, D. E. Blackman, and C. M. Bradshaw (eds) *Behaviour Analysis and Contemporary Psychology*, London: Erlbaum.

— (1986) 'Is operant conditioning sufficient to cope with human behavior?' in P. N. Chase and L. J. Parrott (eds) *Psychological Aspects of Language: The West Virginia Lectures*, Springfield, IL: Charles C. Thomas.

Roberto, C. and Pinson, E. L. (1973) 'Do attitude changes precede behaviour change?' *Journal of Advertising Research* 13: 35–8.

Robertson, T. S. (1967) 'The process of innovation and the diffusion of innovation', *Journal of Marketing* 31:14–19.

— (1971) *Innovative Behavior and Communication*, New York: Holt, Rinehart and Winston.

— (1976) 'Low commitment consumer behavior', *Journal of Advertising Research* 16: 19–24.

Robertson, T. S. and Myers, J. H. (1969) 'Personality correlates of opinion leadership and innovative buying behavior', *Journal of Marketing Research* 6: 164–8.

Robinson, J. (1962) *Economic Philosophy*, London: Watts.

Robinson, P. J., Faris, C. W. and Wind, Y. (1967) *Industrial Buying and Creative Marketing*, Boston, MA: Allyn and Bacon.

Rogers, E. M. (1983) *Diffusion of Innovations*, 3rd edn, New York: Free Press.

Roth, A. E. (ed.) (1987) *Laboratory Experimentation in Economics: Six Points of View*, Cambridge: Cambridge University Press.

Roth, T. P. (1987) *The Present State of Consumer Theory*, Lanham, MD: University Press of America.

Rothschild, M. L. (1979) 'Advertising strategies for high and low involvement situations', in J. C. Maloney and B. Silverman (eds) *Attitude Research Plays for High Stakes*, Chicago: American Marketing Association.

Rothschild, M. L. and Gaidis, W. C. (1981) 'Behavioral learning theory: its relevance to marketing and promotions', *Journal of Marketing* 45: 70–8.

Rotter, J. B. (1954) *Social Learning and Clinical Psychology*, Englewood Cliffs, NJ: Prentice-Hall.

— (1966) 'Generalized expectancies for internal versus external control of reinforcement', *Psychological Monographs: General and Applied* 80 (whole number 609): 1–28.

— (1982) 'Social learning theory', in N. T. Feather (ed.) *Expectations and Actions: Expectancy-Value Models in Psychology*, Hillsdale, NJ: Erlbaum.

Runnion, A., Watson, J. D., and McWhorter, J. (1978) 'Energy savings in interstate transportation through feedback and reinforcement', *Journal of Organizational Behavior Management* 1: 180–91.

Ryan, M. A. and Bonfield, E. H. (1975) 'The Fishbein extended model of consumer behavior', *Journal of Consumer Research* 2: 118–36.

— (1980) 'Fishbein's intentions model: a test of external and pragmatic validity', *Journal of Marketing* 44: 82–95.

Ryle, G. (1949) *The Concept of Mind*, London: Hutchinson.

Scammon, D. (1975) '"Information load" and consumers', *Journal of Consumer Research* 4: 148–55.

Schellenberg, J. A. (1978) *Masters of Social Psychology*, New York: Oxford University Press.

Schiffman, L. G. and Kanuk, L. L. (1983) *Consumer Behavior*, 2nd edn, Englewood Cliffs, NJ: Prentice-Hall.

Schwartz, B. (1984) *Psychology of Learning and Behavior*, 2nd edn, New York: Norton.

Schwartz, B. and Lacey, H. M. (1982) *Behaviorism, Science, and Human Nature*, New York: Norton.

Schwartz, B. and Lacey, H. M. (1988) 'What applied studies of human operant conditioning tell us about humans and about operant conditioning', in G. C. L. Davey and C. Cullen (eds) *Human Operant Conditioning and Behaviour Modification*, New York: Wiley.

Schwartz, B., Schuldenfrei, R., and Lacey, H. (1978) 'Operant psychology as factory psychology', *Behaviorism* 6: 229–54.

Scitovsky, T. (1976) *The Joyless Economy*, New York and London: Oxford University Press.

Scott, W. A., Osgood, D. W., and Peterson, C. (1979) *Cognitive Structure: Theory and Measurement of Individual Differences*, Washington, DC: V. H. Winston and Sons.

Scriven, M. (1973) 'The philosophy of behavior modification', in C. E. Thoresen (ed.) *Behavior Modification in Education*, Chicago: University of Chicago Press.

Searle, J. R. (1983) *Intentionality: An Essay in the Philosophy of Mind*, Cambridge: Cambridge University Press.

— (1984) *Minds, Brains and Science: The 1984 Reith Lectures*, London: BBC.

Seaver, W. B. and Patterson, A. H. (1976) 'Decreasing fuel consumption through feedback and social commendation', *Journal of Applied Behavior Analysis* 9: 147–52.

Seron, X. (1985) 'Behaviour modification and neuropsychology', in C. F. Lowe, M. Richelle, D. E. Blackman, and C. M. Bradshaw (eds) *Behaviour Analysis and Contemporary Psychology*, London: Erlbaum.

Sherman, J. (1988) 'Random drink tests sought', *The Times*, 4 May.

Silver, S. D. (1984) 'A simple mathematical theory of innovative behavior: comment', *Journal of Consumer Research* 10: 441–4.

Simon, H. A. (1959) 'Theories of decision-making in economics and behavioral science', *American Economic Review* 49: 253–83.

— (1976) *Administrative Behavior*, 3rd edn, London: Collier-Macmillan.

— (1983) *Reason in Human Affairs*, Oxford: Basil Blackwell.

Skinner, B. F. (1938) *The Behavior of Organisms*, New York: Appleton-Century.

— (1945) 'The operational analysis of psychological terms', *Psychological Review* 52: 270–7, 291–4.

— (1948a) '"Superstition" in the pigeon', *Journal of Experimental Psychology* 38: 168–72.

— (1948b) *Walden Two*, New York: Macmillan.
— (1950) 'Are theories of learning necessary?' *Psychological Review* 57: 193–216.
— (1953a) *Science and Human Behavior*, New York: Free Press.
— (1953b) 'Some contributions of an experimental analysis of behavior', *The American Psychologist* 8: 69–79.
— (1954) 'A critique of psychoanalytical concepts and theories', *The Scientific Monthly*, September.
— (1955–6) 'Freedom and the control of men', *The American Scholar*, Winter.
— (1957) *Verbal Behavior*, New York: Appleton-Century-Crofts.
— (1958) 'Reinforcement today', *The American Psychologist* 13: 94–9.
— (1963a) 'Operant behavior', *The American Psychologist* 18: 503–15.
— (1963b) 'Behaviorism at fifty', *Science* 140: 951–9.
— (1969) *Contingencies of Reinforcement: A Theoretical Analysis*, Englewood Cliffs, NJ: Prentice-Hall.
— (1971) *Beyond Freedom and Dignity*, New York: Alfred A. Knopf.
— (1972a) *Cumulative Record*, 3rd edn, New York: Appleton-Century-Crofts.
— (1972b) 'A lecture on "having" a poem', in *Cumulative Record*, 3rd edn, New York: Appleton-Century-Crofts.
— (1974) *About Behaviorism*, New York: Alfred A. Knopf.
— (1977) 'Why I am not a cognitive psychologist', *Behaviorism* 5: 1–10.
— (1978) 'Can we benefit from our discovery of behavioral science?', *Reflections on Behaviorism and Society*, Englewood Cliffs, NJ: Prentice-Hall.
— (1983) *A Matter of Consequences*, New York: New York University Press.
— (1984a) 'The evolution of behavior', *Journal of the Experimental Analysis of Behavior* 41: 217–21.
— (1984b) 'Coming to terms with private events', *Behavioral and Brain Sciences* 7: 572–81.
— (1985) 'Cognitive science and behaviorism', *British Journal of Psychology* 76: 291–301.
— (1986) 'What is wrong with daily life in the western world?' *American Psychologist*, May, 568–74.
— (1987) 'Why we are not acting to save the world', in *Upon Further Reflection*, Englewood Cliffs, NJ: Prentice-Hall.
— (1988) 'Reply to Catania', in A. C. Catania and S. Harnad (eds) *The Selection of Behavior. The Operant Behaviorism of B. F. Skinner: Comments and Consequences*, Cambridge: Cambridge University Press.
Skinner, J. H. (1977) 'Effects of reuse and recycling of beverage containers', *Proceedings*, 1975 Conference on Waste Reduction, Washington, DC: US Environmental Protection Agency.
Slama, M. E. and Tashchian, A. (1985) 'Selected socioeconomic and demographic characteristics associated with purchasing involvement', *Journal of Marketing* 49: 72–82.

Smith, V. L. (1982) 'Microeconomic systems as an experimental science', *American Economic Review*, 72.

Staats, A. W. (1975) *Social Behaviorism*, Homewood, IL: Dorsey Press.

— (1983) 'Paradigmatic behaviorism: unified theory for social-personality psychology', *Advances in Experimental Social Psychology*, New York and London: Academic Press.

Staats, A. W. and Staats, C. W. (1963) *Complex Human Behavior*, New York: Holt, Rinehart and Winston.

Staddon, J. E. R. and Simmelhag, V. L. (1971) 'The "superstition" experiment: a re-examination of its implications for the principles of adaptive behavior', *Psychological Review* 78: 3–43.

Stevenson, L. (1974) *Seven Theories of Human Nature*, New York: Oxford University Press.

Stigler, G. J. (1949) *Five Lectures on Economic Problems*, London: Longmans, Green and Co.

Stone, J. R. N. (1954) *The Measurement of Consumers' Expenditure and Behaviour in the United Kingdom*, Cambridge: Cambridge University Press.

Stuart, E. W., Shimp, T. A., and Engle, R. W. (1987) 'Classical conditioning of consumer attitudes: four experiments in an advertising context', *Journal of Consumer Research* 14: 334–40.

Summers, J. O. (1971) 'Generalized change agents and innovativeness', *Journal of Marketing Research* 8: 313–16.

Tarr, D. G. (1976) 'Experiments in token economies: a review of the evidence relating to assumptions and implications of economic theory', *Southern Economic Journal*, 43.

Tarver, J. L. and Haring, R. C. (1988) 'Improving professional selling: a social exchange approach', *Marketing Intelligence and Planning* 6, 2: 15–20.

Tauber, E. M. (1981) 'Utilization of concept testing for new product forecasting', in Y. Wind, V. Mahajan, and R. N. Cardozo (eds) *New Product Forecasting*, Lexington, MA: D. C. Heath.

Thelen, H. and Withal, J. (1949) 'Three frames of reference: the description of climate', *Human Relations*, April, 159–76.

Thibaut, J. W. and Kelley, H. H. (1959) *The Social Psychology of Groups*, New York: Wiley.

Thorelli, H. B. (1986) 'Networks: between markets and hierarchies', *Strategic Management Journal* 7: 37–51.

Thoresen, C. E. (1973) 'Behavioral humanism', in C. E. Thoresen (ed.) *Behavior Modification in Education*, Chicago: Chicago University Press.

Todd, J. T. and Morris, E. K. (1983) 'Misconception and miseducation: presentations of radical behaviorism in psychology textbooks', *The Behavior Analyst* 6: 153–60.

Tolman, E. C. (1932) *Purposive Behavior*, New York: Century.

Trice, A. D. (1983) 'On mentalistic terms: another view', *The Behavior Analyst* 6: 189–90.

Troye, S. V. (1985) 'Situationist theory and consumer behavior', in J. N.

Sheth (ed.) *Research in Consumer Behavior*, 1: 285–321, Greenwich, CT: JAI Press.

Tuck, M. (1976) *How Do We Choose?* London: Methuen.

Tunstall, J. and Walker, D. (1981) *Media Made in California: Hollywood, Politics and the News*, New York: Oxford University Press.

Valentine, E. R. (1982) *Conceptual Issues in Psychology*, London: Unwin.

Van Hooten, R., Nau, P. A. and Merrigan, M. (1981) 'Reducing elevator energy use: a comparison of posted feedback and reduced elevator convenience', *Journal of Applied Behavior Analysis* 14: 377–87.

Van Raaij, W. F. (1984) *Affective and Cognitive Reactions to Advertising*, Working Paper 84–111, Cambridge, MA: Marketing Science Institute.

Van Raaij, W. F., Van Veldhoven, G. M. and Waerneryd, K. E. (1988) (eds) *Handbook of Economic Psychology*, Amsterdam: North Holland.

Veblen, T. (1979) *The Theory of the Leisure Class*, Harmondsworth: Penguin. (First published 1899).

Watson, J. B. (1913) 'Psychology as the behaviorist views it', *Psychological Review* 20: 158–77.

Wearden, J. H. (1988) 'Some neglected problems in the analysis of human operant behaviour', in G. C. L. Davey and C. Cullen (eds) *Human Operant Conditioning and Behaviour Modification*, Chichester: Wiley.

Wessells, M. G. (1981) 'A critique of Skinner's views on the explanatory adequacy of cognitive theories', *Behaviorism* 9: 153–70.

—— (1982) 'A critique of Skinner's views on the obstructive character of cognitive theories', *Behaviorism* 10: 65–84.

Whaley, D. L. and Malott, R. W. (1971) *Elementary Principles of Behavior*, New York: Appleton-Century-Crofts.

Wilkie, W. L. (1986) *Consumer Behavior*, New York: Wiley.

Williams, M. (1985) 'Wittgenstein's rejection of scientific psychology', *Journal for the Theory of Social Behaviour* 15: 203–23.

Williamson, O. E. (1975) *Markets and Hierarchies: Analysis and Antitrust Implications*, New York: Free Press.

Wilson, D. T., Mathews, H. L., and Harvey, J. W. (1975) 'An empirical test of the Fishbein behavioral intentions model', *Journal of Consumer Research* 1: 39–48.

Wilson, G. T. (1982) 'The relationship of learning theories to behavior theories: problems, prospects and preferences', in J. C. Boulougouris (ed.) *Learning Theory Approaches to Psychiatry*, Chichester: Wiley.

Winett, R. A. (1977) 'Promoting turning out lights in unoccupied rooms', *Journal of Environmental Systems* 1: 237–41.

Winett, R. A. and Kagel, John H. (1984) 'The effects of information presentation format on consumer demand for resources in field settings', *Journal of Consumer Research* 11: 655–67.

Winett, R. A., Hatcher, J. W., Fort, T. R., Leckliter, I.N., Love, S. Q., Riley, A. W., and Fishback, J. F. (1982) 'The effects of videotape modeling and daily feedback on residential electricity conservation, home temperature, and humidity, perceived comfort, and clothing worn: winter and summer', *Journal of Applied Behavior Analysis* 15: 381–401.

Winett, R. A., Kaiser, S., and Haberkorn, G. (1977) 'The effects of monetary rebates and feedback on electricity consumption', *Journal of Environmental Systems* 6: 329–41.

Winett, R. A., Kramer, K. D., Walker, W. B., Malone, S. W. and Lane, M. K. (1988) 'Modifying food purchases in supermarkets with modeling, feedback, and goal-setting procedures', *Journal of Applied Behavior Analysis* 21: 72–9.

Winett, R. A., Leckliter, I. N., Chinn, D. E., Stahl, B., and Love, S. Q. (1985) 'Effects of television modeling on residential energy conservation', *Journal of Applied Behavior Analysis* 18: 33–44.

Winett, R. A., Neale, M. S., and Grier, H. C. (1979) 'Effects of self-monitoring and feedback on residential energy consumption ', *Journal of Applied Behavior Analysis* 12: 173–84.

Winkler, R. C. (1980) 'Behavioral economics, token economies, and applied behavior analysis', in J. E. R. Staddon (ed.) *Limits to Action: The Allocation of Individual Behavior*, New York: Academic Press.

Winkler, R. C. and Winett, R. A. (1982) 'Behavioral interventions in resource conservation: a systems approach based on behavioral economics', *American Psychologist* 37: 421–35.

Wiseman, J. (1983) (ed.) *Beyond Positive Economics?* London: Macmillan.

Witmer, J. F. and Geller, E. S. (1976) 'Facilitating paper recycling: effects of prompts, raffles, and contests', *Journal of Applied Behavior Analysis* 9: 315–22.

Woodworth, R. S. (1938) *Experimental Psychology*, London: Wiley.

Wright, P. (1979) 'Concrete action plans in TV messages to increase reading of drug warnings', *Journal of Consumer Research* 6: 256–69.

Wrigley, N. (1988) (ed.) *Store Choice, Store Location and Market Analysis*, London and New York: Routledge.

Zaichkowsky, J. L. (1986) 'Conceptualizing involvement', *Journal of Advertising* 15: 4–15.

Zuriff, G. E. (1979) 'Ten inner causes', *Behaviorism* 7: 1–8.

— (1985) *Behaviorism: A Conceptual Reconstruction*, New York: Columbia University Press.

Author index

Subject index

active interplay 3, 6, 21–3, 97, 169
adoption of innovation 64, 132; *see also*
    innovation; innovativeness; new
    products
advertising 13, 14, 15, 90, 91; and
    choice 69–70, 72; in marketing mix
    73–6; point of sale 73, 75–6;
    postmodern 150; presentation of
    social rules 149; as reward and
    reinforcer 150
affective change 9, 128
amusement 128
animal behaviour 24–5, 28, 32, 48–50;
    choice 51–2; economic 82–90;
    laboratory 82–3, 86–90, 97
approach behaviour 41, 43; consumer
    behaviour as 65–9
arousal 128
assumptions of theory 17, 19, 24, 39,
    57, 64, 170
attention span 150
attitude 2, 3, 4, 8, 10–13, 21, 27, 56; and
    behaviour 36–7, 55, 124; brand 14,
    15; change 9; and choice 70;
    consumer 18; strength 12
attitude-behaviour relationship 2, 8, 13
automated cash dispenser 47
autonomy 3, 108
avoidance behaviour 41, 43, 65–9, 78
awareness 15
awareness-trial-repeat model (ATR)
    15–16, 72

barter 76
baseline 91, 92–5, 154–9
behaviour: analysis 2; animal 24–5;
    change 9, 71, 102, 151–9, 161–4; *see
    also* consumer behaviour
    modification; as choice 71; collateral

114; consistency 114; continuity of
    28, 69; control of 4–5, 39, 56, 101–5;
    economic as operant 26, 119; human
    1, 2, 44–5, 61; instrumental 26;
    innovative 60–3; novel 107–8;
    prediction of 4, 13, 24, 27, 36–7, 39,
    56, 71, 117; primary determinants of
    34–6; reflex 53–4; theory 4, 90; social
    80; superstitious 106–7; verbal 21,
    46–7, 55, 98–103, 104–6; voluntary
    vs. involuntary 53–4; private 46–7;
    public 37, 47
behaviour setting 38, 56, 105, 109–10,
    126; in Behavioural Perspective
    Model of purchase and consumption
    125–39; closed 109–10, 121, 125, 130–
    9; continuum of 110, 124; closure
    147–8, 153, 155, 156; complex 114,
    116; open 109–10, 121, 125, 130–9;
    and response generalization 63;
    relatively closed 124, 126, 133, 134–9;
    relatively open 124, 126–7, 130–2,
    133–5, 137–8; and remote causes of
    behaviour 114, 116; store 106–7, 121,
    130–9
behavioural contrast 87–8
behavioural demarketing 153–4;
    examples 154–9
behavioural induction 87–8
Behavioural Perspective Model of
    purchase and consumption (BPM) 5,
    29, 31, 125–38; and brands 143;
    causal sequence 130; closed vs. open
    settings 125, 126–7; and consumer
    involvement 143–6, 150; Contingency
    Categories 129, 130–9; empirical
    testing 151–9; evaluation 159–64,
    165–7; and extended problem-solving
    (EPS) 139–40; hedonic and

219